The Rhetoric of Concealment

The Rhetoric of Concealment

Figuring Gender and Class in Renaissance Literature

Rosemary Kegl

Cornell University Press
Ithaca and London

First published 1994 by Cornell University Press.

Printed in the United States of America

⊗ The paper in this book meets the minimum requirements of the American National Standard for Information Sciences—Permanence of Paper for Printed Library Materials, ANSI Z39.48–1984.

Library of Congress Cataloging-in-Publication Data

Kegl, Rosemary, b. 1960
    The rhetoric of concealment : figuring gender and class in
 Renaissance literature / Rosemary Kegl.
        p.   cm.
    Includes bibliographical references (p.   ) and index.
    ISBN 0-8014-3016-X (alk. paper)
    1. English literature–Early modern, 1500-1700–History and
 criticism.   2. Literature and society–England–History–16th
 century.   3. Women and literature–England–History–16th century.
 4. Social classes in literature.   5. Sex role in literature.
 6. Renaissance–England.   7. Rhetoric–1500-1800.   I. Title.
 PR418.S64K44   1994
 820.9′003–dc20
                                                         94-16225

To my parents

🍒 Contents

❦ Acknowledgments

An earlier version of Chapter 1 was published in *English Literary Renaissance* ("'Those Terrible Aproches': Sexuality, Social Mobility, and Resisting the Courtliness of Puttenham's *The Arte of English Poesie*," 20:2 [Spring 1990]: 179–208). Arthur F. Kinney, editor of *English Literary Renaissance*, has kindly granted me permission to reprint that essay. I also thank Cambridge University Press, which is allowing me to cite at length from Gladys Doidge Willcock and Alice Walker's edition of George Puttenham's *The Arte of English Poesie* (Cambridge: Cambridge University Press, 1936), reprinted with the permission of Cambridge University Press; Houghton Mifflin, which is allowing me to cite at length from *The Merry Wives of Windsor*, in G. Blakemore Evans (editor), *The Riverside Shakespeare*, copyright ©1974 by Houghton Mifflin Company, used with permission; and Indiana University Press and Oxford University Press, which are allowing me to cite at length from Merritt E. Lawlis's edition of *Jack of Newbury*, in *The Novels of Thomas Deloney*, ed. Lawlis (Bloomington: Indiana University Press, 1961), by permission of Indiana University Press and by permission of Oxford University Press.

This book is the result of many efforts on my behalf. Its writing was facilitated by a Newberry Library/National Endowment for the Humanities Fellowship, a Newberry Library Short-Term Resident Fellowship, and a University of Rochester Junior Faculty Leave. I am grateful to these institutions for their financial support. I am particularly grateful to the fellows and staff at the Newberry Library and to my colleagues in the Department of English and the Susan B. Anthony Center for Women's Studies at the University of Rochester. In seminars and in informal conversations, they have contributed more to the writing of this book than they probably realized.

Several people have read portions of this project, including Harry Berger Jr., Richard Burt, Walter Cohen, Frances E. Dolan, Richard Halpern, Phillip Harper, Stacy Hubbard, Christopher Kendrick, Mary Ann Radzinowicz, and Julie Solomon. Without their questions and insights, my work would have been greatly diminished. In addition, I thank Ann Rosalind Jones and Wendy Wall, the readers for Cornell University Press, for their generous comments and criticisms, and Sheryl Drobny for her research assistance. I cannot acknowledge all the intellectual debts that I accrued before I considered writing this book. But I thank, in particular, Margaret Eggenberger, John Wheeler, and Lawrence Breitborde, because my good fortune began a very long time ago.

Most important, I thank my parents. They are my most reliable models; I work always with them in mind.

R. K.

The Rhetoric of Concealment

Introduction:
Accounting for Social Struggle

For more than a decade, new historicism has provided an occasion for debates within Renaissance studies about the relationship between literature and other forms of culture and about how reading Renaissance texts might help us assess, more generally, the most persuasive methods of cultural analysis. These debates often turn on the role of history in literary criticism, the limits of formalism, the most viable forms of individual and collective agency, and the relative explanatory power of synchronic and diachronic accounts of social struggle.[1] In this way, they

1. Walter Cohen, "Political Criticism of Shakespeare," in *Shakespeare Reproduced: The Text in History and Ideology*, ed. Jean E. Howard and Marion F. O'Connor (New York: Methuen, 1987), 18–46; David Cressy, "Foucault, Stone, Shakespeare, and Social History," *English Literary Renaissance* 21:2 (Spring 1991): 121–33; Anthony B. Dawson, "*Measure for Measure*, New Historicism, and Theatrical Power," *Shakespeare Quarterly* 39:3 (Autumn 1988): 328–41; Jonathan Dollimore and Alan Sinfield, "Introduction: Shakespeare, Cultural Materialism and the New Historicism," in *Political Shakespeare: New Essays in Cultural Materialism*, ed. Dollimore and Sinfield (Ithaca: Cornell University Press, 1985), 2–17; Catherine Gallagher, "Marxism and the New Historicism," in *The New Historicism*, ed. H. Aram Veeser (New York: Routledge, 1989), 37–48; Jonathan Goldberg, "The Politics of Renaissance Literature: A Review Essay," *ELH* 49:2 (Summer 1982): 514–42; Stephen Greenblatt, introduction to *Renaissance Self-Fashioning: From More to Shakespeare* (Chicago: University of Chicago Press, 1980), 1–9, *Shakespearean Negotiations: The Circulation of Social Energy in Renaissance England* (Berkeley: University of California Press, 1988), 1–20, and "Towards a Poetics of Culture," in Veeser, *New Historicism*, 1–14; Barbara Leah Harman, "Refashioning the Renaissance," *Diacritics* 14:1 (Spring 1984): 52–65; James Holstun, "Ranting at the New Historicism," *English Literary Renaissance* 19:2 (Spring 1989): 189–225; Jean E. Howard, "The New Historicism in Renaissance Studies," *English Literary Renaissance* 16:1 (Winter 1986): 13–43; Louis A[drian] Montrose, "Professing the Renaissance: The Poetics and

have made prominent within Renaissance literary criticism those issues that are central to my project.

This book analyzes how struggles over gender and over class were mediated through the formal properties of English Renaissance writing. I develop my argument through close readings of works by George Puttenham, Philip Sidney, William Shakespeare, and Thomas Deloney. Those readings incorporate discussions of Renaissance gynecological and obstetrical texts, misogynist tracts, defenses of women, royal proclamations, legal disputes, town histories and town charters, and narratives written by women and travelers. I organize each chapter around an author's recurrent rhetorical gesture—riddling disclosure in Puttenham's *The Arte of English Poesie*, the logic of architecturally unsound bodies and buildings in Sidney's *Arcadia*, the network of insults in Shakespeare's *The Merry Wives of Windsor*, and the collection of proverbial wisdom in Deloney's *Jack of Newbury*. I ask what sorts of relationships to gender and to class these rhetorical gestures help to promote, and I analyze how these gestures conceal possible sites and forms of Renaissance collective politics.

By claiming that literary production is one among a series of cultural practices that shape and are shaped by Renaissance society, new historicists have emphasized the dynamic role of Renaissance literature. My somewhat different understanding of Renaissance social praxis is influenced by Fredric Jameson's work on the interaction between literary form and social struggle. For Jameson, form designates, first, what he variously describes as the style, gestures, or "verbal thrusts" of a text. This rubric encompasses a range of formal properties, including genre, recurring gaps in a narrative, characteristic sentence structure, and figures that convey sensory perceptions. Second, form designates the process by which these properties influence how the text's more general organizing logic might relate to other practices within society. By aligning form with process, Jameson suggests that form is not simply a short-

Politics of Culture," in Veeser, *New Historicism*, 15–36, and "Renaissance Literary Studies and the Subject of History," *English Literary Renaissance* 16:1 (Winter 1986): 5–12; Edward Pechter, "The New Historicism and Its Discontents: Politicizing Renaissance Drama," *PMLA* 102:3 (May 1987): 292–303; Alan Sinfield, "Power and Ideology: An Outline Theory and Sidney's *Arcadia*," *ELH* 52:2 (Summer 1985): 259–77; Don E. Wayne, "Power, Politics, and the Shakespearean Text: Recent Criticism in England and the United States," in Howard and O'Connor, *Shakespeare Reproduced*, 47–67; and Valerie Wayne, introduction to *The Matter of Difference: Materialist Feminist Criticism of Shakespeare*, ed. Valerie Wayne (Ithaca: Cornell University Press, 1991), 1–26.

hand for a textual or social structure. Instead, form mediates our experience of the shifting and uneven relationships among the cultural, the economic, and the political. Thus a formal reading describes not a textual or social system but, instead, the textual process through which we live our relationship to our material conditions. Third, form designates not simply a process to *be* interpreted but also the process of interpretation itself. In Jameson's formulation, history is accessible only as a text—through the mediations of form. And criticism is one instance of that formal, that ideological mediation.[2]

My book's title, *The Rhetoric of Concealment: Figuring Gender and Class in Renaissance Literature*, alludes to all three definitions of form. First, I am interested in the gestures through which Puttenham, Sidney, Shakespeare, and Deloney figure gender and class relations. As my earlier list of these gestures indicates, I select formal properties that operate in very different registers—from the logic of an individual sentence to the organizing logic of an entire work. Second, I analyze each gesture as a process that participates in social struggle by promoting a particular experience of Renaissance material conditions in England. Third, as the present participle in the subtitle implies, each chapter is a process of refiguring both these sixteenth-century representations of gender and class and those more general notions of literary form and Renaissance social relations through which critics have approached this writing. Finally, I do not want the term "concealment" to be misleading. I am not unveiling the "real" social relations that lurk behind the recurrent gestures of Puttenham, Sidney, Shakespeare, and Deloney. Instead, I ask what sorts of social relations these gestures might have helped promote. I refer to that process as the rhetoric of concealment because I am particularly interested in those sites and forms of collective politics which this writing attempts to make unimaginable. In other words, by analyzing how these recurrent gestures attempt to foreclose emerging utopian impulses, I consider how members of late-sixteenth-century society might have envisioned social change.

I have selected works from approximately one decade near the end

2. Fredric Jameson, "Baudelaire as Modernist and Postmodernist: The Dissolution of the Referent and the Artificial 'Sublime,'" in *Lyric Poetry: Beyond New Criticism*, ed. Chaviva Hošek and Patricia Parker (Ithaca: Cornell University Press, 1985), 247–63; *Marxism and Form: Twentieth-Century Dialectical Theories of Literature* (Princeton: Princeton University Press, 1971; paperback ed., 1974); and *The Political Unconscious: Narrative as a Socially Symbolic Act* (Ithaca: Cornell University Press, 1981; paperback ed., 1982). Unlike Jameson, I analyze how form mediates both struggles over class and struggles over gender.

of the sixteenth century in order to examine how they were located very differently within the shifting conjuncture of forces that comprised the dominant culture and the relationships among dominant and subordinate groups. In so doing, I draw on Antonio Gramsci's concept of hegemony, which, in Raymond Williams's words, "supposes the existence of something which . . . saturates the society to such an extent" that it "even constitutes the substance and limit of common sense. . . . For if ideology were merely some abstract, imposed set of notions, if our social and political and cultural ideas and assumptions and habits were merely the result of specific manipulation, of a kind of overt training which might be simply ended or withdrawn, then the society would be very much easier to move and to change than in practice it has ever been or is." Although I focus on how the rhetorical gestures of Puttenham, Sidney, Shakespeare, and Deloney perform a legitimizing function, I also focus on the range of gender and class relations that these gestures attempt to make dominant. "We have to emphasize that hegemony is not singular; indeed that its own internal structures are highly complex, and have continually to be renewed, recreated and defended; and by the same token, that they can be continually challenged and in certain respects modified," Williams adds. "That is why instead of speaking simply of 'the hegemony', 'a hegemony', I would propose a model which allows for this kind of variation and contradiction, its sets of alternatives and its processes of change."[3] I account for the variation Williams describes by locating my local analyses within larger narratives about sixteenth- and seventeenth-century class and gender struggle.

Most Renaissance literary critics define class sociologically—distinguishing among classes on the basis of differences in rank, status, or authority. I define class in terms of exploitation and the relations of

---

3. For discussions of hegemony, see Antonio Gramsci, "The Modern Prince" and "State and Civil Society," in *Selections from the Prison Notebooks*, ed. and trans. Quintin Hoare and Geoffrey Nowell Smith (New York: International Publishers, 1971), 123–276; Stuart Hall, *The Hard Road to Renewal: Thatcherism and the Crisis of the Left* (London: Verso, 1988), 93–173; Peter Stallybrass, "The World Turned Upside Down: Inversion, Gender, and the State," in Wayne, *Matter of Difference*, 201–20; and Raymond Williams, "Base and Superstructure in Marxist Cultural Theory," in *Problems in Materialism and Culture: Selected Essays* (London: Verso, 1980), 31–49. Ernesto Laclau and Chantal Mouffe, *Hegemony and Socialist Strategy: Towards a Radical Democratic Politics* (London: Verso, 1985), 93–148, offer an account of hegemony in which there is no predictable agent of social change and in which the shifting and unstable relationship between dominant and subordinate groups need not, at all historical conjunctures, entail the political primacy of class struggle. Quotations are from Williams, "Base and Superstructure," 37, 38.

production—distinguishing among classes on the basis of their structural role in the production and extraction of surplus value.[4] Yet, within this paradigm, I assume that rank, status, and authority were categories through which members of late-sixteenth-century society often experienced their relationship to economic exploitation and through which they often articulated their political demands for social change. In this way, I find the Renaissance criticism that is based on the more prevalent sociological definition of class to be a valuable resource when I situate the late-sixteenth-century rhetorical gestures of Puttenham, Sidney, Shakespeare, and Deloney within larger narratives about shifting structures of exploitation.

In analyzing the social relations that these rhetorical gestures promote, I am indebted to a number of historians—including several who are sometimes grouped among revisionists because of their focus on local or regional history. Although revisionist history is not itself central to my analyses, I have shaped this project with the debates surrounding that history in mind. The most controversial revisionist historians frame their accounts of local or regional history within a larger challenge to Marxist and liberal paradigms about sixteenth- and seventeenth-century England. Their work often assumes that members of Renaissance society—even during the seventeenth-century revolution—experienced national politics primarily through their regional identities and insists that no coherent and collective opposition to the government emerged before, during, or after the war. In fact, for many revisionists, this lack of coherent opposition implies that, particularly prior to the war, the government maintained a rough social consensus; that Renaissance social struggle was local, short-lived, and incidental; and that the revolution and interregnum produced no lasting changes in English society. Although revisionist history has centered on the nature of social conflict during the seventeenth century, its polemic often extends more generally to accounts of social struggle—particularly class struggle—during the earlier Renaissance and the eighteenth century. I do not read this work as a convincing challenge to Marxist accounts of social struggle, but I do find it useful for sorting through the factors that contributed to local and regional political alliances. More important, like some critics

4. Robert Brenner, "The Social Basis of Economic Development," in *Analytical Marxism*, ed. John Roemer (Cambridge: Cambridge University Press, 1986), 23–53, offers an argument about class whose discussion of rational self-interest and of the relations of production is particularly useful for analyzing Renaissance society.

of revisionist history and of the new historicism, I also find it crucial, particularly within Renaissance studies, to emphasize how the cultural, the economic, and the political operate within a range of possibilities that they impose on one another.[5]

Each of my chapters addresses one instance of this conjuncture of the cultural, the economic, and the political. For example, I analyze how all four authors' rhetorical gestures help to mediate the relationship between, on the one hand, shifting structures of economic exploitation and, on the other, absolutism, popular rebellion, social mobility, the jurisdiction of ecclesiastical and secular courts, the organization of guilds, and the composition and relative authority of town government. I organize each chapter around the larger methodological assumptions about local phenomena that make it possible for these four Renaissance writers and their critics to conceal potential sites and forms of collective politics. In the Puttenham chapter, I consider how struggles within individual institutions relate to larger social struggles. In the Sidney chapter, I address the political logic of apparently contradictory local alliances, and I discuss the unstable relationship between dominant and subordinate groups within any hegemonic bloc. In the Shakespeare and De-

5. I am particularly indebted to the critiques of revisionist history by Richard Cust and Ann Hughes, "Introduction: After Revisionism," in *Conflict in Early Stuart England: Studies in Religion and Politics, 1603–1642*, ed. Cust and Hughes (London: Longman, 1989), 1–46; Mary Fulbrook, "The English Revolution and the Revisionist Revolt," *Social History* 7:3 (October 1982): 249–64; Tim Harris and Christopher Husbands, "Talking with Christopher Hill: Part II," in *Reviving the English Revolution: Reflections and Elaborations on the Work of Christopher Hill*, ed. Geoff Eley and William Hunt (London: Verso, 1988), 343–45; Cynthia Herrup, "The Counties and the Country: Some Thoughts on Seventeenth-Century Historiography," in Eley and Hunt, *Reviving the English Revolution*, 289–304; Christopher Hill, "A Bourgeois Revolution?" in *Three British Revolutions: 1641, 1688, 1776*, ed. J. G. A. Pocock (Princeton: Princeton University Press, 1980), 109–39, and "Parliament and People in Seventeenth-Century England," *Past and Present* 92 (August 1981): 100–124; James Holstun, "'God Bless Thee, Little David!': John Felton and His Allies," *ELH* 59:3 (Fall 1992): 513–52; Ann Hughes, "Local History and the Origins of the Civil War," in Cust and Hughes, *Conflict in Early Stuart England*, 224–53; Lawrence Stone, "The Bourgeois Revolution of Seventeenth-Century England Revisited," *Past and Present* 109 (November 1985): 44–54; and David Underdown, *Revel, Riot, and Rebellion: Popular Politics and Culture in England, 1603–1660* (Oxford: Oxford University Press, 1985; paperback ed., 1987), 1–8.

My analyses of ideology and of the overdetermined relationships among the cultural, the economic, and the political are indebted to Louis Althusser, "Contradiction and Overdetermination: Notes for an Investigation," in *For Marx*, trans. Ben Brewster (London: New Left Books, 1977; London: Verso, 1979), 87–128, and "Ideology and Ideological State Apparatuses (Notes towards an Investigation)," in *Lenin and Philosophy and Other Essays*, trans. Ben Brewster (New York: Monthly Review Press, 1971), 127–86.

loney chapters, I read the "middle class" not as a thing to be defined but as a process of constructing identities among groups characterized by their multiple and often contradictory short- and long-term interests. And I demonstrate how Shakespeare's insults and Deloney's proverbs participate in Renaissance class struggle precisely by defining the possible relationships among regional and national alliances.

My focus on hegemony and social struggle has a somewhat different inflection when I discuss gender. In her 1977 essay "Did Women Have a Renaissance?" Joan Kelly argues that Europe's gradual transition from feudalism to capitalism disempowered women, particularly aristocratic women. And she argues, more generally, that taking gender as a central category of analysis troubles both the critical priorities and the assumptions about periodization that have defined Renaissance studies.[6] Feminist historians and literary critics have often challenged Kelly's particular analysis of women's "fall" into capitalism. Yet, by taking seriously her more general claims about gender as an analytical category, they have offered compelling accounts of the relationship between Renaissance structures of economic exploitation and the oppression of women. For example, some have analyzed how Renaissance women were located within the relations of production. Others have examined the various positions that these women occupied within political and cultural systems that were compatible with the feudal and emerging capitalist modes of production. And others have focused on the gendered language through which a range of Renaissance social relations were represented, including language based on the analogy between domestic and state order. I draw on this work not only in my Deloney chapter where I most directly address the issue of women and labor but throughout the book where I demonstrate how orderly and disorderly gender relations intersect with Puttenham's depiction of social mobility, with Sidney's notion of popular rebellion, and with Shakespeare's and Deloney's constructions of "middle-class" identities. My readings assume that there is no inevitable political alliance between those oppressed by gender and those exploited by class. Such alliances are produced within a range of possibilities at any one historical moment.

Yet my larger project is designed to retain a provisional separation between my analysis of struggles over gender and my analysis of

6. Joan Kelly, "Did Women Have a Renaissance?" in *Women, History, and Theory: The Essays of Joan Kelly* (Chicago: University of Chicago Press, 1984; paperback ed., 1986), 19–50.

struggles over class. I select rhetorical gestures that are located quite differently in relation to each of these struggles and that emphasize the disparate forces that comprise the dominant culture. In this way, each chapter divides into two sections that highlight the very different nature of these struggles within Renaissance society and the very different ways in which they have been addressed by both historians and literary critics. Unwilling to "dispense with [women] as an organizing political focus," Michèle Barrett explains that "feminism is very hard to conceive without the experiential dimensions of women's sense of oppression and without a vision of change." This conception of feminism demands not only that the critic "recognize the independent character of women's oppression and avoid explanations that reduce . . . it to other factors" but also that she recognize the "significant difference between feminism as a historical movement . . . and Marx's conception of revolutionary emancipation." Barrett acknowledges that there are—and have been—a range of possible feminisms yet refers here to that nineteenth- and twentieth-century liberal political movement in Europe and the United States which has most frequently identified itself, and which has most frequently been identified, as feminism.[7] This movement was not present in English Renaissance society, of course. Yet, by provisionally separating my analysis of gender from my analysis of class, I am able to attend to the particular structures both of oppression and of exploitation which *were* present in that society. And I am able to ask the very different questions about collectivity which were central to gender struggle and to class struggle during the sixteenth and seventeenth centuries.

My understanding of Renaissance gender struggle is indebted to a range of feminist historians and literary critics who have asked how Renaissance women understood their relationships to one another and to the conditions that helped shape their lives. These writers do discuss Renaissance women who wrote pro-women arguments, who filed defamation charges in ecclesiastical courts, and who petitioned guild authorities, town officials, and, eventually, parliament. Yet they suggest that these women seldom located their specific demands within larger arguments about women's structural oppression. And they suggest that these women generally described their behavior as exceptional, as motivated by individual rather than collective concerns, and as ultimately in keep-

7. Michèle Barrett, "Introduction to the 1988 Edition," in *Women's Oppression Today: The Marxist/Feminist Encounter*, rev. ed. (London: Verso, 1988), v–xxxiv. Quotations are from v, xiii, and xxiii.

ing with accepted definitions of the proper sphere and nature of women's activity. In short, they argue that Renaissance women's subordination tended not to be experienced as oppression, and that gender tended not to serve as a political identity—particularly as an identity that might organize any sort of collective politics.

This study examines how the rhetorical gestures of Puttenham, Sidney, Shakespeare, and Deloney mediate the relationship between Renaissance women and their conditions of existence and asks how those gestures help conceal women's structural position within Renaissance society. Those gestures attempt to make unimaginable any sort of collective struggle for social change, including one that might address the differences among women. My local analyses of those gestures consider, more generally, the shifting cultural, economic, and political positions of Renaissance women during England's sixteenth and seventeenth centuries. Each chapter focuses on sites that historians and literary critics have identified as particularly conflictual. At these sites, the subordination of women did threaten to become recognizable as a form of oppression which was neither natural nor logically coherent—a form of oppression which unevenly distributed benefits to and unevenly oppressed its gendered subjects. Within this framework, I address the language surrounding Elizabeth's rule, the prescriptive literature and practices surrounding companionate marriage, the pro-women writing about misogyny and about equity, the gendered division of skilled and unskilled labor, the opportunities afforded to and the limitations imposed on propertied widows, and the prosecution of women's verbal and sexual excess in ecclesiastical courts and in shaming rituals. I want to stress, first, that women who were situated quite differently in Renaissance society also would have been located quite differently in relation to each of these sites and, second, that each site threatened to make possible, more generally, what Merry E. Wiesner defines as a feminist politics—a politics based on the explicit understanding that women are subject to certain forms of oppression precisely *because* they are women.[8]

Finally, as this introduction suggests, many of the questions that motivate this project emerge from my reading of contemporary cultural criticism. The book thus concludes with an afterword in which I analyze recent writing by two contemporary Renaissance critics—Karen New-

8. Merry E. Wiesner, "Women's Defense of Their Public Role," in *Women in the Middle Ages and the Renaissance: Literary and Historical Perspectives*, ed. Mary Beth Rose (Syracuse: Syracuse University Press, 1986), 22.

man and Richard Halpern. I place in tension Newman's feminist account and Halpern's Marxist account of a single rhetorical gesture—
Renaissance *copia*—in order to analyze how their reading practices
might comment on each another. In this way, I discuss what their versions of historical criticism and cultural analysis might tell us about how
Renaissance rhetorical gestures mediate the relationships among the
cultural, the economic, and the political. And I discuss, more generally,
what their reading practices might tell us about the peculiar role that
Renaissance historical criticism occupies within contemporary cultural
studies.

❦ Chapter One

"Those terrible approches": Sexuality, Social Mobility, and Resisting the Courtliness of Puttenham's *The Arte of English Poesie*

In the first chapter of *The Arte of English Poesie*, George Puttenham promises to explain "what a Poet and Poesie is, and who may be worthily sayd the most excellent Poet of our time" (3).[1] Puttenham begins by offering Homer as proof that some combination of divine instinct, excellency of nature and complexion, subtlety of spirits and wit, and experience and observation of the world allows poets to perfect their art of making and imitating. "Otherwise how was it possible," he asks, "that *Homer* being but a poore priuate man, and as some say, in his later age blind, should so exactly set foorth and describe, as if he had bene a most excellent Captaine or Generall, the order and array of battels, the conduct of whole armies, the sieges and assaults of cities and townes?" (4). Puttenham duplicates the structure of this query in the questions that follow—first asking how, if not for the combination of divine and human traits, the exemplary poet could write *as if he had been*, in turn, some great prince's majordomo, a surveyor in court, and a politician and, second, outlining the expertise that prompts each comparison between the private man and these public officials. Yet Puttenham alters this format when he concludes, "Finally how could he so naturally paint out the speeches, countenance and maners of Princely persons and priuate?" (4). Here he carefully avoids saying what the structure of the preceding questions makes clear—that Homer's perfected poetry

---

1. All citations are from George Puttenham, *The Arte of English Poesie*, ed. Gladys Doidge Willcock and Alice Walker (1589; reprint, Cambridge: Cambridge University Press, 1936).

allows him to write *as if he had been* not only a private but also a princely person.

Read in conjunction with the earlier passage about Homer, the chapter's final paragraphs suggest, again without stating directly, that all poets usurp the prerogatives of royalty. Puttenham describes their poetic overreaching as an imitation of royalty's countenance—of the queen's inseparable beauty and royal authority. Although he later will praise the queen's "learned, delicate, noble Muse" (63), here Puttenham claims that the celebrated qualities of poetic making and imitating which characterize his greatest of contemporary poets mark not her skills at verse but, instead, the expertise with which she performs her public functions. "Forsooth," he explains, "by your Princely purse fauours and countenance, making in maner what ye list, the poore man rich, the lewd well learned, the coward couragious, and vile both noble and valiant. Then for imitation no lesse, your person as a most cunning counterfaitor liuely representing *Venus* in countenance, in life *Diana*, *Pallas* for gouernement, and *Iuno* in all honour and regall magnificence" (4–5). Puttenham implies but stops short of saying, then, that Homer's exemplary poetic ability to "paint out the speeches, countenance and maners of Princely persons" (4) marks the poet's characteristic usurpation of royal imitating and making. Poets counterfeit from princes the very countenance that Elizabeth I counterfeits from Venus and by which royalty countenances, or authorizes, not only the transformation of the poor, the lewd, the cowardly, and the vile but also the elevation of the private poet to public status. Within his first chapter, then, Puttenham carefully avoids saying what the structure of his repeating questions makes clear; he suggests and retreats; he implies but refuses to state explicitly. In each instance, he constructs a transparent riddle whose solution he discloses yet will not utter. This chapter analyzes the politics of that particular form of indirect revelation.

In *Poetry and Courtliness in Renaissance England*, Daniel Javitch argues that the indirection of Renaissance court verse is not part of an apolitical, ahistorical aesthetic but, rather, part of an aesthetic that responds to the dangers and demands within a court that revolved around Elizabeth's absolute authority. Javitch explains, for example, that poetry's indirect revelation operates within the court either as a politic strategy for conveying dangerous sentiments or, alternately, as a method for creating an aesthetic pleasure that renders irrelevant any particular meaning or message. The first explanation underscores the wisdom of avoiding dangerous commitments; the second underscores the artful transparency of such an avoidance and its ability to please readers and auditors familiar, in their own courtliness, with precisely that sort of transparent gesture.[2] Extending Javitch's claims about verse, Louis Adrian Montrose and Heinrich F. Plett have read the *Arte* not only as a manual that outlines for the fledgling poet-courtier the rules of Elizabethan courtliness but also as itself a courtly bid for favor. The structure of that bid, they add, both determines and is determined by the cultural politics of Elizabethan England.[3] Together with recent discussions of Shakespeare's, Sidney's, and Spenser's relationships to the court,[4] their readings have refined our understanding of the historical

2. Daniel Javitch, *Poetry and Courtliness in Renaissance England* (Princeton: Princeton University Press, 1978), 50–106. Javitch argues that the *Arte* is not simply a handbook of rhetorical terms or a treatise on poetry but is, in addition, a handbook of courtly conduct. By stressing this combination of rhetorical, poetic, and courtly handbook, Javitch explains the flourishing of verse in Tudor England.

3. For discussions of Puttenham by Louis Adrian Montrose, see his "Celebration and Insinuation: Sir Philip Sidney and the Motives of Elizabethan Courtship," *Renaissance Drama* 8 (1977): 6–7, 10, 22, 23, 28–29; "'Eliza, Queene of shepheardes,' and the Pastoral of Power," *English Literary Renaissance* 10:2 (Spring 1980): 153–54; and, for his most extensive treatment, "Of Gentlemen and Shepherds: The Politics of Elizabethan Pastoral Form," *ELH* 50:3 (Fall 1983): 433–52. See also Heinrich F. Plett, "Aesthetic Constituents in the Courtly Culture of Renaissance England," *New Literary History* 14:3 (Spring 1983): 610–11, and "The Place and Function of Style in Renaissance Poetics," in *Renaissance Eloquence: Studies in the Theory and Practice of Renaissance Rhetoric*, ed. James J. Murphy (Berkeley: University of California Press, 1983), 364–75. In "Puttenham's Perplexity: Nature, Art, and the Supplement in Renaissance Poetic Theory," in *Literary Theory/Renaissance Texts*, ed. Patricia Parker and David Quint (Baltimore: Johns Hopkins University Press, 1986), 257–79, Derek Attridge agrees that the *Arte* is itself an instance of courtliness. His article concentrates, however, on Puttenham's attempt to maintain a strict distinction between nature and art and, to a lesser extent, on the culturally specific uses of that distinction. In *Hidden Designs: The Critical Profession and Renaissance Literature* (New York: Methuen, 1986), 19–34, 120–29, Jonathan Crewe considers the professional and, ultimately, psychic motives for Renaissance critics' obsession with "detecting" cultural narratives within literature's courtly codes. His own readings enact that impulse to detect and, when discussing Puttenham's relation to the queen, detect the necessity for politic courtliness. In *Literary Fat Ladies: Rhetoric, Gender, Property* (London: Methuen, 1987), 99, 108–10, 130–31, Patricia Parker explains that many of the *Arte*'s rhetorical figures correspond to particular sixteenth-century notions of gender and class. The nature of this correspondence—the relationship between the rhetoricity and the historicity of gender—is the subject of Jacques Lezra's "'The Lady Was a Litle Peruerse': The 'Gender' of Persuasion in Puttenham's *Arte of English Poesie*," in *Engendering Men: The Question of Male Feminist Criticism*, ed. Joseph A. Boone and Michael Cadden (New York: Routledge, 1990), 53–65.

4. In addition to the work by Montrose cited in the previous note, see his "The Elizabethan Subject and the Spenserian Text," in Parker and Quint, *Literary Theory/Renaissance Texts*, 303–40; "*A Midsummer Night's Dream* and the Shaping Fantasies of Elizabethan Cul-

milieu of Elizabethan courtliness and of the relationship between courtly practices and literary texts.

Like Puttenham's riddling disclosures, these interpretations of courtly literature stress the perils among which politic courtiers negotiate. Elizabethan courtiers did confront danger, yet the emphasis on politic courtliness tends to filter all social struggles for meaning and for control over material conditions, all dissent and all alliances, through a narrative about relations among courtiers or about relations between those courtiers and their queen. Discussions of gender, for example, have focused on the interchangeability of and structural parity between erotic discourse and that of court politics, on the ability of erotic discourse to act out and sublimate courtly desires for power, and on the imagery employed by courtiers and the queen in order to manage the contradiction they experience between a cultural belief in female subservience and the courtly reality of Elizabeth's rule.[5] Discussions of class have focused on

ture," in *Rewriting the Renaissance: The Discourses of Sexual Difference in Early Modern Europe*, ed. Margaret W. Ferguson, Maureen Quilligan, and Nancy J. Vickers (Chicago: University of Chicago Press, 1986), 65–87; and "'The perfecte paterne of a Poete': The Poetics of Courtship in *The Shepheardes Calender*," *Texas Studies in Literature and Language* 21:1 (Spring 1979): 34–67. For a sampling of relevant discussions about Shakespeare, Sidney, Spenser, and their relationship to Elizabeth and the court, see also Francis Barker, *The Tremulous Private Body: Essays on Subjection* (London: Methuen, 1984), 21–40; Crewe, *Hidden Designs*, 35–118; Patricia Fumerton, "'Secret' Arts: Elizabethan Miniatures and Sonnets," *Representations* 15 (Summer 1986): 57–97; Jonathan Goldberg, *Endlesse Worke: Spenser and the Structures of Discourse* (Baltimore: Johns Hopkins University Press, 1981), 122–74; Stephen Greenblatt, *Renaissance Self-Fashioning: From More to Shakespeare* (Chicago: University of Chicago Press, 1980), 157–92; Richard Helgerson, "The New Poet Presents Himself: Spenser and the Idea of a Literary Career," *PMLA* 93:5 (October 1978): 893–911; Clark Hulse, "Stella's Wit: Penelope Rich as Reader of Sidney's Sonnets," in Ferguson, Quilligan, and Vickers, *Rewriting the Renaissance*, 272–86; Leah S. Marcus, "Shakespeare's Comic Heroines, Elizabeth I, and the Political Uses of Androgyny," in *Women in the Middle Ages and the Renaissance: Literary and Historical Perspectives*, ed. Mary Beth Rose (Syracuse: Syracuse University Press, 1986), 135–54; Plett, "Aesthetic Constituents," 597–621; and Leonard Tennenhouse, *Power on Display: The Politics of Shakespeare's Genres* (New York: Methuen, 1986), 17–122. In *Shakespearean Negotiations: The Circulation of Social Energy in Renaissance England* (Berkeley: University of California Press, 1988), 4, Greenblatt comments on the inevitable centrality of the monarch in discussions of Renaissance society.

5. See Montrose, "Celebration and Insinuation," 4–5, 21–22, 26–27, 29–31, 33; "'Eliza, Queene of shepheardes,'" 157, 166–67; "Elizabethan Subject," 325–28; "Shaping Fantasies," 77, 86–87; "Of Gentlemen and Shepherds," 440–43; and "'The perfecte paterne of a Poete,'" 39–40. See also Crewe, *Hidden Designs*, 120–29; Fumerton, "'Secret' Arts," 57–66; Greenblatt, *Renaissance Self-Fashioning*, 169–73; Tennenhouse, *Power on Display*, especially 102–4; and Marilyn L. Williamson, *The Patriarchy of Shakespeare's Comedies* (Detroit: Wayne State University Press, 1986), 27–32.

social mobility within the court; on the specific courtly forms with which courtiers negotiate their own ambiguous status during a period of social change; and on those particular interactions between the queen and her politic courtiers which legitimize Tudor rule, foster England's identity as a harmonious nation, and promote imperialism and colonialism.[6] These readings of relations within the court—however thoroughly contextualized—neglect to analyze how both Elizabethan and present-day preoccupations with courtly peril reinforce a monolithic notion of social struggle. The *Arte*, invariably cited as a touchstone for politic courtliness, is an appropriate point from which to reconsider these readings.

Because ideology is produced within social struggle, critics have claimed that institutions, such as the court, are a site of gender or class conflict. In theory I agree: the beliefs and practices of courtliness do not simply reproduce a social system but, instead, are shaped by and participate in struggles over the possible character of that system. In practice, however, these claims have supported readings of courtly literature which assume not simply that courtliness participates in ongoing gender and class struggles but, in addition, that those larger struggles are represented by courtly relations. Courtly relations, when not read as homologies for a larger system of social relations, are read as one privileged piece within a seamless social puzzle and courtly struggles as one front within a seamless social battle. In short, critics tend to read one site of intervention within ongoing gender and class struggles as a stage on which those struggles actually are played out and won or lost. By contrast, I assume that the court continually reproduces itself as an institution and, at the same time, is continually produced within social struggles—for the purposes of this · chapter, gender and class struggles—which are not circumscribed by the boundaries of any single institution. In other words, Puttenham's courtly literature might reproduce courtly beliefs and practices, but those institutional relations are not necessarily homologies for a larger network of social relations. Nor does their reproduction guarantee the reproduction of that larger social system.[7]

6. See Montrose, especially "Celebration and Insinuation," 4–7, 21–22, 29; "Elizabethan Subject," 319–21; and "Of Gentlemen and Shepherds," 421–33. See also Attridge, "Puttenham's Perplexity," 269–70; Crewe, *Hidden Designs*, 19–34; Greenblatt, *Renaissance Self-Fashioning*, 182–92; Helgerson, "New Poet Presents Himself," 893–97, 900–902, 907–8; Plett, "Aesthetic Constituents," especially 597, 612; and Frank Whigham, *Ambition and Privilege: The Social Tropes of Elizabethan Courtesy Theory* (Berkeley: University of California Press, 1984), especially 1–62.

7. See Louis Althusser, "Ideology and Ideological State Apparatuses (Notes towards an

By reinforcing a monolithic notion of social struggle, critics reaffirm Puttenham's attempt to obscure the relationship between a single institution and the larger society. Riddling disclosure is a form of politic courtliness that reproduces courtly relations and, in the process, offers the court's internal struggles as a model for larger struggles over gender and over class. Puttenham's disclosing participates in larger gender struggles by filtering the contradictory positions assigned to all Renaissance women through Elizabeth's claims for a paradoxical double existence. It participates in larger class struggles by attempting to relocate within the dynamics of the court the threat that social mobility poses to the absolutist state.[8]

Investigation)," in *Lenin and Philosophy and Other Essays*, trans. Ben Brewster (New York: Monthly Review Press, 1971), 127–86. My reading relies on Althusser's definition of ideology and on his description, emphasized in the essay's April 1970 postscript, of the ways in which ideology is realized within institutional rituals and practices and is produced within class struggles that extend beyond any single institution. My notion of social struggle, of course, is not restricted to class struggle; nor is it based on a unified underlying social structure or source of domination. Pierre Bourdieu, in *Outline of a Theory of Practice*, trans. Richard Nice (Cambridge: Cambridge University Press, 1977), and in *Reproduction in Education, Society, and Culture*, trans. Richard Nice (London: Sage Publications, 1977), has stressed the mechanisms that facilitate an institution's reproduction; he has also stressed the distance, due to what Althusser would call the institution's "relative autonomy," between institutional reform and larger social change. I would argue that relative autonomy, social phenomena that exist within several institutions, and shifting configurations of social domination actually suggest that the reproduction of institutions cannot guarantee the reproduction of a larger social structure and its forces of oppression. For further descriptions, by Althusser, of ideology and of the mediated relationship between an ideological institution and the larger social system, see also "Contradiction and Overdetermination: Notes for an Investigation" and "Marxism and Humanism," in *For Marx*, trans. Ben Brewster (London: New Left Books, 1977; London: Verso, 1979), 87–128, 219–47, especially 109–16, 231–36. For a helpful discussion of Althusser, particularly of the 1970 postscript to "Ideology and Ideological State Apparatuses," see Michael Sprinker, *Imaginary Relations: Aesthetics and Ideology in the Theory of Historical Materialism* (London: Verso, 1987), 177–205, 227–36, 267–76.

For explicit references to courtly literature as a site of social struggle, see Stephen Greenblatt, introduction to *Representing the English Renaissance*, ed. Greenblatt (Berkeley: University of California Press, 1988), vii–xiii; Montrose's discussion of *The Shepheardes Calender* as product and production of culture in "Elizabethan Subject," especially 322, 332–33; Montrose's discussion of the shaped and shaping character of *A Midsummer Night's Dream* and of the play's role as a courtly entertainment in "Shaping Fantasies," especially 69–70; Plett, "Aesthetic Constituents," 597–98, 615; and Alan Sinfield, "Power and Ideology: An Outline Theory and Sidney's *Arcadia*," *ELH* 52:2 (Summer 1985): 259–77.

8. Perry Anderson, *Lineages of the Absolutist State* (London: New Left Books, 1974; London: Verso, 1979), 113–42, discusses royal efforts to establish absolute rule in England. He stresses the relatively brief and limited character of English absolutism; it is that limited absolutism to which this chapter refers.

The Laughing Lamenting Spouse

Puttenham depicts women who speak simultaneously yet without contradiction from several traditionally incompatible subject positions and aligns his own politic disclosing with their speech. He is not, in the language of Renaissance criticism, the protean courtier who maintains favor by remaining ambiguous or oscillating or vacillating or suspending himself between two choices or arguing *in utramque partem*.[9] Nor does he construct a voice which claims the autonomy, the centeredness, or the unity whose persistence and spuriousness have been identified as the trademark of that increasingly bourgeois male selfhood which emerged during the Renaissance transition into capitalism.[10] Instead, Puttenham attempts to speak simultaneously from several otherwise discrete positions. He would offer his diverse readership, at any one time, multiple potential points of identification and multiple opportunities to obtain pleasure from his text.[11] Puttenham proposes to speak from a destabilized, decentered subject position not in the name of a radical gender or class politics but as a means of advancing his own position within the court by reinforcing his readers' identities and retaining the status quo.

9. See Montrose, "Celebration and Insinuation," 6, 11, 13; "'Eliza, Queene of shepheardes,'" 160; "Of Gentlemen and Shepherds," 438–40, 443–52; and "'The perfecte paterne of a Poete,'" 47. See also Joel B. Altman, *The Tudor Play of Mind: Rhetorical Inquiry and the Development of Elizabethan Drama* (Berkeley: University of California Press, 1978); Greenblatt, *Renaissance Self-Fashioning*, especially 162–64; Helgerson, "New Poet Presents Himself," 907–8; Hulse, "Stella's Wit," 279–81, 285–86; Javitch, *Poetry and Courtliness*, 1–105; and Plett, "Aesthetic Constituents," 600–607, 610–11, 613.

10. Readings of Renaissance individuality generally are traced to Jacob Burckhardt's 1860 work *The Civilisation of the Renaissance in Italy*. Recent discussions stress either Renaissance authors' attempts to construct the effect of this autonomy, centeredness, and unity (Belsey, Easthope, Ferry, and Greenblatt) or, alternately, the literary "pathos" (Barker and Fineman) inherent when the Renaissance subject is constituted precisely through its nostalgia for that less dispersed selfhood. Neither seems applicable to the courtly simultaneity celebrated within the *Arte*. See Catherine Belsey, *The Subject of Tragedy: Identity and Difference in Renaissance Drama* (London: Methuen, 1985); Antony Easthope, *Poetry as Discourse* (London: Methuen, 1983), especially 94–109; Anne Ferry, *The "Inward" Language: Sonnets of Wyatt, Sidney, Shakespeare, Donne* (Chicago: University of Chicago Press, 1983); Joel Fineman, *Shakespeare's Perjured Eye: The Invention of Poetic Subjectivity in the Sonnets* (Berkeley: University of California Press, 1986); and Greenblatt, *Renaissance Self-Fashioning*, and, more recently, *Shakespearean Negotiations*, especially 1–20. Barker, *Tremulous Private Body*, discusses this as a phenomenon that begins in the seventeenth century.

11. For an analysis of Puttenham's *Arte* which addresses this multiplicity by attending to the historicity of sexuality, see Jonathan Goldberg, *Sodometries: Renaissance Texts, Modern Sexualities* (Stanford: Stanford University Press, 1992), 29–61.

Women are his vehicle for claiming that this sort of simultaneity is possible.

For example, in Puttenham's account, the epithalamion discloses a woman's cry that issues, at once, from two traditionally exclusive positions. The first third of the wedding ritual, which takes place outside the bedroom during the first sexual encounter between bride and groom, occurs only when the bride is a virgin. He explains, "This ceremony was omitted when men maried widowes or such as had tasted the frutes of loue before, (we call them well experienced young women) in whom there was no feare of daunger to their persons, or of any outcry at all, at the time of those terrible approches" (53). Here the physical threat to virginity and the woman's responding cry authorize the ceremony. Yet Puttenham complicates the nature of that cry when he defines the purpose of this first encounter—"the husband to rob his spouse of her maidenhead and saue her life, the bride so lustely to satisfie her husbandes loue and scape with so litle daunger of her person" (52–53). Robbing the bride's maidenhead, as Puttenham's elocution makes clear, demands that she lustily engage in intercourse. The cry of the "laughing lamenting spouse" (51) is, at once, the cry of physical danger and the cry of a desire that has been unfettered by the woman's first sexual partner. That cry marks the coexistence of endangered *virgo* and desiring *mulier*.

Issuing simultaneously from *virgo* and *mulier*, the ritual cry subverts one conventional Renaissance classification of women according to the discrete, successive physiological stages—*virgo, mulier, mater*—in which it is precisely the loss of virginity that defines the woman as *mulier*. The Renaissance woman who claimed most famously to occupy several incompatible stages was, of course, Elizabeth. She spoke simultaneously as *virgo* and *mater* yet never as *mulier* and, invoking an alternate paradigm that defined women according to their marital status, as maid and wife yet never as widow.[12] Like the queen, Puttenham does not dismantle these traditionally discrete categories yet claims for them a paradoxical simultaneity—offering here, for example, a cry that issues, at once, from the physiological *virgo* and the physiological *mulier*. In the end that cry becomes a means of propelling the woman into the third stage, motherhood. "The first embracementes neuer bred barnes, by reason of their ouermuch affection and heate, but onely made passage for children and

---

12. See, for example, Allison Heisch, "Queen Elizabeth I: Parliamentary Rhetoric and the Exercise of Power," *Signs* 1:1 (Autumn 1975): 31–55.

enforced greater liking" (52), Puttenham later explains, borrowing loosely from popular beliefs about gynecology.[13] Here Puttenham retains the original physiological paradigm yet suggests that the groom's terrible approach does not end the woman's existence as *virgo* and initiate her existence as *mulier* but instead provokes a cry that issues at once from those mutually exclusive stages. In short, the terrible approach that conventionally places the woman within a single position along the physiological continuum here destabilizes those positions and allows their simultaneous existence.

The epithalamion, an "ancient guise in old times vsed at weddings" (51), customarily clothes the cry that marks the unwieldy coexistence of endangered *virgo* and desiring *mulier*. That veiling, Puttenham suggests, actually discloses the cry's existence. He describes the first part of the epithalamion:

The first breach was song at the first parte of the night when the spouse and her husband were brought to their bed & at the very chamber dore, where in a large vtter roome vsed to be (besides the musitiēs) good store of ladies or gētlewomen of their kinsefolkes, & others who came to honor the mariage, & the tunes of the songs were very loude and shrill, to the intent there might no noise be hard out of the bed chāber by the skreeking & outcry of the young damosell feeling the first forces of her stiffe & rigorous young man, she being as all virgins tender & weake, & vnexpert in those maner of affaires. For which purpose also they vsed by old nurses (appointed to that seruice) to suppresse the noise by casting of pottes full of nuttes round about the chamber vpon the hard floore or pauemēt, for they vsed no mattes nor rushes as we doe now. So as the Ladies and gentlewomen should haue their eares so occupied what with Musicke, and what with their handes wantonly scambling and catching after the nuttes,

13. See Audrey Eccles, *Obstetrics and Gynaecology in Tudor and Stuart England* (Kent: Kent State University Press, 1982), especially 26–42, 74–85; Thomas Laqueur, "Orgasm, Generation, and the Politics of Reproductive Biology," *Representations* 14 (Spring 1986): 1–41; Angus McLaren, *Reproductive Rituals: The Perception of Fertility in England from the Sixteenth Century to the Nineteenth Century* (London: Methuen, 1984), 13–87; and Ian Maclean, *The Renaissance Notion of Woman: A Study in the Fortunes of Scholasticism and Medical Science in European Intellectual Life* (Cambridge: Cambridge University Press, 1980), 28–46. These authors discuss Renaissance theories of gynecology and obstetrics—including the belief that the couple's first sexual encounter seldom results in pregnancy because one or both have not yet developed strong enough seed and the belief that the virgin must develop a greater desire and capacity for pleasure before her seed is released and is strong enough for procreation.

that they could not intend to harken after any other thing. This was as I said to diminish the noise of the laughing lamenting spouse. (51)

The presence and power of the woman's outcry are confirmed by the musicians who must ritually ward off that sound by enacting it with their loud, shrill music. In order to avoid exposure to the bride's cry of simultaneity, the "Ladies and gentlewomen" outside must attend to its musical surrogate as they ceremonially enact both her sense of endangerment and her wanton desire. The association between the musicians and female auditors, on the one hand, and their counterpart within the chamber, on the other, ends precisely at midnight when, after all the ladies have "gone to their rest," the musicians must "refresh the faint and weried bodies and spirits" (52) of the bridal couple so that they might now engage in the epithalamion's second, less heated procreative embrace.

The bride's initial cry replaces process with simultaneity. The paired tales of Sir Andrew Flamock suggest why the courtier might find that simultaneity attractive. Here Puttenham's riddling disclosure both links the two tales and reveals Flamock's terrible tendency to place his auditor within a single courtly position. In addition, that same riddling disclosure points to another woman, who—in Puttenham's narrative—again speaks simultaneously and yet without contradiction from two traditionally discrete positions. In this way, Puttenham grounds his own riddling form of revelation as a politic alternative to Flamock's. By offering his audience multiple positions from which to obtain pleasure from his text, the disclosing Puttenham assures his own courtly decorum, which "for the delight it bringeth comming towardes vs . . . may be called [*pleasant approche*]" (262).

Puttenham frames the two Flamock tales as a lesson in distinguishing decorous from indecorous scurrility in those "cases whereof no generall rule can be giuen, but are best knowen by example" (268). In the first tale Flamock, standard-bearer for King Henry VIII, follows the king into the park at Greenwich. "The king blew his horne," Puttenham writes. "*Flamock* hauing his belly full, and his tayle at commaundement, gaue out a rappe nothing faintly, that the king turned him about and said how now sirra? *Flamock* not well knowing how to excuse his vnmanerly act, if it please you Sir quoth he, your Maiesty blew one blast for the keeper and I another for his man. . . . So was *Flamocks* action most vncomely, but his speech excellently well becōming the occasion"

(268). Although Flamock's indiscreet "rappe" appears to challenge the hierarchy which placed him at the heels of his king as they entered the park, the standard-bearer enlists his "rappe" in an effort to reinforce that same hierarchy. By pairing the king's blast for the keeper with his for the keeper's man, he decorously claims that even his potentially subversive "rappe" actually occurred at the command not of his belly but of his king.

"But at another time and in another like case," Puttenham explains, "the same skurrillitie of *Flamock* was more offensiue, because it was more indecent" (268). In this second tale the less decorous Flamock scurrilously completes a poem that the king has been composing for his beloved. Puttenham writes:

> The/king . . . being disposed to be merry, said, *Flamock* let vs rime: as well as I can said *Flamock* if it please your grace. The king began thus:
>
> > *Within this towre,*
> > *There lieth a flowre,*
> > *That hath my hart.*
>
> *Flamock* for aunswer: *Within this hower, she will, &c.* with the rest in so vncleanly termes, as might not now become me by the rule of *Decorum* to vtter writing to so great a Maiestie. (268–69)

The phrase "the same skurrillitie of *Flamock*," which introduces this second tale, serves less to link the natures of what are, after all, quite different witticisms than to suggest that readers might replace Puttenham's "*&c.*" with the missing rhyming word if only they remember Flamock's earlier "rappe." Here Puttenham fastidiously circumvents uttering, yet riddlingly discloses, Flamock's obscenely "fastidious aunswer" (269).

When parsing the second tale about Flamock, Puttenham explains that the standard-bearer risked his position at court not simply because he uttered an obscenity in the king's presence but, more precisely, because he endangered Henry's perception that he controlled his own desires. "But the very cause [of the king's anger] in deed," Puttenham writes, "was for that *Flamocks* reply answered not the kings expectation, for the kings rime commencing with a pleasant and amorous propositiō: Sir *Andrew Flamock* to finish it not with loue but with lothsomnesse, by termes very rude and vnciuill, and seing the king greatly fauour that

Ladie for her much beauty by like or some other good partes, by his fastidious aunswer to make her seeme odious to him, it helde a great disproportion to the kings appetite, for nothing is so vnpleasant to a man" (269). Here Flamock not only forces Henry to witness explicitly his lover's comic degradation and to witness her exposure to his servant but, in addition, he forces the king to become an ally in that hostile exposure. Making her "vulgar for all English mens vse" (24), Flamock can no longer speak as an unthreatening and subservient comic figure whose scurrility is decorous because, in Puttenham's words, he "is knowne to be a common iester or buffon, such as take vpon them to make princes merry" (268).[14] Revealing the possibility that power might lie not in wielding the scepter but in wielding wit, the standard-bearer's rhyme is a terrible approach which offers the king a single, and untenable, position and thus labels Flamock a courtly usurper.

Within these paired tales Flamock, who attempts to "please your grace" (268), is no more in control of the effects produced by his witticisms than he is of his initial "rappe." The scurrility in question here— shared by the standard-bearer's decorous and indecorous wit, which defeats Puttenham's attempt to create a general rule for the politic courtier to follow—is the scurrilous form of jokes. Answering not their auditor's expectation, jokes release an energy that inevitably places the auditor in a single and often unpredictable position.[15] For the courtier, that position's decorum or indecorum is determined solely by the eventual reaction of the king.

Refusing "by the rule of *Decorum* to vtter" (269) Flamock's obscenity, Puttenham refuses to utter a joke. This riddling replacement of Flamock's "rappe" also gestures toward another riddling "&c."—one that discloses a speech issuing simultaneously from two otherwise incompatible positions. With that gesture Puttenham attempts to rescue not only his fastidiously careful riddle but, more generally, riddling disclosure and its form of inexplicit revelation from the effects pro-

14. See Sigmund Freud, *Jokes and Their Relation to the Unconscious* (reprinted from *The Standard Edition of the Complete Psychological Works of Sigmund Freud*), trans. and ed. James Strachey (New York: Norton, 1963), 97–102. Freud's own theories about joking assert a notion of simultaneity whose resistance to temporal process, interestingly enough, he grounds with what I have been calling riddling disclosure and, at one juncture, with a riddling "etcetera." See *Jokes*, 41–45.

15. Similarly, Freud defines and categorizes jokes partially according to their effects— the degree of laughter they produce. Here scurrilous jokes figure prominently. See *Jokes*, 17, 82, 92, 96, 117–39.

duced by Flamock's fastidiously scurrilous joking. In the anecdote that precedes the paired tales of Flamock, Puttenham's "&c." replaces an obscenity uttered not by the king's servant but by a princess. He writes:

> A daughter of Fraunce and next heyre generall to the crowne (if the law *Salique* had not barred her) being set in a great chause by some harde words giuen her by another prince of the bloud, said in her anger, thou durst not haue said thus much to me if God had giuē me a paire of, &c./and told all out, meaning if God had made her a man and not a woman she had bene king of Fraunce. The word became not the greatnesse of her person, and much lesse her sex, whose chiefe vertue is shamefastnesse, which the Latines call *Verecundia*, that is a naturall feare to be noted with any impudicitie. (267)

One popular version of Renaissance gynecology taught that the woman's reproductive organs were identical to the man's but internalized. The product of inferior seed—not well-enough heated during procreation—the woman needed her body's extra warmth to keep her organs healthy and their seed fertile. Theoretically, according to Renaissance conflations of gender and sex, excessive heat might externalize those organs.[16] Puttenham writes, of course, not that the woman's anger literally turned her organs outward and made visible a transformation but that she "told all out" (267). Whatever the princess might have meant, Puttenham offers an image neither of biological female nor of biological male but of a woman whose speech not only issues from but actually summons forth their simultaneity. Like the disclosing courtier— who implies but refuses to state explicitly—she maintains her precarious double existence precisely because she is not explicitly "noted with any impudicitie" (267).

In his conclusion to the *Arte*'s second book, Puttenham refers to Aesop's tale of the rattlemouse—or bat—in order to define the courtly advantages of that sort of simultaneity. After describing the courtier Philino's oracular riddling disclosure, Puttenham explains that

16. See Eccles, *Obstetrics and Gynaecology*, 26–44, 74–85; Laqueur, "Politics of Reproductive Biology," especially 4–16; Maclean, *Renaissance Notion of Woman*, 28–46, especially 38–39; and Hilda Smith, "Gynecology and Ideology in Seventeenth-Century England," in *Liberating Women's History: Theoretical and Critical Essays*, ed. Berenice A. Carroll (Urbana: University of Illinois Press, 1976), 97–114.

howsoeuer the oracle had bene construed, he could not haue receiued blame nor discredit. . . . [A]nd so by this meane *Philino* serued all turnes and shifted himselfe from blame, not vnlike the tale of the Rattlemouse who in the warres proclaimed betweene the foure footed beasts, and the birdes, beyng sent for by the Lyon to be at his musters, excused himselfe for that he was a foule and flew with winges: and beyng sent for by the Eagle to serue him, sayd that he was a foure footed beast, and by that craftie cauill escaped the danger of the warres, and shunned the seruice of both Princes. (135–36)

It would be more than one hundred years after the *Arte*'s publication before John Ray, somewhat hesitantly, would decide whether bats were birds or beasts by classifying them as the only mammals known to fly.[17] Both flying and moving quickly on four legs, bats, like courtiers, avoid danger by uttering incompatible claims that emerge not from an oscillation between traditionally discrete positions but from an ability to inhabit these positions simultaneously. Puttenham's riddling disclosures offer his courtly readers, at any one time, an opportunity for multiple and shifting identifications.

In addition, because Puttenham aligns his courtly simultaneity with women's speech, his riddling also participates in gender struggles that extend beyond the court. Catherine Belsey has argued that the contradictory legal positions assigned to women in both the Renaissance state and the Renaissance family left them no single recognized voice with which to speak. She reminds us, for example, that married women were defined as children who had no rights to property and as adults who were required to answer alone for their crimes; they were mothers who shared equally with their husbands the rule over their children and also wives who, like the children, were ruled by those husbands. In short, women were expected to inhabit simultaneously positions whose logics were mutually exclusive—positions, then, that could actually be inhabited only discontinuously, and whose coexistence would produce contradictions. She concludes that any explicit acknowledgment of women's contradictory existence threatened to expose the precariousness of male claims to stability, autonomy, and unity. As a result, authors often consigned women to silence or represented their radically discontinuous

17. See Glover Morrill Allen, *Bats* (Cambridge: Harvard University Press, 1940), 3–13, and John E. Hill and James D. Smith, *Bats in Natural History* (Austin: University of Texas Press, 1984), 161, 182. Bats are still classified as the only known flying mammal.

speech—the lived effect of their multiple and incompatible subject positions—as incoherent or morally duplicitous.[18]

I want to extend Belsey's observations, first, by emphasizing that the incompatible positions assigned to Renaissance women are both a reinforcement and a lived effect of their oppression and, second, by suggesting that Renaissance representations of women attempt to prevent an experience of subordination from becoming an awareness of oppression. Such an awareness would make palpable not only that the subordination of women to men is neither "natural" nor logically coherent but, in addition, that it is a construct which unevenly distributes benefits to and unevenly oppresses its gendered subjects. That awareness, I caution, is a condition for political action yet guarantees neither the existence nor the efficacy of that action.[19]

Within this paradigm, Puttenham's politic disclosures rewrite the lived incompatibilities and impossibilities—the uncomfortably contradictory and discontinuous nature—of Renaissance women's existence as an experience of simultaneity. His own tale of the rattlemouse is an emblem of that rewriting. When Puttenham refers to the legendary battle between beasts and birds, he rewrites Aesop's popular tale in which the bat's lack

18. Belsey, *Subject of Tragedy*, 149–91. For a slightly different argument, which emphasizes that a brief opening for subversion occurs when the sixteenth-century public or dynastic marriage is unsettled and the seventeenth-century private nuclear family is not yet consolidated, see Belsey's "Disrupting Sexual Difference: Meaning and Gender in the Comedies," in *Alternative Shakespeares*, ed. John Drakakis (London: Methuen, 1985), 166–90. Ann Rosalind Jones, "Nets and Bridles: Early Modern Conduct Books and Sixteenth-Century Women's Lyrics," in *The Ideology of Conduct: Essays on Literature and the History of Sexuality*, ed. Nancy Armstrong and Leonard Tennenhouse (New York: Methuen, 1987), 39–72, discusses the contradictions inherent in the feminine ideal that was celebrated by the poet-courtiers of Renaissance Italy: "The metaphors and paradoxes of love poetry, its nets of desire and silent eloquence, produce a model that few women readers could have put into practice. Guazzo's reverie reveals the tensions built into court life between the call for women's purity and the flirtatious volubility they were expected to provide for their male companions" (48).

19. For the distinction between relations of subordination and oppression (and domination), I rely on Ernesto Laclau and Chantal Mouffe, *Hegemony and Socialist Strategy: Towards a Radical Democratic Politics* (London: Verso, 1985), 152–59. Here Laclau and Mouffe suggest that, beginning roughly with the French Revolution, the notion of organizing societies around the category of democracy suggested that equality and liberty were "natural" goals. Acting, in their words, as a "fermenting agent," discourses of equality often made palpable the oppression inhering within relations of subordination. For a discussion of Renaissance pro-women discourses of equality, and the limited opportunity for political change that they offered, see Constance Jordan, *Renaissance Feminism: Literary Texts and Political Models* (Ithaca: Cornell University Press, 1990), 286–307.

of a single place results from, rather than enables, its attempt to avoid danger. In 1484, William Caxton translated and published an edition of Aesop's fables whose tale of warfare among the birds and beasts describes the punishment inflicted on a duplicitous woman. There a bird, the bat, deserts her fellow birds because she believes that the beasts will prevail. "And for the treason that the backe [bat] made," Aesop explains, "she was condempned to never see the day / and never flee but only by nyght / And also she was despoylled of alle her fethers." Punished for her inconstancy, the bat becomes not, like the "rattlemouse" Philino, a doubly placed creature, both bird and beast, but a creature placed in dark exile, neither entirely feathery bird nor flightless beast. Aesop moralizes: "None may doo no good to two lordes at ones / whiche ben contrary one to that other."[20] In Puttenham's version, the rattlemouse avoids the danger of serving either lord only by converting his female predecessor's lack of any coherent position into a simultaneously held multiplicity of positions.

I do not mean to suggest that Puttenham directly addresses the particular instances of lived contradiction and discontinuity which are central to Renaissance women's oppression. Irresolvably incompatible definitions of authority, for example, applied to the woman who was both a parent in the physiological paradigm of *virgo, mulier,* and *mater* and a wife in the marital paradigm of maid, wife, and widow. When the *Arte's* bride cries out simultaneously as both *virgo* and *mulier,* she might be overturning the first of these paradigms, but she is not crying from two incompatible positions whose coexistence was actually expected of women. Yet, as Belsey's own examples demonstrate, the Renaissance representation of incoherent and duplicitous women does not confine itself to depicting the particular contradictory and discontinuous positions that women actually were forced to inhabit. Like his contemporaries, Puttenham addresses that gendered social structure more generally; unlike his contemporaries, he does so by creating female voices that are able to issue simultaneously from several otherwise incompatible positions and are able to maintain that simultaneity without dismantling those positions. The bride's cry as endangered *virgo* and desiring *mulier,* for example, retains both the woman's virginity and her heated or even errant desire. Both female virginity and female desire were categories that conventionally reinforced patrilineal descent, safeguarded patrimony,

20. Aesop, *Fabulae,* trans. William Caxton in 1484; reprint, *Caxton's Aesop,* ed. R. T. Lenaghan (Cambridge: Harvard University Press, 1967), 107.

and cemented marriage, especially during the renewed vigor of debates over divorce in the 1590s.[21] And the androgynous princess—angered by her inability to succeed to the throne under the conveniently "other" Salic law—speaks simultaneously as man and woman yet challenges neither category. By definition unrepresentable, the princess's androgyny approaches, yet avoids, the fixed image of a hermaphrodite—the woman with visible male genitalia.

Moreover, Puttenham's inexplicit image of the androgynous princess suggests not a lack of sexual differentiation but a woman whose simultaneous existence as man and woman actually fulfills her gender's apparently contradictory imperatives. In keeping with Renaissance legal writing, Puttenham defines women as possessing *verecundia*—a Latin term which suggests that they paradoxically exist, at once, as shamefaced women and as instances of that very shamefulness to which their modesty is opposed.[22] Within the *Arte's* narratives, men—the groom with his "terrible approches" (53) and the prince with his "harde words" (267)—elicit women's voices that express this reassuring paradoxical simultaneity. Puttenham's riddling disclosures enact that same sort of simultaneity. In this way, his politic courtliness belies women's lived discontinuities and, in so doing, elides their oppression under Renaissance patriarchy.

As my earlier discussion of the *Arte's* first chapter implies, not all of Puttenham's disclosures refer specifically to women or to simultaneity, yet Puttenham figures each use of riddling disclosure as the simultaneous clothing and stripping of Elizabeth. Through this figure, riddling disclosure itself is grounded with a woman—the queen—who speaks simultaneously from incompatible positions. The importance of

21. See, for example, Belsey, *Subject of Tragedy*, 129–48, 185; Eccles, *Obstetrics and Gynaecology*, especially 76–84; Martin Ingram, *Church Courts, Sex, and Marriage in England, 1570–1640* (Cambridge: Cambridge University Press, 1987), 144–50; McLaren, *Reproductive Rituals*, especially 16–27, 38–42, 49–50, 60, 66, 78; Maclean, *Renaissance Notion of Woman*, especially 14–15, 19–22, 29; Smith, "Gynecology and Ideology," 104–5; and Williamson, *Patriarchy of Shakespeare's Comedies*, 32–53.

22. *Verecundia* is defined both as "*the natural feeling of shame*, by whatever cause produced, *shamefastness, bashfulness, shyness, coyness, modesty*" and, "with an implication of censure," as "*over-shyness, bashfulness, sheepishness, timidity*." In keeping with this latter definition, *verecundia* can actually refer to a "*shame*" or "*disgrace*" (*A Latin Dictionary: Founded on Andrew's Edition of Freund's Latin Dictionary*, revised by Charlton T. Lewis and Charles Short [Oxford: Clarendon Press, 1879]). See also Maclean, *Renaissance Notion of Woman*, 78, for a brief discussion of the Renaissance legal implications of what he calls "the (quasi-)virtue of *verecundia* or shame."

Puttenham's clothing and stripping will become clearer if we turn briefly
to Elizabeth's use of the doctrine of the king's two bodies. Responding to
challenges to her female rule, Elizabeth invoked that doctrine when she
claimed for herself a fantastically double existence as "one Bodye natu-
rallye Considered though by his [God's] permission a Bodye Politique to
Governe." According to the logic of the king's two bodies, at the moment
of the monarch's death, the perpetual body politic passes into the natural body of the genealogical successor, where it will continually wash
away any imperfections that might otherwise weaken the successor's ability to rule—imperfections, for example, of youth and age, of gender
and foreign citizenship. Always an adaptable doctrine at best, the notion
of a body politic and a body natural was instrumental not only in reinforcing Elizabeth's royal control but also in justifying her father's appro-
priation of church land, in strengthening the authority of the young
Edward, in claiming the throne for the Scottish Mary, and in ensuring
the passage of the throne to James. Yet in her speeches Elizabeth underscored, as her male counterparts did not, her weak and imperfect body
natural. She stressed that she existed simultaneously as a woman who
was subject to the authority of men and, by the greater authority of God,
as a monarch whose corporate body transcended the limitations of any
individual and encompassed the nation and its citizens. Clothed within
the *Arte*, then, Elizabeth is a governing figure of royal authority who is
"more beautiful than the natural"; stripped, she is a naturally naked
body that is never quite available for our consideration. Gender concerns inflected not only her emphasis on the body natural but also the
nature of its transcended limitations. In defending her female rule, for
example, Elizabeth claimed that she was simultaneously a passive virgin
mother on whom the "burthen" of rule had fallen, an unmarried maid,
and a wife in that marriage of "Rulinge" and "Service" which promises to
comfort the citizen "posteritye."[23]

23. Heisch, "Queen Elizabeth I," 33. Marcus, "Shakespeare's Comic Heroines," also
emphasizes Elizabeth's gendered articulation of the "king's two bodies." Yet she discusses
the queen's stress on her naturally weak female body and her claim to a male, often
"princely," body politic. Elizabeth certainly does make that claim; for the purposes of this
chapter, however, I am interested in her alternate claim that her body politic, the corporate
body which authorizes her rule, allows the coexistence of a naturally weak female with a
transformed, unwieldy woman. For a discussion of the doctrine of the king's two bodies
and of Elizabeth's inflection of that doctrine, see Marie Axton, *The Queen's Two Bodies:
Drama and the Elizabethan Succession* (London: Swift Printers for the Royal Historical Society,
1977), 11–37. For rhetoric emphasizing Elizabeth's weak natural body and rhetoric empha-

Critics generally suggest that courtiers, made anxious by Elizabeth's rule, either minimized her unwieldy transcendence of conventional womanliness or celebrated her unwieldiness as the exception that proved the gender rule.[24] Yet within the *Arte*, the queen's double existence grounds Puttenham's own riddling disclosures, and individual instances of that courtly practice construct, as their local ground, women whose fantastic simultaneity is modeled on her claims. By insistently filtering all women's sexuality through the royal discourse of Elizabeth, Puttenham's courtliness transforms the contradictory and discontinuous positions assigned to women within Renaissance patriarchy into reassuringly unwieldy cases of simultaneity.

With Elizabeth's doubleness we also return to another feature of the *Arte*'s first chapter—the uneasy relationship between the disclosing poet and the queen. Although disclosure has seemed to enable a politic simultaneity that would serve the courtier Puttenham well, the image of clothing and stripping suggests that each use of that riddling form also threatens Elizabeth and thereby endangers his position within the court.

The Manner of Life of a Craftsman

In order to analyze that threat, we must first examine the relationship between riddling—as defined by Puttenham—and the gesture that I have been calling riddling disclosure. Although I have focused on the *Arte*'s characteristic disclosures, the rhetorical gesture that Puttenham actually *recommends* to courtiers is not disclosure, which he associates with Elizabeth's royal authority, but dissemblance—the ability to "speake otherwise then we thinke" (186). Puttenham lists riddling as a version of that dissemblance:

---

sizing her unwieldy womanliness, see also Heisch, "Queen Elizabeth I," 32, 34–39, 54–55; Montrose, "Shaping Fantasies," 66–67, 79–81; and speeches excerpted or reprinted by J. E. Neale in *Elizabeth I and Her Parliaments, 1559–1581* (London: Jonathan Cape, 1953), 107–9, 126–27, 364–67, and in *Elizabeth I and Her Parliaments, 1584–1601* (London: Jonathan Cape, 1957), 126–29, 391.

24. See Montrose, "Elizabethan Subject," 309, and "Shaping Fantasies," especially 77–84. See also Greenblatt, *Shakespearean Negotiations*, 69; Marcus, "Shakespeare's Comic Heroines," 137–39, 146–48; Peter Stallybrass, "Patriarchal Territories: The Body Enclosed," in Ferguson, Quilligan, and Vickers, *Rewriting the Renaissance*, 123–42, especially 128–32; and Tennenhouse, *Power on Display*, 102–3.

We dissemble againe vnder couert and darke speaches, when/we speake by way of riddle (*Enigma*) of which the sence can hardly be picked out, but by the parties owne assoile, as he that said:

> *It is my mother well I wot,*
> *And yet the daughter that I begot.*

Meaning it by the ise which is made of frozen water, the same being molten by the sunne or fire, makes water againe.

My mother had an old womā in her nurserie, who in the winter nights would put vs forth many pretty ridles, whereof this is one:

> *I haue a thing and rough it is*
> *And in the midst a hole Iwis:*
> *There came a yong man with his ginne,*
> *And he put it a handfull in.*

The good old Gentlewoman would tell vs that were children how it was meant by a furd glooue. Some other naughtie body would peraduenture haue construed it not halfe so mannerly. (188)

Here the first riddle is an example of one sort of dissemblance in which all meaning is "couert and darke" (186) or inaccessible. The nurse's riddle, paired with her lesson to the children, is an example of a more representative sort of dissemblance in which the "wordes beare contrary countenaunce to th'intent" (186). Puttenham's presentation of that riddle and its never entirely exposed author, however, is an example of riddling disclosure in which he maintains a precarious coexistence of several meanings by drawing attention to an interpretation he refuses to utter.

Philino's oracle similarly functions not as riddling or dissembling but, instead, as riddling disclosure. When the honest but naive Polemon arrives at court and asks the courtier Philino how best to obtain the king's favor, Philino

brings him into a place where behind an arras cloth hee himselfe spake in manner of an Oracle in these meeters. . . .

> *Your best way to worke—and marke my words well,*
> *Not money: nor many,*
> *Nor any: but any,*
> *Not weemen, but weemen beare the bell.*

(135)

Understandably unsure of the oracle's meaning, Polemon "conceyued in his head the pleasanter construction, and stacke to it" (135). Puttenham explains to his readers the riddle's possible constructions: "And the sub-tiltie lay in the accent and Ortographie of these two words [*any*] and [*weemen*] for [*any*] being deuided sounds [*a nie* or *neere* person to the king: and [*weemen*] being diuided soundes *wee men*, and not [*weemen*]" (135). Presumably, then, Polemon imposes his own "pleasanter" interpretation—that "weemen beare the bell" or carry off the prize—when he offers his eighteen-year-old daughter for inspection to Philino and the lords who, "perceiuing her great beauty and other good parts, brought her to the King, to whom she exhibited her fathers supplica-tion, and found so great fauour in his eye, as without any long delay she obtained her sute at his hands" (135). Not surprisingly, even when wom-en "beare the bell," it is men, in the end, who carry off the prize: Pole-mon obtains his suit and Philino a promised reward. In order to make sense of Philino's actions, we must remember that Puttenham ostensibly draws this anecdote from his comedy *Ginecocratia*, in which a king, ruled by his attraction to women, makes himself womanly. Although Philino cannot guarantee that Polemon's daughter will succeed, he is neverthe-less more likely to receive his reward if Polemon sends a woman to persuade the king. Puttenham emphasizes both the doubleness of the riddle and its attempt to elicit Polemon's "pleasanter construction" when he explains, "For euery waies it would haue proued true, whether *Pole-mons* daughter had obtayned the sute, or not obtained it" (135). The line *"Not money: nor many"* (135) establishes a pattern which suggests that Polemon might conclude the oracle, "Nor a nie: but any, / Not wee men: but weemen beare the bell." The oracle, then, is a riddling disclosure that speaks at once from several positions yet suggests one particularly pleasurable meaning which it refuses to utter.

Why does the *Arte* recommend riddling, or dissemblance, and yet enact what I call riddling disclosure? Puttenham identifies Elizabeth with a rhetorical figure that he calls "Gorgious." "Gorgious" is the figure of the queen's beautiful countenance and of the riddling disclosures whose distance from her earlier politic dissemblance reveals her royal authority. Throughout the *Arte*, Puttenham characteristically usurps the queen's gorgeous authority by moving from the politic dissemblance he advocates to the royal disclosure he enacts. Nor is he a lone overreacher; all poet-courtiers, he maintains, usurp the queen's gorgeous figure. However indirect the revelations within his riddling disclosures and

however multiple the positions offered to his readers, each use of riddling disclosure is itself a direct commitment to subversion. Yet, as I will
demonstrate, when Puttenham and his fellow poet-courtiers usurp Elizabeth's courtly power, they actually reassert the power of the absolutist
state. Through an elaborately tangled relationship between craftsmen
and poet-courtiers, Puttenham relocates the threat which social mobility
poses *to* the absolutist state as a threat which arises *within* and is restricted
to the court. Because he figures that courtly threat as the poet's imitation
of the queen's gorgeous countenance, each instance of riddling
disclosure—whatever its local function—not only usurps Elizabeth's authority but also, in the process, relocates threatening social mobility within the politics of courtliness. Here Puttenham attempts to transform a
struggle among classes into a struggle between courtiers and their
queen.

In order to understand that process of relocation, we first must turn
briefly to the politics of social mobility at court—a politics expressed best
by the ambivalent implications of singularity. During the Renaissance,
singularity implied the uniqueness and solitude that characterized a
public position of superiority and also the privateness that accompanied
being denied a government position.[25] Associating singularity not only
with visible signs of class superiority but also with a visible attempt to
move between class boundaries, Puttenham writes that singular conduct
is "as for one man to march or iet in the street more stately, or to looke
more solēpnely, or to go more gayly & in other coulours or fashioned
garmēts then another of the same degree and estate" (287). Yet, as he
admits in the tale of Dinocrates (287–88), when royalty sanctions an
attempt at social elevation, such singularity loses any taint of overreaching. Within the tale, royal authorization transforms singularity into a
sign of the courtier's natural, if previously unrecognized, distance from
former peers. The politics of courtly social mobility depends on an economy of control between courtiers and royalty in which prudent courtiers
decorously dissemble their portion of that control.

Dissemblance allows the poet-courtier to appear singularly worthy
of advancement while avoiding the dangers of visibly attempted and
*un*sanctioned social mobility—the self-authorized singularity—which

25. *The Oxford English Dictionary* defines "singular" both as "unique, . . . separate from
others by reason of superiority or pre-eminence, distinguished, notable" and as "alone,
solitary, . . . peculiar, strange, odd, . . . holding no office, having no special position"—all
in use in sixteenth-century England.

would, in its threat to royal control, risk a singularly private exclusion from royal favor and public office. Like the printer who writes the *Arte's* prefatory address, the poet-courtier, offering a "vewe of this mine impression (a feat of mine owne simple facultie)," risks making an impression without being able to dissemble the impression of its craft. Puttenham warns the poet that "being now lately become a Courtier he shew not himself a crafts man, & merit to be disgraded, & with scorne sent back againe to the shop, or other place of his first facultie and calling, but that so wisely & discreetly he behaue himselfe as he may worthily retaine the credit of his place, and profession of a very Courtier, which is in plaine termes, cunningly to be able to dissemble" (299). Here he advises that courtly poets dissemble their humble beginnings and the unnatural craft with which they obtained their current social positions.

Yet although he *advises* the courtier to dissemble, to "speake one thing and thinke another . . . that our wordes and our meanings meete not" (186), Puttenham—like the printer who reveals but avoids stating explicitly that his patron is as much a craftsman as he—actually *proceeds* not by concealing but, instead, by disclosing yet refusing to utter explicitly the terms that would complete his transparent riddles. As I suggested earlier, by moving from the dissemblance he advocates to the disclosure he enacts, Puttenham ritually usurps the queen's gorgeous authority. Puttenham dubs "Gorgious" the "last and principall figure of our poeticall Ornament" and reserves that figure for the queen and for her verse— "her selfe beyng the most bewtifull" (247). The name "Gorgious," Puttenham explains, is transferred from those "polishers of marble or porphirite, who after it is rough hewen & reduced to that fashiō they will, do set vpon it a goodly glasse, so smoth and cleere as ye may see your face in it, or otherwise as it fareth by the bare and naked body, which being attired in rich and gorgious apparell, seemeth to the common vsage of th'eye much more comely & bewtifull then the naturall" (247). Describing the queen's "Gorgious" poetry, he continues, "And this was the occasion: our soueraigne Lady perceiuing how by the Sc. Q. residence within this Realme at so great libertie and ease . . . bred secret factions among her people. . . . The Queene our soueraigne Lady to declare that she was nothing ignorāt in those secret practizes, though she had long with great wisdome and pacience *dissembled it*, writeth this ditty most sweet and sententious, *not hiding* from all such aspiring minds the daunger of their ambition and disloyaltie" (247–48, my emphases). Like the printed abbreviation for "Scottish Queen," the ditty that reveals Elizabeth's long-dissembled knowledge and power is itself a riddling disclosure which suggests but refuses to state either the nature of the English subjects' ambition or the object of their loyalty. As I have also suggested, "Gorgious" is the figure of the queen's beautiful countenance and of the poetic disclosures whose *distance* from her earlier politic dissemblance reveals her control over her subjects and thus empowers her royal countenancing. By enacting her movement from politic dissemblance to royal disclosure, Puttenham ritually usurps that control. Yet all poet-courtiers usurp the queen's countenance. By demanding that poets not "follow the steps, and maner of life of a craftes man, shepheard or sailer" (41), poetic decorum actually guarantees their Homeric "following and counterfeyting" (304) of royalty's "speeches, countenance and maners" (4). Poets routinely usurp the queen's "most bewtifull and gorgious" (247) figure and the royal power which that figure authorizes.

Riddling disclosure was actually one strategy by which Elizabeth negotiated with Parliament throughout her reign. And as Puttenham implies, riddling disclosure became prominent as she attempted to retain her personal power and to assert the absolute power of the monarch during the arrest, trial, and execution of Mary, Queen of Scots, in the years immediately prior to the *Arte*'s publication in 1589. Between 1584 and 1586, Elizabeth spoke repeatedly to Parliament—carefully revising her speeches for delivery and for their supposedly accidental public circulation. Her revisions display a careful circumspection that habitually reveals without explicitly stating. In November 1586, between Mary's trial and her execution, while the Scottish queen's fate remained uncertain, Elizabeth addressed the controversies surrounding her cousin: "I have Griued more this day then euer in my life whither I shold speake or vse silence. If I speake and not complaine I shall dissemble, If I hold my peace your labor taken weare ful vaine. For me to make my mone weare strange and rare . . . : Yet such I protest hath bene my greedie desire and hungry will, that of your consultation might haue falne out some other meanes to work my saftie ioyned with youre assurance (then that for which Youe are become so ernest suitors) as I protest I must needes vse complaint." In an earlier draft of the speech, Elizabeth had asked if she should "hold my peace." Here she also asks if she should "vse silence." The revision emphasizes her royal authority by maintaining that even her earlier silence was not simply restraint but a politic dissembling which she now admits was used, and useful, for a time. Yet her decision to abandon that silence is not a decision to speak out but, more precisely, a decision to disclose—to refer to "that for which Youe are become so ernest suitors" without explicitly mentioning either her cousin's execution or the Bond of Association with which Parliament sought to obtain for itself the royal authority necessary to assassinate traitors such as Mary and to rule England during an interregnum should attempts on Elizabeth's life prove successful.[26]

In the *Arte*'s final chapter, Puttenham uses a complicated system of shifting affiliations between courtier and craftsman in order to rewrite the threat *to* absolutism as the courtly poet's threatening embrace of Elizabeth's royal disclosure. After he initially warns the dissembling poet-courtier to "shew not himself a crafts man" (299), Puttenham relegates to foreign courtiers the dissemblance of "not onely his countenances & cōceits, but also all his ordinary actions of behauiour" (300). He restricts his English courtier to poetic dissemblance: "We doe allow our Courtly Poet to be a dissembler only in the subtilties of his arte: that is, when he is most artificiall, so to disguise and cloake it as it may not appeare, nor seeme to proceede from him by any studie or trade of rules, but to be his naturall" (302). Adding that he actually wants to avoid "irkesome" and "schollerly affectation," Puttenham qualifies even this restricted dissemblance. "For all that our maker may not be in all cases restrayned," he writes, "but that he may both vse, and also manifest his arte to his great praise, and need no more be ashamed thereof, than a shomaker to haue made a cleanly shoe, or a Carpenter to haue buylt a faire house" (302–3). First, Puttenham warns socially mobile poets to dissemble both their humble background among craftsmen and the craft that secured their social advancement. Then he condemns as foreign or scholarly this *nonpoetic* dissembling of the socially mobile courtier even as he domesticates, as constitutive of poetry, an artistry whose announcement celebrates the once-dissembled link between poets and laboring artisans. By celebrating that link, Puttenham divorces craftsmen from the foreigners and scholars with whom they once shared an exclusion from the court and its poetry.

Earlier in the *Arte*, defining ideal poetic language by its sociogeographic inclusion in the urban English court, Puttenham had banished not only the speech of foreigners or affected scholars but also the speech of dwellers in marshes and outlying villages and the speech "of a

---

26. See Heisch, "Queen Elizabeth I," 45–54. These versions of Elizabeth's speech are quoted by Heisch (52).

craftes man or carter, or other of the inferiour sort, though he be inhabitant or bred in the best towne and Citie in this Realme" (144). Like their counterparts, these craftsmen signaled the limits not only of the court's generosity but, increasingly, of English absolutism. Printed in 1589, Puttenham's *Arte* emerged during an era in which social mobility was marked by a relative decline in aristocratic wealth, an increase in social differentiation among peasants and craftsmen, and an increase in wealth and landholding not only among gentry but also among yeomen and merchants, who often acceded to the status of gentlemen. Within this unstable social system, urban craftsmen actually designated both free and unfree laborers—free laborers referring both to the wealthier craftsmen who operated shops and to the wage laborers whom they employed. For contemporaries, the ambiguity of the category underscored not only social mobility itself but also the economic shifts which both enabled that mobility and threatened absolutism's control. In his 1577 *An Historical Description of the Island of Britain*, for example, William Harrison writes, "We in England divide our people commonly into four sorts, gentlemen, citizens or burgesses, yeoman, and artificers or laborers." Within the *Description*, however, he identifies laborers, alternately, with all artificers and with only "the common sort of artificers." In his revised and expanded 1587 edition of this work, Harrison amends his sentence from "yeoman, *and* artificers or laborers" to "yeoman, *which are* artificers" (my emphases). In addition, for Harrison, artificers—or craftsmen—summon up not only their own ambiguous, shifting social status but also, by their very multiplication, the royal economic policies that, established "to the great gain and commodity of our merchants," grant merchants social mobility and help to create market alliances. After initially grouping merchants among citizens and burgesses, Harrison corrects himself parenthetically, "although they [merchants] often change estate with gentlemen as gentlemen do with them, by a mutual conversion of one into the other."[27]

Social mobility among Elizabethan craftsmen and merchants was somewhat more restricted than contemporary accounts suggest. Labor-

27. William Harrison printed his *An Historical Description of the Island of Britain* in 1577. In 1587 he printed a revised and expanded version—reserving the original title for the new edition's first book and calling its second and third books *The Description of England*. See Harrison's "Of Degrees of People in the Commonwealth of England," in *The Description of England*, ed. Georges Edelen (Ithaca: Cornell University Press for the Folger Shakespeare Library, 1968), 94–123. Edelen describes Harrison's 1587 revisions of the 1577 version of this text. Quotations appear on 94, 94 n. 2, 117, 116, 115.

ing craftsmen who were not master artisans and shop owners, for example, had little opportunity to advance their positions, and merchants
who were connected with London companies were far more likely to
benefit from Elizabeth's policies than their less fortunate counterparts.
Nor was there always an obvious parallel between the fortunes of merchants and those of craftsmen; as the two groups consistently vied for
economic control, Elizabeth's policies generally enabled merchants to
emerge victorious. Nonetheless craftsmen did symbolize a very real increase in social mobility, and the distinctions among craftsmen—
determined by a combination of freedom and wealth—actually underscored the urban economy's growing distance from the crown's feudal
ethic of service and obligation. Forming market ties with merchants and
gentry, craftsmen became increasingly resentful of the fines, monopo-
lies, tolls, and taxes by which the crown continued to extract surplus
from direct producers and, as contemporaries unfailingly noted, increasingly sympathetic to the Puritan rejection of absolute royal authority.[28] Whatever the local intent of Elizabeth's policies, her economic support of merchants partially enabled, first, an increase in social mobility—
including that of craftsmen—and, eventually, the creation of new ave-
nues of social advancement and new criteria for designating social position. As this discussion suggests, social mobility was one symptom of a
more general threat to the absolutist state. Puttenham's riddling disclosures attempt to disarm that threat. By advising that poet-courtiers no
longer dissemble the link between themselves and craftsmen, Puttenham
subsumes those representative laborers within the world of courtly
artistry—ending their exclusion *from* the court so that he might reinstate
them *within* royal control.

    Finally, Puttenham inscribes *within* the announced artistry of the poet-
craftsman the founding distinction *between* the newly domesticated

28. Anderson, *Lineages*, 113–42; Alan Everitt, "Social Mobility in Early Modern England," *Past and Present* 33 (April 1966): 56–73; Christopher Hill, *The World Turned Upside
Down: Radical Ideas during the English Revolution* (Aldershot, Hants.: Maurice Temple Smith,
1972; Harmondsworth, Middlesex: Penguin Books, 1975), 13–56, 287–305; R. J. Holton,
The Transition from Feudalism to Capitalism (New York: St. Martin's Press, 1985); Lawrence
Stone, *The Causes of the English Revolution, 1529–1642* (New York: Harper and Row, 1972),
58–117, and "Social Mobility in England, 1500–1700," *Past and Present* 33 (April 1966):
16–55; and George Unwin, *Industrial Organization in the Sixteenth and Seventeenth Centuries*
(Oxford: Clarendon Press, 1904; reprint, New York: Augustus M. Kelley, 1963), 1–125.
See also *The Transition from Feudalism to Capitalism* (London: New Left Books, 1976; Lon-
don: Verso, 1978), especially essays by Maurice Dobb, Christopher Hill, Rodney Hilton,
Eric Hobsbawm, and John Merrington.

craftsmen and crafty foreign courtiers. That inscription now implies that a threat arises neither from laboring craftsmen nor from within foreign courts but from the courtly social mobility of the English poet. Discussing the four components of any verse project, Puttenham writes that "because our maker or Poet is to play many parts and not one alone . . . it is not altogether with him as with the crafts man, nor altogither otherwise then with the crafts man" (306). Reminding the reader that the English poet-courtier is, in some cases, restricted to *poetic* dissemblance, he initially relies on a straightforward division between the craftsman's announced artistry and the dissembler's concealed artistry. Creating metrics, fashioning a poem, and uttering figures to please and delight—these are tasks that demand the poet-craftsman's announced artistry, he implies. But the fourth verse component, devising a subject, demands *poetic* dissemblance and will be "most admired when he [the poet] is most naturall and least artificiall" (307). Yet Puttenham undercuts this straightforward definition of craftsmen when, listing the forms of artistry that poets should announce proudly, he inscribes *within* the craftsman's announced poetic artistry, the distinction *between* craftsmen's labor and foreign courtiers' crafty dissemblance of their own countenances and "ordinary actions of behauiour" (300). Here he distinguishes carpenters, joiners, tailors, and smiths, whose unnatural crafts use nature's products to produce effects contrary to hers, from crafty painters and carvers, whose "bare" imitation counterfeits nature's effects "as the Marmesot doth many countenances and gestures of man" (304). Enabled by nature but proceeding according to an alternate logic, the sanctioned labors of the carpenter, joiner, tailor, and smith parallel the social mobility of the urban artisan, which is fostered by the policies of the absolutist state but also proceeds according to an alternate logic. When these craftsmen resurface once more in the *Arte,* they perform only the uncontroversial task of creating metrics. By contrast, the two remaining verse components—uttering figures to please and delight and fashioning a poem—allow crafty poets to counterfeit royal countenances and, thereby, threaten royal authority from *within* the courtly economy.

When poets utter figures, Puttenham writes, they resemble the rhetorician who "doth as the cunning gardiner that using nature as a coadiutor, furders her conclusions & many times makes her effectes more absolute and straunge" (307).[29] Earlier, listing two forms of gardening

---

29. Here Puttenham locates poet-courtiers within that literary garden terrain from

artistry that poets should announce, Puttenham had distanced rhetoric from the singular gardening which alters and surmounts nature and placed it within the domain of that gardening which simply aids and furthers nature. The courtier's defective natural persuasion, he suggested, is corrected by rhetorical artistry "as th'eye by his spectacle, I say relieued in his imperfection, but not made more perfit then the naturall" (306). There Puttenham defined rhetoric as an announced singular artistry that, founded on the courtier's own insufficiency, risked no overreaching. In his gardening metaphor for uttering figures, however, he collapses the distinction embodied by the earlier rhetorician between, on the one hand, the gardener who reinforces "the causes wherein shee [nature] is impotent and defectiue" (303) and, on the other, the more subversive gardener who alters and even surmounts nature "so as by meanes of it her owne effects shall appeare more beautifull or straunge and miraculous" (303). Making nature "appeare more beautifull" (303), poets apply the ornamental polish which makes the queen "more comely & bewtifull then the naturall" (247) and which allows them to see their faces reflected as gorgeous disclosers in her "goodly glasse" (247). Elizabeth's most gorgeous status is produced by poets at the same time that it enables their self-transformation into gorgeous disclosers. The queen's disclosing figure, itself a copious "masse of many figurative speaches" (247), actually is constituted by a collective of singular courtier figures "all running upon one point & to one intēt" (247). That intent is to impress their disclosing craft upon the queen in order to maintain the impression that subversive social mobility is a courtly affair.

Alluding to the popinjay and marmesot that hover over the "bare immitatour" (304), Puttenham reduces his comments about the final component of verse, fashioning a poem, to a warning against the Homeric telling of another's tale—against the poet's bare imitation of the

---

which authors, over the next half century, would debate royal privilege and social mobility. In so doing, he also offers poets the prerogative that those authors generally would accord to the monarch—an ability to perfect and extend the natural boundaries which govern social class. See Francis Bacon, "Of Gardens," *The Essays,* ed. John Pitcher (Harmondsworth, Middlesex: Penguin, 1985), 197–98, 202; Thomas Browne, *The Garden of Cyrus: or The Quincunciall, Lozenge, or Net-work Plantations of the Ancients, Artificially, Naturally, Mystically Considered,* orig. pub. 1658, reprinted in *The Prose of Sir Thomas Browne,* ed. Norman Endicot (New York: Doubleday, in the Doubleday Anchor Seventeenth-Century Series, 1967; New York: New York University Press, 1968), 295–96; Harrison, *Description of England,* 263–71; and William Shakespeare, *The Winter's Tale,* in *The Riverside Shakespeare,* ed. G. Blakemore Evans (Boston: Houghton Mifflin, 1974), IV.iv.79–108.

queen's gorgeous countenance and manners. When poets usurp Elizabeth's gorgeous countenance and authority, that warning reminds us, they simultaneously undermine their own singular status. By moving from the courtier figure of dissembling allegory to the royal figure of gorgeous disclosing, poets transform themselves from the "chief ringleader and captaine of all other figures" (186) to their embodiment—from a singular appointed position to royalty's most singular position. Yet the poet's crafty imitation of the queen's gorgeous countenance and disclosing manner not only usurps her authority but, in so doing, strips her of her gorgeous garments. Earlier Puttenham compared poetry whose artifice clothes the "lymme" of naked speech until it is "somwhat out of sight" (137) and whose figures are set upon "language by arte, as the embroderer doth his stone and perle, or passements of gold vpon the stuffe of a Princely garment" (138) to "great Madames of honour" (137) who, "if they want their courtly habillements or at leastwise such other apparell as custome and ciuilitie haue ordained to couer their naked bodies, would be halfe ashamed or greatly out of countenaunce" (137). Elizabeth's disclosing figure is the most gorgeous among such "gallant or gorgious" (137) artifices, her countenance the most beautiful among such "comely and bewtifull" (137) madames. When deprived of that singular figure, Elizabeth is, like the unclothed or poorly clothed madames, "out of countenaunce" (137). Stripping the queen by usurping royalty's "gorgious apparell" (247), the poets' naked imitation actually removes the beautiful clothing that is provided by those same poets in the garden of poetic figures and reveals that she is their "rough hewen" (247) construct. In other words, Puttenham's exemplary poet-courtiers—those bare imitators of royal disclosure—strip the queen of her "gorgious apparell" (247) and, in so doing, strip the very polish with which they clothe themselves in the robes of royalty. That stripping unveils their truly unsingular membership among a mass of exposed overreachers.

I am not suggesting that the politic Puttenham performs his courtly duty by usurping Elizabeth's authority and that—subversive only in the service of a mutual desire to reinforce her absolute control—he bows in the end to the impossibility of ever truly obtaining her power without losing his own. That would imply that his disruption of the courtly economy functions unproblematically as merely a clever facade for managing a more genuine social and economic class conflict. Yet uttering figures and fashioning a poem designate neither discrete options among which the politic poet may choose nor discrete stages in a poetic process that ultimately reinforces courtly hierarchies. Instead, Puttenham insists, these poetic components coexist. Poets create the queen as a gorgeous discloser in whose singular image they are reflected. At the same time, disclosing poets strip the queen of her gorgeous figure and are themselves revealed as overreachers. He does not relinquish the position of subversive yet successful discloser which allows him to relocate social mobility within the court. Nor does he relinquish his exposure as an impolitic imitator—an exposure that both endangers his status and reasserts royal control over the courtly economy. Instead, *as a form*, riddling disclosure allows Puttenham to speak simultaneously as a singularly favored courtier and as a singularly endangered overreacher.

Puttenham's double position within the court might make more sense if we remember that his riddling disclosures usurp the queen's gorgeous body politic, a body which is "more comely & bewtifull then the naturall" (247). In order to maintain Elizabeth's royal authority, her gorgeous disclosing must announce that she combines the singularly gorgeous royal body which encompasses the nation and its citizens and the singularly common body of a woman who is naturally subject to male domination. As I suggested earlier, Elizabeth maintains her authority by neither entirely abandoning her body natural nor entirely transforming it. When courtiers usurp her royal form, they simultaneously clothe and strip the queen—creating a royal marble statue, at once polished and unpolished, whose perpetual multiplicity reinforces Elizabeth's rhetoric of the queen's two bodies and, within that rhetoric, her stress on the weakness of her womanly body natural and the unwieldiness of her womanly body politic. And, perhaps, their marble work also supplants that other royal rhetoric—less amenable to Puttenham's needs—with which she gravely fixed herself in a single position, claiming, "And in the end this shalbe for me sufficient that a marble stone shall de[clare, that a] Qu[ene h]aving ra[i]gn[ed such] a time [l]y[ved and] dyed a vargin." Through the logic of simultaneity, then, the disclosing courtier reproduces the courtly economy that compels Elizabeth to acknowledge her natural subjection to male domination at the very moment when she asserts the royal inviolability and ultimate authority of her body politic. In 1566, addressing a Parliament ever anxious for her to marry and produce an heir, Elizabeth both speculates that she would probably thrive "yf I were turned owte of the Realme in my pettycote" and announces, "I am yor anoynted *Queene* / I wyll neuer be by vyolence constreyned to doo any thynge."[30] Through his riddling disclosure, Puttenham reproduces courtly relations. In the process, he attempts to impose his own constraints on struggles over gender and over class by locating those struggles within the realm of the court.

30. For this paragraph's quotations, see Heisch, "Queen Elizabeth I," 55, 34–36.

Chapter Two

"Altogether like a falling steeple": The Politics of Sidney's Rebellions

In the previous chapter, I argued that *The Arte of English Poesie* both reinforces the Elizabethan court and, at the same time, relocates, within that court, larger struggles over gender and over class. In this way, Puttenham's riddling disclosures accord one culturally dominant institution a sort of structural hegemony: Elizabethan *courtly* struggles provide a model for Elizabethan *social* struggles. By suggesting that gender and class struggles can be played out—and won or lost—on the terrain of a single institution, Puttenham obscures the fact that *any* institution, even a powerful one, is actually only a single intervention within those struggles and thus that the reproduction of the court does not imply the reproduction of Elizabethan society at large. In this chapter, I turn my analysis of the rhetoric of concealment from Puttenham's riddling disclosures to Philip Sidney's depiction of architecturally unsound bodies and buildings. In so doing, I examine how Sidney's rhetorical gesture, like Puttenham's, helps shape the possible sites and forms of collective politics in late-sixteenth-century England.

Although frequently described—both by his contemporaries and by ours—as the paradigmatic courtier, Sidney often merits that status as much for embodying the ideal of the courtier as for displaying that ideal as an anachronistic and ineffective method of influencing Queen Elizabeth's domestic and foreign policy. For example, one enduring account of Sidney's life emphasizes that he was a friend to François Hotman and Philippe du Plessis-Mornay, was godfather to du Plessis-Mornay's son, and, like du Plessis-Mornay, was a friend and protégé of Hubert

Languet. These men were among the French Huguenots who, governed by a Catholic king yet writing in support of Protestantism, advocated various versions of a limited or constitutional monarchy. They argued that the monarch's absolute power should be limited by the consent of aristocratic magistrates. Individually those magistrates are subject to their monarch; together they supersede the monarch's authority. Although these men generally advised magistrates to exercise their collective authority only when monarchs became tyrants, not surprisingly the implications of their arguments made European royalty apprehensive. According to this account of Sidney's life, then, Elizabeth became wary of his ties both with the French Huguenots and with England's powerful Leicester family. Interpreting as a form of rebellion his criticism of her potential marriage to the Duke of Alençon and, more generally, of her lukewarm support for the Protestant cause in the Netherlands and in the Americas, Elizabeth denied Sidney most of the influential and lucrative appointments he sought. In articles spanning over sixty years, critics have disagreed about the extent to which Sidney actually supported the right of aristocrats to rebel against a tyrannical monarch and about the precise nature of his notoriously vexed relationship to Elizabeth.[1] Yet these

1. For a sampling of articles that analyze Sidney's relationship to Queen Elizabeth and his thoughts about rebellion in France and in England, see Doris Adler, "Imaginary Toads in Real Gardens," *English Literary Renaissance* 11:3 (Autumn 1981): 235–60; Edward Berry, "Hubert Languet and the 'Making' of Philip Sidney," *Studies in Philology* 85:3 (Summer 1988): 305–20, "The Poet as Warrior in Sidney's *Defence of Poetry*," *Studies in English Literature* 29:1 (Winter 1989): 21–34, and "Sidney's 'Poor' Painter: Nationalism and Social Class," in *Literature and Nationalism*, ed. Vincent Newey and Ann Thompson (Liverpool: Liverpool University Press, 1991), 1–10; William Dinsmore Briggs, "Political Ideas in Sidney's *Arcadia*," *Studies in Philology* 28:2 (April 1931): 137–61, and "Sidney's Political Ideas," *Studies in Philology* 29:4 (October 1932): 534–42; Simon Groenveld, "'In the Course of His God and True Religion': Sidney and the Dutch Revolt," in *Sir Philip Sidney's Achievements*, ed. M. J. B. Allen, Dominic Baker-Smith, and Arthur F. Kinney, with Margaret M. Sullivan, AMS Studies in the Renaissance, no. 28 (New York: AMS Press, 1990), 57–67; Dennis Kay, "'She was a Queen, and Therefore Beautiful': Sidney, His Mother, and Queen Elizabeth," *Review of English Studies*, new series, 43:169 (February 1992): 18–39; Arthur F. Kinney, "Puritans versus Royalists: Sir Philip Sidney's Rhetoric at the Court of Elizabeth I," in Allen, Baker-Smith, and Kinney, *Sir Philip Sidney's Achievements*, 52–56, and "Sir Philip Sidney and the Uses of History," in *The Historical Renaissance: New Essays on Tudor and Stuart Literature and Culture*, ed. Heather Dubrow and Richard Strier (Chicago: University of Chicago Press, 1988), 293–314; Roger Kuin, "Sir Philip Sidney: The Courtier and the Text," *English Literary Renaissance* 19:3 (Autumn 1989): 249–71; Richard C. McCoy, *Sir Philip Sidney: Rebellion in Arcadia* (New Brunswick, N.J.: Rutgers University Press, 1979); Louis Adrian Montrose, "Celebration and Insinuation: Sir Philip Sidney and the Motives of Elizabethan Courtship," *Renaissance Drama* 8 (1977): 3–35; Maureen Quilligan, "Sidney and His Queen," in Dubrow and Strier, *Historical Renaissance*, 171–96; Martin N. Raitière, "Amphialus' Rebellion: Sidney's Use of History in *New Arcadia*," *Journal of Medieval and*

critics *do* agree that, however Sidney felt about aristocratic rebellion against the monarch, he certainly would have condemned any sort of popular insurrection.[2]

In the first section of my chapter, I analyze the logic of dismembered bodies and crumbling buildings—what I refer to as Sidney's rhetoric of rebellion—in order to assess the *form* that this condemnation takes within *The Countess of Pembroke's Arcadia*.[3] I argue that Sidney's rhetoric obscures the degree to which hegemonic formations are always in process. It suggests that popular politics in general and class politics in particular inevitably will collapse into an ineffective anarchy when individual rebels confront their conflicting alliances. And it depicts as predictable the range of possible relationships among subordinate and dominant groups. This chapter does not focus on the particular political identities that the *Arcadia* promotes. Instead, I consider, more generally, how its *model* of collective politics helps shape England's late-sixteenth-century political terrain.

Renaissance Studies 12:1 (Spring 1982): 113–31, and *Faire Bitts: Sir Philip Sidney and Renaissance Political Theory* (Pittsburgh: Duquesne University Press, 1984); Irving Ribner, "Sir Philip Sidney on Civil Insurrection," *Journal of the History of Ideas* 13:2 (April 1952): 257–65; Alan Sinfield, "The Cultural Politics of the *Defence of Poetry*," in *Sir Philip Sidney and the Interpretation of Renaissance Culture: The Poet in His Time and in Ours, a Collection of Critical and Scholarly Essays*, ed. Gary F. Waller and Michael D. Moore (Totowa, N.J.: Barnes and Noble, 1984), 124–43, and "Power and Ideology: An Outline Theory and Sidney's *Arcadia*," *ELH* 52:2 (Summer 1985): 259–77; Robert E. Stillman, "The Politics of Sidney's Pastoral: Mystification and Mythology in *The Old Arcadia*," *ELH* 52:4 (Winter 1985): 795–814; and John L. Sutton, Jr., "A Historical Source for the Rebellion of the Commons in Sidney's *Arcadia*," *English Language Notes* 23:4 (June 1986): 6–11.

2. In addition to the work cited in the preceding note, see Stephen Greenblatt, "Murdering Peasants: Status, Genre, and the Representation of Rebellion," *Representations* 1:1 (February 1983): 14–19, and Richard M. Berrong, "Changing Attitudes toward Material Wealth in Sidney's *Arcadias*," *Sixteenth Century Journal* 22:2 (Summer 1991): 331–53, and "Changing Depictions of Popular Revolt in Sixteenth-Century England: The Case of Sidney's Two *Arcadias*," *Journal of Medieval and Renaissance Studies* 19:1 (Spring 1989): 15–33. Berrong argues that the revised *Arcadia* demonstrates a greater understanding of the conditions that prompted the lower orders to rebel. In Berrong's account, these revisions suggest that aristocrats can no longer afford to mock and dismiss popular revolt, although, he stresses, they do not convey sympathy either for the plight of the lower orders or for their rebelliousness.

3. All citations are from Philip Sidney, *The Countess of Pembroke's Arcadia*, ed. Maurice Evans (Harmondsworth, Middlesex: Penguin Books, 1977). I have selected this edition because it attempts to approximate—for the modern reader—the Countess of Pembroke's 1593 edition of the *New Arcadia*. Because Sidney's revisions break off midsentence in Book Three, William Alexander added, for an early seventeenth-century edition, a bridge between the unfinished action of the *New Arcadia* and the resumption of the *Old Arcadia* text. Evans's edition includes Alexander's bridge; my chapter does not address that material.

Although the *Arcadia* is interested in female rulers and in purported Amazons, its rebellious collectives do not include groups of women. Instead it associates popular rebellion with any individual woman who would challenge her husband's domestic authority. In the second section of this chapter, I analyze how the *Arcadia* depicts that challenge. I focus on the logic of equity and equality within the *Arcadia*'s companionate marriages, including the narrative's idiosyncratic version of the analogy between order within the family and order within the state. In this way, I locate Sidney's rhetoric of rebellion at one particularly contested site within the writing about and practices surrounding companionate marriage—contested precisely because it was a site at which Renaissance women's subordination threatened to become recognizable as a form of oppression. I argue that Sidney's rhetoric attempts to foreclose that recognition and the collective politics it might have produced. That collective politics, some contemporaries feared, might have undermined not only the hierarchy of men over women but also the system of status and authority which defined membership within and the hierarchies among what I refer to as "social classes." As I explained in this book's introduction, I distinguish among classes on the basis of their structural role in the production and extraction of surplus value and *not* on the basis of differences in rank, status, or authority. Yet, as I also explained, it is through the latter, sociological categories—discussed in this chapter in terms of social class—that members of late-sixteenth-century society often experienced their relationship to economic exploitation and often articulated their political demands for social change.

My arguments about class and gender address issues raised in the Countess of Pembroke's 1593 edition of the *New Arcadia*. Sidney produced and circulated an unprinted version of the *Arcadia* during the early 1580s. At the time of his death in 1586, he had revised the first two chapters and a portion of the third chapter from that earlier manuscript; Fulke Greville published a 1590 edition of Sidney's revised work. In 1593, Mary Sidney and Hugh Sanford published an edition that appended the remaining, unrevised, portions of the *Old Arcadia* to the revised 1590 material. It is their 1593 version that, until the beginning of this century, was the only available text of Sidney's work. More important, it is the 1593 edition of the *Arcadia* which was quite popular among and, by 1599, was inexpensive enough to be widely available to those Elizabethans who purchased books.[4]

---

4. For essays that address the initial production, the reception, and the recent editing

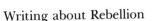

Writing about Rebellion

In the third book of the *Arcadia*, Musidorus writes an elegy to his beloved, Pamela. Sidney stresses the prince's tortured process of composition:

---

of the various versions of the *Arcadia*, see Maurice Evans, "Divided Aims in the *Revised Arcadia*," in Waller and Moore, *Interpretation of Renaissance Culture*, 34–43; Margaret P. Hannay, *Philip's Phoenix: Mary Sidney, Countess of Pembroke* (New York: Oxford University Press, 1990), 59–83; Mary Ellen Lamb, *Gender and Authorship in the Sidney Circle* (Madison: University of Wisconsin Press, 1990), 72–114; Nancy R. Lindheim, "Vision, Revision, and the 1593 Text of the *Arcadia*," in *Sidney in Retrospect: Selections from "English Literary Renaissance*," ed. Arthur F. Kinney and the editors of *ELR* (Amherst: University of Massachusetts Press, 1988), 169–80; Michael McCanles, *The Text of Sidney's Arcadian World* (Durham: Duke University Press, 1989), 1–14, 134–43; Jean Robertson, general introduction and textual introduction to *The Countess of Pembroke's Arcadia (The Old Arcadia)*, ed. Robertson (Oxford: Oxford University Press, 1973), xv–lxxi; Victor Skretkowicz, "Building Sidney's Reputation: Texts and Editors of the *Arcadia*," in *Sir Philip Sidney: 1586 and the Creation of a Legend*, ed. Jan Van Dorsten, Dominic Baker-Smith, and Arthur F. Kinney (Leiden, Netherlands: E. J. Brill/Leiden University Press for the Sir Thomas Browne Institute, 1986), 111–24; and general introduction and textual introduction to *The Countess of Pembroke's Arcadia (The New Arcadia)*, ed. Victor Skretkowicz (Oxford: Oxford University Press, 1987), xiii–lxxxii; and Laura Caroline Stevenson, *Praise and Paradox: Merchants and Craftsmen in Elizabethan Popular Literature* (Cambridge: Cambridge University Press, 1984), 14–15. Hannay and Lamb emphasize Mary Sidney's role in preparing the 1593 edition. Lamb discusses how she helps to create for her brother an enduring reputation as an author, courtier, and Protestant martyr. W. A. Ringler, Jr., "Sir Philip Sidney: The Myth and the Man," in Dorsten, Baker-Smith, and Kinney, *Creation of a Legend*, 3–15, locates that project within the larger process of mythmaking that surrounded Sidney even before his death.

Many editors and critics decide which is the most authentic version of the *Arcadia* on the basis of evidence about Sidney's authorial intent. Annabel Patterson, "'Under . . . Pretty Tales': Intention in Sidney's *Arcadia*," in *Sir Philip Sidney: An Anthology of Modern Criticism*, ed. Dennis Kay (Oxford: Clarendon University Press, 1987), 265–85, analyzes how the question of intention is produced by Sidney's writing, by the threat of censorship under which he wrote, and by the late-sixteenth- and seventeenth-century publication history of the *Arcadia*.

For debates about the nature of the sixteenth- and early-seventeenth-century book-buying population and about those who were likely to have been able to read or to have books read to them, see Patricia Crawford, "Women's Published Writings, 1600–1700," in *Women in English Society, 1500–1800*, ed. Mary Prior (London: Methuen, 1985), 211–31; David Cressy, *Literacy and the Social Order: Reading and Writing in Tudor and Stuart England* (Cambridge: Cambridge University Press, 1980); Hilda L. Smith, *Reason's Disciples: Seventeenth-Century English Feminists* (Urbana: University of Illinois Press, 1982), 19–38; Margaret Spufford, "First Steps in Literacy: The Reading and Writing Experiences of the Humblest Seventeenth-Century Spiritual Autobiographers," *Social History* 4:3 (October 1979): 407–35, and *Small Books and Pleasant Histories: Popular Fiction and Its Readership in Seventeenth-Century England* (Athens: University of Georgia Press, 1982); Stevenson, *Praise and Paradox*, 11–39, 51–74; and Keith Thomas, "The Meaning of Literacy in Early Modern England," in *The Written Word: Literacy in Transition (Wolfson College Lectures 1985)*, ed. Gerd Baumann (Oxford: Oxford University Press, 1986), 97–131. Crawford, "Women's Pub-

Never pen did more quakingly perform his office; never was paper more double-moistened with ink and tears; never words more slowly married together, and never the Muses more tired than now with changes and rechanges of his devices; fearing how to end before he had resolved how to begin, mistrusting each word, condemning each sentence. This word was not significant; that word was too plain: this would not be conceived; the other would be ill-conceived: here sorrow was not enough expressed; there he seemed too much for his own sake to be sorry: this sentence rather showed art than passion; that sentence rather foolishly passionate than forcibly moving.

At last, marring with mending and putting out better than he left, he made an end of it and being ended, was divers times ready to tear it, till his reason assuring him the more he studied the worse it grew. (437)

Here, and throughout the *Arcadia*, Sidney depicts the limitations of po-etry making, particularly the writing of verse. In the second book, for example, Pyrocles, disguised as Zelmane, attempts to sing out his sorrow, but the "ending of the song served but for a beginning of new plaints, as if the mind, oppressed with too heavy a burden of cares, was fain to discharge itself of all sides and, as it were, paint out the hideousness of the pain in all sorts of colours" (215). Strephon and Claius attempt, in their sestina, to relieve their minds, yet, again, the song proves insuffi-cient. It is "but the taking of a taste of their wailings" (415), and they follow that taste with the crown whose end seems no more a relief. In fact, Sidney suggests that this lack of relief is constitutive of the lovers' verse. When Pyrocles fails to sing out his sorrow, he claims that his song actually forces him to dwell on his pain. He identifies his emotional failure with the artistic success of his verse making, asking his lute, "'Alas, what is then thy harmony but the sweet-meats of sor-row?' . . . And thus much spoken, instead of a conclusion was closed up with so hearty a groaning that Gynecia could not refrain to show her-self" (215–16). In a series of puns on the word "refrain," Sidney corre-lates the insufficiencies of the lovers' verse with an uncontrollable yield-ing to violent excesses of meaning and passion. This yielding to excess—from which Gynecia cannot refrain—is the refrain that is inseparable from the lovers' verse precisely because it never can be versified.

---

lished Writings"; Spufford, "First Steps in Literacy"; and Thomas, "Meaning of Literacy," offer analyses that challenge Cressy's description of literacy.

The *Arcadia*'s violently uncontrollable excesses coalesce for both poet and auditor in Sidney's flood metaphors. He not only describes Zelmane's song as a yielding "to the flood of her own thoughts" (632) but also writes that the disguised Pyrocles' verse "opened some great floodgate of sorrow whereof her [Gynecia's] heart could not abide the violent issue" (216). With these metaphors, Sidney links the limitations of poetry making to the rebels' attack on Pyrocles, Gynecia, and Gynecia's daughter, Philoclea, at the end of the second book: "Yet before they could win the lodge by twenty paces, they were overtaken by an unruly sort of clowns and other rebels which, like a violent flood, were carried they themselves knew not whither. . . . [Y]et so many as they were, so many almost were their minds, all knit together only in madness. Some cried 'Take'; some 'Kill'; some, 'Save'; but even they that cried 'Save' ran for company with them that meant to kill. Everyone commanded; none obeyed" (379). The rebels' contradictory impulses to "take" and "save" parallel Musidorus's vacillating editorial decisions. And their rebellion, like his verse, is knit together by a series of confused and, at best, provisional impulses over which they have only intermittent control. "So many as they were," Sidney writes of the rebels, "so many almost were their minds" (379). They are the "many-headed multitude" (387), a "confused rumour" (378). They are a single movement composed of many disparate desires, a single common voice composed of a confusing plenitude of meanings. In the second section of this chapter, I return to the connections among the insufficiencies of the lovers' verse, an excess of passion, and popular rebellion in the *Arcadia*. For the moment, however, I want to focus on the logic of the *Arcadia*'s assertion—made explicit in these flood metaphors—that popular rebellion is incoherent.

Sidney's "many-headed multitude" was one common sixteenth- and seventeenth-century European idiom for describing that incoherence.[5] For example, after outlining the conditions under which subjects might rebel against a tyrannical monarch, the author of *Vindiciae contra Tyrannos*—a 1579 treatise variously attributed to du Plessis-Mornay and Languet—imagines a typical objection to his claims: "Do you really mean, it will be said, that the entire multitude, that many-headed monster, should go rushing into matters of this sort like a raging flood? Can order be expected from the mob? Or wisdom for settling affairs?" He

---

5. See Christopher Hill, *Change and Continuity in Seventeenth-Century England* (London: Weidenfeld and Nicolson, 1974), 181–204.

answers these objections by distinguishing between the private people and their public magistrates. "When we speak of the people collectively," he writes, "we mean those who receive authority from the people, that is, the magistrates below the king who have been elected by the people or established in some other way. These take the place of the people assembled as a whole." Adopting the plural "we," the author distances himself from private individuals who "are not to be regarded as basic parts of a community any more than planks, nails, and pegs are taken as the parts of a ship; or stones, beams, and mortar as the parts of a house." Not surprisingly, the consent with which the people endorse their contract with the monarch can be offered or withdrawn only by public magistrates. Yet, more important, magistrates obtain their public authority precisely by embodying some sanctioned—some recognized—segment of private individuals and their collective will. As the author's odd metaphor suggests—after all, planks, nails, and pegs are literally the *most* basic parts of a ship—people constitute a "basic part of a community" only after they coalesce into a recognizable group. According to the author of the *Vindiciae*, private individuals coalesce into a recognizable group by virtue of their regional identities: "We are speaking rather of a province or a town, which is a part of the kingdom in the same way the prow, deck, and rudder are the parts of a ship, or the roof, walls, and foundation are the parts of a house. And we are also speaking of the magistrate who is in charge of that province or town."[6]

Although the *Arcadia* is not interested in promoting the regional authority of aristocratic magistrates, it *is* interested in outlining the conditions under which private people might coalesce into recognizable groups and thus obtain public authority. In the next few pages, I analyze the unraveling of the *Arcadia*'s madly knit rebellions. I demonstrate how Sidney depicts the multiple and even contradictory alliances that often characterize collective politics as an absurd tendency toward the dismemberment of individual rebels' bodies. In this way, his rhetoric of rebellion dismisses the possibility that England's marginalized and oppressed might offer any successful challenge to the dominant culture.

Asked by Pyrocles, disguised as Zelmane, to choose "someone who may relate your griefs or demands" (383), the rebellious common people

---

6. *Vindiciae contra Tyrannos*, orig. pub. 1579, in *Constitutionalism and Resistance in the Sixteenth Century: Three Treatises by Hotman, Beza, and Mornay*, trans. and ed. Julian H. Franklin (New York: Pegasus, 1969), 149, 152.

in the *Arcadia*'s second book fail to select a representative and, instead,
display how little they actually have in common:

> But when they began to talk of their griefs, never bees made such a
> confused humming: the town dwellers demanding putting down of im-
> posts; the country fellows, laying out of commons: some would have the
> prince keep his court in one place, some in another. All cried out to have
> new counsellors, but when they should think of any new, they liked them
> as well as any other that they could remember. . . . At length they fell to
> direct contrarieties. For the artisans, they would have corn and wine set at
> a lower price, and bound to be kept so still: the ploughmen, vine-
> labourers and farmers would none of that. The countrymen demanded
> that every man might be free in the chief towns: that could not the bur-
> gesses like of. The peasants would have all the gentlemen destroyed; the
> citizens (especially such as cooks, barbers, and those other that lived most
> on gentlemen) would but have them reformed. And of each side were like
> divisions, one neighbourhood beginning to find fault with another.
> . . . The finer sort of burgesses, as merchants, prentices and cloth-
> workers, because of their riches disdaining the baser occupations, and
> they because of their number as much disdaining them; all they scorning
> the countrymen's ignorance, and the countrymen suspecting as much
> their cunning. (383–84)

Here Sidney fantasizes that, with a little prodding, popular alliances
obligingly will self-destruct. Eventually the rebellion disintegrates into
two feuding groups—those "that would yield to Basilius" and those "that
would not yield" (389). Thus the rebels, "being divided in minds and not
divided in companies, . . . converted their ungracious motion into their
own bowels, and by a true judgement grew their own punishers" (388–
89). Even the alliances within each of these groups are quickly broken
when "many times it fell out that they killed them that were of their own
faction" (389).

Basilius, Musidorus, and Pyrocles make literal the rebellion's inevitable disintegration with a series of macabre slaughters. Those slaughters
inscribe upon each rebel's corpse the rapid movement from delusions of
alliance to the reality of self-division. For example, Sidney writes, "But
Dorus . . . with his two-hand sword strake off another quite by the waist
who the night before had dreamed he was grown a couple, and, interpreting it that he should be married, had bragged of his dream that

morning among his neighbours" (381). Individual bodies split apart along class fault lines when "arms and legs go complain to the earth how evil their masters had kept them" (380) and when Pyrocles strikes a butcher across the face, leaving "nothing but the nether jaw, where the tongue still wagged, as willing to say more if his master's remembrance had served" (380). Severed from the body, the arms and legs and tongues retain a life of their own—the parts outliving the whole and thus accentuating their disconnection from it. By correlating each rebel's fate with his occupation, Sidney emphasizes rebellion's tendency, in his own terminology, not merely to *be* disemboweled but actually to disembowel itself. The unlucky butcher is dismembered by his own cleaver, and a tailor dies pursuing his occupational impulse to mend. After Basilius strikes off the tailor's nose, the man stoops "down, because he had heard that if it were fresh put to, it would cleave on again. But as his hand was on the ground to bring his nose to his head, Zelmane with a blow sent his head to his nose" (380).

Yet here, oddly enough, the disguised prince not only decapitates the tailor but also, in so doing, reunites the man's nose with his head. Sidney depicts this same curious doubling of dismemberment and reunion when Musidorus later fights the "scummy remnant of those rebels" (753), who, when asked their motive for attacking Pamela and the prince, respond with characteristic self-division, "'Pardon,' said one. 'Reward,' cried another" (761). Sidney writes, "But the first he overtook as he ran away, carrying his head as far before him as those manner of runnings are wont to do, with one blow, strake it so clean off that—it falling betwixt the hands, and the body falling upon it—it made a show as though the fellow had had great haste to gather up his head again" (754–55). If the litany of dismembered rebels has displayed how they "by a true judgement grew their own punishers" (389), what is the significance of this double-edged "show"? Why is this gruesomely ludicrous portrait of a decapitation paradoxically imagined best as a *re*capitation— this dispersal of the rebels best depicted as a reunion?

In part, this doubled image is appropriate for Basilius, Musidorus, and Pyrocles, who respond to the rebels by "sometimes seeking to draw together those of their party, sometimes laying indifferently among them" (389). They find that forming new, less threatening coalitions might be as effective as simply dispersing the rebels—that a multitude with one royal head is as unthreatening as individuals who retain their many heads yet remain isolated from one another. In short, they are not entirely certain how best to combat rebellion, and the *Arcadia* does not entirely endorse either pole of their royal ambivalence. More importantly, however, the doubled image of decapitation and recapitation suggests that the *Arcadia does* agree on one principle: whether Basilius and the disguised princes decide to reunite or to disperse the rebels, their maneuvers and the rebellion's disintegration are best depicted by way of individual bodies. Sidney emphasizes the absurdity of popular rebellion by defining it as a litany of squabbling class and occupational constituencies. When he recasts rebellion as a litany of each rebel's squabbling body parts, its absurdity, as the startled rebels attest, is even more horrifyingly—and humorously—clear.

Not surprisingly, popular rebellion in late-sixteenth-century England actually *did* consist of an often bewildering array of shifting alliances and demands. Groups that Sidney—and we—might want to identify with particular political and economic interests often were divided internally, or they formed seemingly anomalous provisional alliances overdetermined by familial, religious, or regional affiliations.[7] For example, the enclosure of common land removed land rights from agricultural workers and thus denied them control over their means of production. Without that control, both rural workers and those forced into the city became wage laborers who were increasingly dependent on their employers. Uprisings against enclosure, however, included varying constituencies. When the enclosers were London courtiers and merchants, local gentry and yeomen often sanctioned—or even organized—rioting smallholders and landless peasants. When the enclosers were local gentry, such regional alliances were understandably less relevant to rioters than was the distinction between large landowners and the agricultural workers they exploited.[8] Within this framework, individual rioters often occupied multiple and even contradictory positions.

7. Roger B. Manning, *Village Revolts: Social Protest and Popular Disturbances in England, 1509–1640* (Oxford: Clarendon Press, 1988), and David Underdown, *Revel, Riot, and Rebellion: Popular Politics and Culture in England, 1603–1660* (Oxford: Oxford University Press, 1985; paperback ed., 1987), 1–145.

8. Manning, *Village Revolts*, 31–107, and Underdown, *Revel, Riot, and Rebellion*, 107–16. Enclosure refers to a variety of social practices—including encroachment, overpopulation, and the actual hedging in of common land. Manning suggests that between 1590 and 1610 it was more likely than earlier in the sixteenth century that rioting lesser gentry, smallholders, and landless peasants would include among their targets those local aristocratic landlords who were attempting to rationalize their estates by encroaching on wastes,

Yet such contradictions are not *necessarily* an impediment to social change. In the previous paragraph, I discussed shifting alliances through the example of enclosure. I choose this example because anti-enclosure riots were one prominent and well-organized form of rebellion during the mid-sixteenth century and during the late sixteenth and early seventeenth centuries,[9] and because a discussion of class, one of my central categories of analysis, will allow me to outline my more general assumptions about hegemony and collective politics. First, a class's struggle should be considered successful when the society's economic *structure* has been changed and conditions have improved for members of that class—even if individuals who participate in the struggle do not recognize their class alliances or experience other, locally conflicting cultural affiliations as more compelling. For instance, the seventeenth-century revolution—whatever the class allegiances of its actual supporters—structurally reinforced England's increasingly capitalist economy.[10] Second, structural changes in a society are not the result of an inexorable economic logic that supersedes all political alliances. Instead, the economy and those alliances operate within a range of possibilities that they create for one another. As my discussion of the middle

---

commons, and woodlands; rack-renting; and converting customary tenures into fixed-term leases. These rioters often were willing to articulate their resistance to large capitalist landlords not only as a reassertion of their own feudal rights but also, increasingly, as a more general attack on aristocratic privilege. Manning excludes from this paradigm the anti-enclosure activity that occurred between 1548 and 1552.

9. Underdown, *Revel, Riot, and Rebellion*, 107–16, discusses the planning and cooperation that characterized anti-enclosure riots before the civil war; he focuses on the early seventeenth century. For one excellent analysis of that planning and cooperation during the mid-sixteenth century, see Diarmaid MacCulloch, "Kett's Rebellion in Context," *Past and Present* 84 (August 1979): 36–59. Manning, *Village Revolts*, 31–107, distinguishes among Tudor anti-enclosure riots before the 1590s, the anomalous riots between 1548 and 1552, and the riots between 1590 and 1610. In his analysis of late Elizabethan and early Jacobean anti-enclosure activity, Manning stresses the sustained and united character of an opposition whose members raised common purses to pay litigation costs.

10. Mary Fulbrook, "The English Revolution and the Revisionist Revolt," *Social History* 7:3 (October 1982): 249–64; Christopher Hill, "A Bourgeois Revolution?" in *Three British Revolutions: 1641, 1688, 1776*, ed. J. G. A. Pocock (Princeton: Princeton University Press, 1980), 109–39; Lawrence Stone, "The Bourgeois Revolution of Seventeenth-Century England Revisited," *Past and Present* 109 (November 1985): 44–54. I cite these particular historians because they formulate their arguments in response to those who claim that the war was not a bourgeois revolution because both royalist and antiroyalist forces held mixed class affiliations and because aristocratic solidarity led antiroyalist landowners to hold in trust the estates confiscated from their royalist counterparts.

class in the next chapter will suggest, even within the parameters of class analysis alone, individuals frequently occupy positions whose cultural and economic instability offers an opportunity for very different political alliances. In spite of Sidney's ridicule, such divided alliances are, again, not necessarily an impediment to social change. In fact, in part because networks of alliances are not a closed system, political identities and larger hegemonic formations are never entirely stable. Finally, the terms of the reciprocity between economic structures and political alliances are themselves always shifting.[11] For example, as I suggested earlier, although economic class structures were central to sixteenth-century English society, economic class was not the political idiom through which members of that society generally voiced their demands for social change. More frequently, people experienced their economic exploitation—and linked that exploitation to other forms of oppression—through the language of social mobility and social status and through the language of authority relations, including relations between rulers and their subjects.[12]

11. For analyses that have influenced my remarks about the overdetermined relationships among the cultural, the economic, and the political, see Louis Althusser, "Contradiction and Overdetermination: Notes for an Investigation," in *For Marx*, trans. Ben Brewster (London: New Left Books, 1977; London: Verso, 1979), 87–128, and "Ideology and Ideological State Apparatuses (Notes towards an Investigation)," in *Lenin and Philosophy and Other Essays*, trans. Ben Brewster (New York: Monthly Review Press, 1971), 134–36. For discussions of hegemony see Antonio Gramsci, "The Modern Prince" and "State and Civil Society," in *Selections from the Prison Notebooks*, ed. and trans. Quintin Hoare and Geoffrey Nowell Smith (New York: International Publishers, 1971), 123–276; Stuart Hall, *The Hard Road to Renewal: Thatcherism and the Crisis of the Left* (London: Verso, 1988), 93–173; Peter Stallybrass, "The World Turned Upside Down: Inversion, Gender, and the State," in *The Matter of Difference: Materialist Feminist Criticism of Shakespeare*, ed. Valerie Wayne (Ithaca: Cornell University Press, 1991), 201–20; and Raymond Williams, "Base and Superstructure in Marxist Cultural Theory," in *Problems in Materialism and Culture: Selected Essays* (London: Verso, 1980), 31–49. My thinking about hegemony and the instability of hegemonic formations has also been influenced by Ernesto Laclau and Chantal Mouffe, *Hegemony and Socialist Strategy: Towards a Radical Democratic Politics* (London: Verso, 1985), 93–148.

12. Christopher Hill, "Parliament and People in Seventeenth-Century England," *Past and Present* 92 (August 1981): 118–22, argues that the absence of a seventeenth-century vocabulary about class presupposes neither the absence of exploitation nor the absence of an experience of exploitation. I derive my understanding of the categories through which people experienced that exploitation from historians such as Susan Dwyer Amussen and Keith Wrightson. Amussen, *An Ordered Society: Gender and Class in Early Modern England* (Oxford: Basil Blackwell, 1988), 34–66, discusses how members of Renaissance society understood their relations to one another through the prevalent analogy between domes-

With this discussion in mind, I return to the *Arcadia*'s rhetoric of rebellion and ask how that rhetoric might have helped to shape the political imaginations not only of those who were subordinate in late-sixteenth-century English society but also of those who were dominant. If hegemonic formations are successful when ruling groups are able to make their political agenda compelling to those over whom they dominate,[13] how does Sidney's rhetoric of rebellion help to set the terms for that hegemonizing process? I begin to answer this question by outlining how rebellion figures within the *Arcadia*'s larger vision of national unity, social status, and social order.

Like the *Vindiciae contra Tyrannos*, the *Arcadia* emphasizes the political benefits of governing by eliciting consent rather than by exercising force. The author of the *Vindiciae* distinguishes between people who have entered into contracts with monarchs under violent coercion and those who have entered into such contracts "freely and willingly." His examples depict a distinction, more accurately, between violent coercion and a consent that is *experienced* as free will. God is perhaps the most adept manufacturer of consent in the *Vindiciae*. In a tale which ostensibly demonstrates God's awareness that all monarchs must obtain the people's consent, the *Vindiciae*'s author describes Israel's transition to a monarchical form of government:

> *The elders of Israel, who represented the people as a whole . . . met with Samuel at Ramah. . . . [T]hey demanded a king of Samuel.* Upon Samuel's request for counsel, God revealed that He had selected Saul to rule the people. And so Samuel anointed Saul. All of this, so far, bears on the selection of a king at the people's request, and it might have seemed sufficient for Samuel to present the people with the king whom God had chosen and to command them to obey. But in order that the king might know that he was established by the people, Samuel called an assembly at Mizpah, and there—*as if the entire transaction had to be redone, as if, that is, the choice of Saul had not occurred*—the lot was drawn. And it fell on someone from the tribe of

---

tic and state models of authority. And Wrightson, *English Society, 1580–1680* (New Brunswick, N.J.: Rutgers University Press, 1982), 17–38, and "Estates, Degrees, and Sorts in Tudor and Stuart England," *History Today* 37 (January 1987): 17–22, discusses how members of Renaissance society conceived of their world through the language of "estates" or "orders" and its attendant emphasis on social function.

13. Gramsci, "Modern Prince," 161, 166, and "State and Civil Society," 244, 249, 257–64, 275–76; Hall, *Hard Road to Renewal*, 123–73; and Stallybrass, "World Turned Upside Down," 217.

Benjamin, and from the family of Matri, and within this family on Saul, whom God had chosen. *Then only, with the acclamation of the people as a whole, was Saul considered king.* But God also willed that royal status should not be attributed solely to lot. After Saul had given a token of his virtue by liberating Jabesh-Gilead from a siege by the Ammonites, he was confirmed as king in the presence of God by the whole people assembled at Gilgal, even though some of them dissented. We see, then, that the king whom God had chosen, who had been selected from all the rest by lot, became king by the votes of the people.[14] (My emphases)

The *Vindiciae* suggests that if the virtuous Saul had not obtained popular consideration, if his subjects had not consented to be ruled, his position as monarch could only have been maintained through the explicit force that characterizes tyranny. The process of manufacturing consent encompasses God's choice of Saul, the temporally (if not narratively) subsequent request from the people's public representatives that a king be selected, and finally the moment when Saul is ultimately "considered king" not solely by lot.

Sidney's letters agree that monarchs must manufacture popular consent if they wish to safeguard their nations; in writing those letters he demonstrates the potential role of public magistrates in securing that consent for their rulers. In a 1577 letter to Walsingham, for example, he reports that "the Emperour is . . . nothinge the manner his father had in winninge men in his behauior, but yet constant in keepinge them" and that the brothers Matthias and Maximilian are "broughte upp togeather, but in Jermany, and in their behauiour fram[ing] of them selues to the lykinge of this contrey people."[15] And in his infamous letter dissuading Elizabeth from her marriage to the Duke of Alençon, Sidney worries that the marriage will divide a realm now united in spite of its "two mighty factions, and factions bound upon the never ending knot of religion." Sidney's letters both describe Elizabeth's command of the people's consent and remind her of its fragility:

Look in your own estate, how willingly they grant, and how dutifully they pay, such subsidies as you demand of them; how they are now less troublesome to your Majesty in certain requests than they were at the beginning

14. *Vindiciae contra Tyrannos*, 159.
15. Philip Sidney, *The Miscellaneous Works of Sir Philip Sidney, knt, with a Life of the Author and Illustrative Notes*, ed. William Gray (Boston: T. O. H. P. Burnham, 1860), 353.

of your reign; and you shall find your Majesty hath a people more than
ever devoted to you. . . .

Virtue and justice are the only bands of the people's love. And as for
that point, many princes have lost their crowns, whose own children were
manifest successors.[16]

Succession alone, he warns, does not secure the people's collective consent. The monarch must constantly labor to subdue factions that might
undermine national unity. Yet, he stresses, she must do so not by tyran-
nically exercising force but by retaining her subjects' willing love and
devotion.

The *Arcadia* emphasizes the *national* character of the unity that this
method of governing would preserve. "But some of the wiser [Phryg-
ians]," Sidney writes, "(seeing that a popular licence is indeed the many-
headed tyranny) prevailed with the rest to make Musidorus their chief"
(270). The foreign prince instates "conditions, and cautions of the conditions" so that "not only that governor . . . but the nature of the government, should be no way apt to decline to tyranny" (271). Yet, although
"the whole estates of the country with one consent gave the crown and all
other marks of sovereignty to Musidorus," he, "having received the full
power to his own hands," resigns the kingdom to the Phrygian nobleman
who was of "the blood royal" (270, 271, 270).

Like Sidney's letters, the *Arcadia* suggests that those monarchs who
obtain the advice of public magistrates might be better able to prevent
the "decline to tyranny" (271) which inevitably threatens national unity.
For example, Arcadia degenerates into "confused and dangerous divisions" (766) not merely because of Basilius's sudden and unexpected
flight but more properly because "public matters had ever been privately
governed" (766) by its monarch. Basilius's solitary method of government, unassisted by public magistrates, produces subjects who are unable to consent to any single leader or to any single form of government.
The "extreme medley of diversified thoughts" (766) that emerge after
Basilius abdicates his royal responsibilities make equally improbable any
effective resistance to a monarchical form of government and any selection of magistrates who might navigate the Arcadians through their
national crisis:

16. Philip Sidney, "A Letter Written by Sir Philip Sidney to Queen Elizabeth, Touching
her Marriage with Monsieur," in *Miscellaneous Prose of Sir Philip Sidney*, ed. Katherine
Duncan-Jones and Jan Van Dorsten (Oxford: Clarendon Press, 1973), 47, 54.

This composition of conceits brought forth a dangerous tumult which yet would have been more dangerous, but that it had so many parts that nobody well knew against whom chiefly to oppose themselves. For some there were that cried to have the state altered and governed no more by a prince: marry, in the alteration, many would have the Lacedaemonian government of few chosen senators; others, the Athenian, where the people's voice held the chief authority. But these were rather the discoursing sort of men than the active, being a matter more in imagination than practice. (767)

This description suggests that vacillating and ineffectual calls both for a republic and for a limited democracy ultimately present the same sort of threat to a nation as "the worst kind of Oligarchy: that is, when men are governed indeed by a few, and yet are not taught to know what those few be to whom they should obey" (254). Deprived of that instruction by Basilius's "private" government, the Arcadians—like their counterparts in Macedon—risk exchanging the "name of a king" for the "dissolution of all estates" (254). In other words, a too private monarchy invites a tyrannical popular rebellion, one that would threaten a nation's unity and, at the same time, unsettle the status relationships among members of that nation.

In keeping with this paradigm, it is not surprising that Arcadia becomes susceptible, as Philanax notes, to an unscrupulous leader—"the waters being (as the proverb saith) troubled and so the better for his fishing" (769). Nor is it surprising that one particularly rebellious segment of the Arcadians find themselves unwittingly ruled by Cecropia's ambassador, Clinias. Clinias "had by his mistress been used, (ever since the strange retiring of Basilius), to whisper rumours into the people's ears: and this time, finding great aptness in the multitude, was one of the chief that set them in the uproar. . . . But now perceiving the flood of their fury begun to ebb, he thought it policy to take the first of the tide, so that no man cried louder than he upon Basilius" (387–88). The rebels prove apt pupils under Clinias's circumspect instruction. He not only helps to provoke their initial rebellion but also prompts them to convert "their ungracious motion into their own bowels" (389) when his vocal and enthusiastic support for Basilius makes visible the division between those who would once more pledge loyalty to the king and those who would continue their revolt.

Finally, the *Arcadia* consistently addresses the relationships among monarchs, public magistrates, and the private people through a pervasive insistence on the "right of birth" (351). Although this work certainly does not present all members of the aristocracy as equally virtuous, it sanctions neither private people nor aristocratic women who would offer their consent to nonnobility. In fact, the *Arcadia* punctuates its rhetoric of rebellion with the specter of an unfixed social order—including, in its discussion of the Helot rebellion, international class alliances that would threaten national unity and the privileges of birth. The narrative emphasizes that the Helots do not confine their armed revolts to the Lacedaemonians but target "all gentlemen" (86) and "nobility" (669). When Palladius arrives in Arcadia during the first of these revolts, he is told that neighboring Laconia is made poor "by a civil war . . . between the gentlemen and the peasants (by them named Helots)" (70). As the story unfolds, it becomes clear that "Helot" is not simply the Laconian word for peasant; instead, the Helot nation was conquered and enslaved by the Laconian nobility, the Lacedaemonians, and its former citizens now are in revolt:

> They were a kind of people who, having been of old freemen and possessioners, the Lacedaemonians had conquered them and laid not only tribute, but bondage upon them; which they had long borne, till of late, the Lacedaemonians through greediness growing more heavy than they could bear, and through contempt less careful how to make them bear, they had with a general consent (rather springing by the generalness of the cause than of any artificial practice) set themselves in arms, and whetting their courage with revenge, and grounding their resolution upon despair, they had proceeded with unlooked-for success. (94)

This passage signals both the generalness and the genuineness of the Helot cause. Yet, in spite of its promising "general consent," the revolt fails when the disguised Musidorus and his fellow soldiers pose as "country-people of Arcadia, no less oppressed by their lords and no less desirous of liberty than they" (96), and when the Helots accept into their camp this Trojan horse and its utopian promise of international class alliances.

Pyrocles, "under the name of Daiphantus" (790), explains to the conquered Helots that they now must merge with the Lacedaemonians into a single nation:

> The towns and forts you presently have are still left unto you, to be kept either with or without garrison, so as you alter not the laws of the country,

and pay such duties as the rest of the Laconians do. Yourselves are made by public decree free men, and so capable both to give and receive voice in election of magistrates. The distinction of names between Helots and Lacedaemonians to be quite taken away, and all indifferently to enjoy both names and privileges of Laconians.

. . . [F]or this is not a peace which is made with them, but this is a peace by which you are made of them. . . . [A]nd as you hated them before like oppressors, so now to love them as brothers; to take care of their estate because it is yours, and to labour by virtuous doing that the posterity may not repent your joining. (102)

In Sidney's account, the Helots readily consent to their absorption within the Laconian state. In fact, they initially rebelled because the Lacedaemonians were greedy and will later rebel because the tyrannical Laconian monarch will refuse to abide by the terms set by Daiphantus (790).

This description of the Helot rebellion is particularly intriguing because it is the one instance in which the *Arcadia* depicts as comprehensible the rebels' grievances. Yet, in spite of the comprehensibility—and even the justice—of their cause, the rebellion disintegrates, as do its simultaneous threats to national unity and to the status relationships among members of the Laconian nation. The narrative inevitability of this disintegration might best be explained by returning to the logic that governs Sidney's description of the troubled Arcadia:

There was a notable example how great dissipations monarchal governments are subject unto. For now their prince and guide had left them, they had not experience to rule, and had not whom to obey. Public matters had ever been privately governed, so that they had no lively taste what was good for themselves, but everything was either vehemently desireful or extremely terrible. Neighbours' invasions, civil dissension, cruelty of the coming prince, and whatsoever in common sense carries a dreadful show, was in all men's heads, but in few how to prevent: hearkening on every rumour, suspecting everything, condemning them whom before they had honoured, making strange and impossible tales of the king's death: while they thought themselves in danger, wishing nothing but safety; as soon as persuasion of safety took them, desiring further benefits as amendment of forepassed faults (which faults, notwithstanding, none could tell either the grounds or effects of); all agreeing in the universal names of liking or misliking, but of what in especial points, infinitely disagreeing: altogether like a falling steeple, the parts whereof—as windows, stones, and pinacles—were well, but the whole mass ruinous. (766)

I find striking the architecture of national politics with which this passage concludes because, in keeping with the earlier images of disintegrating rebels' bodies, it insists not only that there is a single possible coherent configuration of the steeple's "parts" but also that the social groups in question are themselves always already predetermined. In fact, in the *Arcadia*'s metaphor, the "windows, stones, and pinacles" remain stable and "well" even as the mortar that binds them together crumbles. In the same way, whether Sidney's royalty are "seeking to draw together" the rebels or "laying indifferently among them" (389), they are in the process of manipulating individuals who belong to a predetermined set of groups. In the *Arcadia*'s narrative, rebellions disperse when those *recognized* groups do not cohere.

In other words, the *Arcadia*'s rhetoric of rebellion figures the challenge to a dominant culture in terms of disintegrating alliances whose reconfiguration it makes unimaginable. More important, however, it also makes unimaginable a popular politics whose "parts" are not always already given—a politics in which the groups with which rebels identify are themselves shifting and unstable. Sidney's rhetoric of rebellion obscures the nature and the potential strength of collective resistance to a dominant culture. And, by concealing the degree to which hegemonic formations are always in process, that rhetoric also obscures both the shifting character of any dominant culture and the shifting terms through which dominant groups obtain consent. In so doing, it attempts to make unimaginable any radical reshaping of the political terrain—including one that might challenge the *Arcadia*'s particular conjunction of national unity, social status, and social order. And it leaves the dominant culture which is defined by that conjunction ill-equipped to confront what Antonio Gramsci would label its growing "crisis in authority."[17] In the next two chapters, I demonstrate how Shakespeare's insults and Deloney's proverbs promote collective identities that help define the range of possible intersections between local and national affiliations. In order to analyze how these collective identities participate in sixteenth-century class struggle, I consider struggles over absolutism and between commercial and industrial capital, the jurisdiction of ecclesiastical and

17. Gramsci, "State and Civil Society," 275–76, and Hall, *Hard Road to Renewal*, 95–122.

secular courts, the organization of guilds, and the composition and relative authority of town government. In this way, I address the sort of shifting and unstable political terrain that Sidney's rhetoric of rebellion refuses to imagine.

Rebelling as a Woman

This section of my chapter begins with the premise that, in the *Arcadia*, the falling steeple of a disorderly marriage is not altogether like the falling steeple of a disorderly state. I analyze how Sidney's rhetoric of rebellion offers a model of equity and of equality within companionate marriages, including an idiosyncratic version of the analogy between order within the family and order within the state. And I analyze how that model attempts to make unimaginable a collective politics which might have undermined the hierarchy of men over women and, at the same time, undermined the system of status and authority upon which the *Arcadia*'s vision of national unity depends. This analysis considers how Sidney inflects his distinction between consent and force and his depiction of architecturally unsound bodies and buildings when he considers the proper relationship between husband and wife. I begin by returning to an issue I raised in the first section of this chapter and ask precisely what *sort* of emotion could characterize popular rebellion, the lovers' excess passion, and their failed attempts to articulate that passion in verse.

"As soon as they [the rebels] came within perfect discerning of these ladies," Sidney writes in reference to Gynecia, Philoclea, and the disguised Pyrocles, "like enraged beasts, without respect of their estates or pity of their sex, . . . they began to run against them" (379). These "unruly sort of clowns and other rebels" (379) appear when Gynecia yields both to her adulterous yearnings for the disguised Pyrocles and to her unnatural hatred for Philoclea, her daughter and competitor in love. "Then began she to display to Zelmane the store-house of her deadly desires," Sidney writes; "when suddenly the confused rumour of a mutinous multitude gave just occasion to Zelmane to break off any such conference" (378–79). When the "scummy remnant of those rebels" (753) later emerges from the forest, they interrupt not only Pamela's flight, with Musidorus, from her father and her country but, more immediately, the prince's advances toward the sleeping princess:

> But that the roses of her lips . . . now by force drew his sight to mark how prettily they lay one over the other, uniting their divided beauties. . . . And lest this beauty might seem the picture of some excellent artificer, forth there stale a soft breath, carrying good testimony of her inward sweetness . . . which did so tyrannize over Musidorus' affects that he was compelled to put his face as low to hers as he could, sucking the breath with such joy. . . .
>
> But long he was not suffered, being within a while interrupted by the coming of a company of clownish villains. (653–54)

Like the rebels, Musidorus is controlled by a tyrannical force that is more compelling than the laws of his nation. The prince's resemblance to those "clownish villains" suggests the inevitable link between his treason and the "dissolution of all estates" (254).

Euarchus attributes the behavior of Gynecia, Musidorus, and the rebels to an ill-governed passion that is characterized by force rather than by consent:

> Both [princes] remember the force of love and, as it were, the mending up of the matter by their marriage. If that unbridled desire which is entitled love might purge such a sickness as this, surely we should have many loving excuses of hateful mischief. . . . [H]e that rebels, [might allege] the love of greatness, as the adulterer the love of a woman, since they do in all speeches affirm they love that which an ill-governed passion maketh them to follow. But love may have no such privilege. That sweet and heavenly uniting of the minds, which properly is called love, hath no other knot but virtue, and therefore if it be a right love, it can never slide into any action that is not virtuous. (837)

Although the *Arcadia* refuses to characterize as love an emotion "which he [Plangus] rather did take into himself willingly than by which he was taken forcibly" (313), it does not hesitate to condemn those characters who, forcefully overtaken by love, allow that passion to govern their "slide into any action that is not virtuous." Musidorus might have been subject to "love's force" when he fled with Pamela (833), yet, in the words of Euarchus, "it were very barbarous and preposterous that force should be made judge over reason" (829). I am not suggesting, as Musidorus suggests early in the narrative, that Arcadian love is "so unnatural a rebellion," a "womanish" and "base weakness" which must be overthrown by a masculine display of "sound forces" (132–33). Instead, in the *Arcadia*, love tests the boundaries between force and consent precisely because it is actually antithetical to forceful action. In fact, Musidorus fashions a jewel that reads, "By force, not choice" (233), when he wants to signal to Pamela that he does not truly love the gullible Mopsa. Unlike ill-governed passion, love produces gender relations that are governed not by a force that "maketh them to follow" but, rather, by a "sweet and heavenly uniting" whose knot of mutual consent is experienced as free will.

The marriage of Argalus and Parthenia best exemplifies that "sweet and heavenly uniting." Sidney writes that Parthenia's "heart hath vowed her to Argalus with so grateful a receipt in mutual affection that if she desired above all things to have Argalus, Argalus feared nothing but to miss Parthenia" (88–89). Throughout their courtship and marriage, they live without the ill-governed passion that tortures the adulterous Gynecia and Basilius. Free from that rebellious self-division, Argalus and Parthenia are "a happy couple . . . both increasing their riches by giving to each other; each making one life double, because they made a double life one; where desire never wanted satisfaction, nor satisfaction ever bred satiety" (501). This quotation depicts a marriage of mutuality in which husband and wife are indistinguishable. In fact, its second clause enacts that indistinguishability by doubling back upon itself in a near palindrome.

After Argalus is killed in battle, Parthenia recreates the mutuality characteristic of her marriage by disguising herself as the Knight of the Tomb and rushing into a battle where she hopes to obtain "her heart's desire" (530) by following her husband to his grave:

> Himself in an armour all painted over with such a cunning of shadow that it represented a gaping sepulchre: the furniture of his horse was all of cypress branches, wherewith in old time they were wont to dress graves. His bases, which he wore so long as they came almost to his ankle, were embroidered only with black worms, which seemed to crawl up and down, as ready already to devour him. In his shield, for impresa, he had a beautiful child, but having two heads, whereof the one showed that it was already dead; the other alive, but in that case, necessarily looking for death. The word was: "No way to be rid from death, but by death." (526)

Argalus had been "carried away by the tyranny of honour" (503); Parthenia embraces his anachronistic fate both by wearing knightly attire and by riding a horse whose cypress branches "in old time . . . were wont to dress graves" (526). In so doing, she also equates death's attempt to separate her from her husband with her mother's earlier attempt to force her not to marry Argalus: "When the time came that Demagoras, full of proud joy, thought to receive the gift of herself, she, with words of resolute refusal though with tears showing she was sorry she must refuse, assured her mother she would first be bedded in her grave than wedded to Demagoras" (89). After Parthenia's death, she is buried with her husband, and their mingled remains literally form the "blessed relics of faithful and virtuous love" (530). Basilius eulogizes this marriage whose mutuality extends into death:

> His being was in her alone:
> And he not being, she was none.
>
> They joy'd one joy, one grief they griev'd,
> One love they lov'd, one life they liv'd.
> The hand was one, one was the sword
> That did his death, her death afford.
>
> As all the rest, so now the stone
> That tombs the two is justly one.
> ARGALUS AND PARTHENIA
>
> (530)

In each of these passages, the *Arcadia* describes this marriage of mutual consent in general terms that do not distinguish between the spouses.

The *Arcadia*'s more specific descriptions, in which gendered pronouns distinguish the actions of Argalus from those of Parthenia, suggest that the general rubric of mutuality does not eliminate the hierarchy between husband and wife:

The messenger made speed, and found Argalus at a castle of his own, sitting in a parlour with the fair Parthenia, he reading in a book the stories of Hercules, she by him, as to hear him read; but while his eyes looked on the book, she looked on his eyes, and sometimes staying him with some pretty question, not so much to be resolved of the doubt as to give him occasion to look upon her. A happy couple: he joying in her, she joying in herself, but in herself, because she enjoyed him: . . . he ruling, because she would obey, or rather because she would obey, she therein ruling. (501)

In this passage, Sidney constructs skewed palindromes in which both spouses look, both joy, both rule, yet each does so with a different motive and each with a different allotment of power within the marriage. The relationship between husband and wife is bound by a mutual consent that does not eliminate the hierarchy between the partners. Their relationship is equitable, not equal.

In order to sort through the significance of this distinction, I turn to late-sixteenth- and early-seventeenth-century descriptions of marriage. Protestant marriage doctrines in Renaissance England borrowed the language of mutual affection with which Catholic doctrines had defined marital relations. Yet, by endorsing marital love and by viewing the family as a "seminary of the Church," Protestants mobilized the language of mutuality in a way that focused attention more firmly on the woman's role as companion and helpmate within the nuclear family. The Protestant companionate marriage was built on the assumption that men and women are equal in the eyes of God. Not surprisingly, domestic conduct books seldom extended that spiritual equality into political or economic equality. For example, although the initial marriage contract was supposedly predicated on mutual consent, household manuals seldom advised that mutual consent govern the subsequent practices of married life, during which the wife was decidedly subordinated to her husband. It is in this context that women were often accorded equitable rather than equal treatment with men. By emphasizing that the ideal wife served as a companion and helpmate to her husband, however, domestic handbooks were forced to address the sphere and nature of her complementary, yet necessarily ancillary, activity. The defining of that complementary activity through conduct books and through the actual practices of married couples was one site at which Renaissance women's subordination often threatened to become recognizable as a form of oppression. Such a recognition might have produced what Merry E. Wiesner defines as a feminist politics—a politics based on the explicit understanding that women are subject to certain forms of oppression precisely *because* they are women.[18] The *Arcadia* attempts to

18. Amussen, *An Ordered Society*, 34–66; Kathleen M. Davies, "The Sacred Condition of Equality—How Original Were Puritan Doctrines of Marriage?" *Social History* 5 (May 1977): 563–80; Roberta Hamilton, *The Liberation of Women: A Study of Patriarchy and Capitalism* (London: George Allen and Unwin, 1978), 50–75; Constance Jordan, *Renaissance Feminism: Literary Texts and Political Models* (Ithaca: Cornell University Press, 1990), 214–20, 286–97; Lawrence Stone, *The Family, Sex, and Marriage in England, 1500–1800* (New York: Harper

foreclose the possibility of this sort of politics through its depiction of equity and through its idiosyncratic analogy between order within the family and order within the state.

Constance Jordan argues that Renaissance pro-women writing often resisted the celebrations of equity that accompanied descriptions of companionate marriages. Pro-women writers maintained that biological men and biological women were equally capable of possessing what culture had termed masculine and feminine traits. For example, Jordan points out that Renaissance discussions about men who had raped women often described those women as naturally licentious; pro-women writers responded by describing women whose constancy disproved the notion that licentiousness was an inherently female trait.[19] Interestingly enough, given Jordan's framework, although the *Arcadia* does idealize the equitable marriage of Parthenia and Argalus, it also seems to undermine the logic of equity. In keeping with pro-women writing about rape and in keeping, more generally, with pro-women challenges to arguments based on equity, the *Arcadia* maintains that constancy is a trait shared by virtuous males and virtuous females. Pamela is praised for possessing "her mother's wisdom, greatness, nobility, but . . . knit with a more constant temper" (76). And, when Parthenia's mother offers Argalus increasingly dangerous military assignments and insists that her daughter marry Demagoras, Sidney writes that "it was hard to judge

---

and Row, 1977), 135–42, 195–206; and Merry E. Wiesner, "Women's Defense of Their Public Role," in *Women in the Middle Ages and the Renaissance: Literary and Historical Perspectives,* ed. Mary Beth Rose (Syracuse: Syracuse University Press, 1986), 22. The quotation from Protestant literature on marriage is cited in Hamilton, *Liberation of Women,* 56.

19. Jordan, *Renaissance Feminism,* 8, 112, 299–300. Jordan's analysis of the *Arcadia* focuses on Sidney's representations of androgyny. She argues that these representations contribute to Renaissance pro-women writing by suggesting that "masculine and feminine behaviors that are not specifically procreative are not restricted by biological sex" (225) and that "a monarch's responsibility as judge must include respect for . . . equity and mercy"—two aspects of justice that were coded as feminine (239). My analysis focuses on the logic of equity and equality in Sidney's depiction of companionate marriage. Like Jordan, I argue that the *Arcadia* detaches conventionally gendered moral traits—such as constancy—from biology. Yet, unlike Jordan, I also analyze how the *Arcadia* limits the potentially radical nature of this distinction. My analysis considers the very different logics that, according to the *Arcadia,* characterize a harmonious marriage and a harmonious state.

Alan Sinfield, *Literature in Protestant England, 1560–1660* (Totowa, N.J.: Barnes and Noble, 1983), 60–61, compares the marriage of Argalus and Parthenia to the imprisonment of Parthenia by Cecropia and Amphialus. He focuses on Sidney's Protestant critique of "romantic and Ovidian love" and his consequent effort to sort through the potentially contradictory consequences of passion.

whether he in doing or she in suffering shewed greater constancy of affection" (89).

In fact, in the *Arcadia*, it is the evil queen Cecropia who, when advising her son to rape Philoclea, associates women with licentiousness:

> But above all mark Helen, daughter to Jupiter, who could never brook her mannerly-wooing Menelaus, but disdained his humbleness and loathed his softness. But so well she could like the force of enforcing Paris that for him she could abide what might be abidden. But what? Menelaus takes heart: he recovers her by force, by force carries her home, by force enjoys her; and she (who could never like him for serviceableness) ever after loved him for violence. For what can be more agreeable than upon force to lay the fault of desire, and in one instant to join a dear delight with a just excuse? . . .
>
> Truly I have known a great lady, long sought by most great, most wise, most beautiful, most valiant persons, never won, because they did over-superstitiously solicit her: the same lady brought under by another, inferior to all them in all those qualities, only because he could use that imperious masterfulness which nature gives to men above women. For indeed, son, I confess unto you, in our very creation we are servants. . . . Awake thy spirits, good Amphialus, and assure thyself that though she refuseth, she refuseth but to endear the obtaining. . . . Think she would not strive, but that she means to try thy force; and my Amphialus, know thyself a man, and show thyself a man; and, believe me upon my word, a woman is a woman. (533–34)

The narrative consistently satirizes and discredits Cecropia's advice—advice that, as this passage indicates, turns on an absolute distinction between men's and women's behavior.

Earlier in the narrative, Cecropia links this behavioral difference to sexual difference. Philoclea, fearing that she will be forced to marry Amphialus, claims to have promised God that she will remain a virgin. Cecropia counters her niece's Catholic championing of celibacy by referring to a prior vow made for Philoclea by nature. "A vow, quoth you?" Cecropia asks, "No, no, my dear niece, Nature, when you were first born, vowed you a woman, and as she made you child of a mother, so to do your best to be mother of a child" (460). The woman simply must do her best to fulfill the contract made for her and without her consent. Yet, in Cecropia's account, it is precisely in fulfilling this contract that the woman demonstrates that her refusal is a form of consent that "endear[s] the obtaining" (534):

> "Tush, tush, son," said Cecropia. "If you say you love but, withal, you fear, you fear lest you should offend. Offend? And how know you that you should offend? Because she doth deny? Deny! Now by my truth, if your sadness would let me laugh, I could laugh heartily to see that yet you are ignorant that 'No' is no negative in a woman's mouth. My son, believe me, a woman speaking of women. . . . Each virtue hath his time. . . . Let examples serve. Do you think Theseus should ever have gotten Antiope with sighing and crossing his arms? He ravished her, . . . but having ravished her, he got a child of her. And I say no more, but that, they say, is not gotten without consent of both sides." (532–33)

One version of Renaissance gynecology argued that reproduction was possible only if the seeds of both partners were heated by their desire. As Cecropia's anecdote illustrates, this theory often disproved women's charges of rape.[20] In Cecropia's scenario, the woman's consent is predetermined because, however she behaves and whatever she says, she means "yes"; even her body betrays that truth. Philoclea's constancy disproves this cliché.

Yet if the *Arcadia* seems to challenge arguments based on equity by detaching moral traits, such as constancy, from biology, it also deflects what might be one radical implication of this separation: it refuses to extend its challenge beyond the moral realm. The *Arcadia*'s female characters are accorded moral equality without being accorded political or economic equality. In fact, the *Arcadia* associates the political equality of men and women with popular rebellion and with a threat to the distinctions among private people, their public magistrates, and the monarch. For example, the rebels alternately lust after, attack, and curse the supposed Amazon Zelmane after she displays unwomanly skills in both combat and public oration. "An unused thing it is," she had admitted before being attacked, "and I think not heretofore seen, O Arcadians, that a woman should give public counsel to men, a stranger to the country people, and that lastly in such a presence, by a private person the

20. Angus McLaren, *Reproductive Rituals: The Perception of Fertility in England from the Sixteenth Century to the Nineteenth Century* (London: Methuen, 1984), 20–21, 27, explains that the Renaissance link between procreation and women's pleasure was often used to disprove women's charges of rape.

regal throne should be possessed" (384). In short, the *Arcadia* reinforces the logic of companionate marriages by appropriating the language with which pro-women writers had challenged both that logic and the larger system of social inequalities it fostered.

In addition, by associating such challenges with the specter of popular rebellion, Sidney offers a model for imagining women's economic and political rights that would have been familiar to the audience of pro-women writing. Jordan explains: "The failure of sixteenth-century feminist debate to produce any social change was due to a variety of factors, one of which may have been the ambivalence that women could be made to feel toward the prospect of securing rights as representatives of their sex irrespective of rank. Any interest that women might have in securing equality of the sexes could be depicted as if it threatened privileged social status."[21] Although I am not convinced that Renaissance pro-women writing was unable to contribute to any sort of social change, Jordan's work does persuade me that much of the sixteenth-century audience for pro-women arguments might have understood alliances among women as a threat to the privileges they enjoyed on the basis of their family's social status. Such an understanding would have emerged from a variety of cultural forces—including, as I have been arguing, the *Arcadia*. Thus, even though Renaissance pro-women writing generally addressed the concerns of and certainly would have made political rights available to only a limited number of Renaissance women, it was nonetheless unlikely to prompt even that limited group of female readers and auditors to articulate their oppression in terms of gender.

Yet the *Arcadia* also associates challenges to companionate marriage with an unsettling of the distinctions among private people, their public magistrates, and the monarch. In this way, it acknowledges that the definition of a woman's complementary role within marriage was one site at which women's more general social subordination threatened to become visible as a form of oppression. Susan Amussen explains that

> the analogy between the household and the state was available to all those interested in authority and the enforcement of order in early modern England. It must be understood as an analogy, however, not an equation. As an analogy it could be used in many different ways. Those who employed the analogy were not all in agreement on the fundamental nature

21. Jordan, *Renaissance Feminism*, 301.

of faith, the family or the state, and few of them . . . actually dealt with the assumptions that others made.

This passage stresses the uneven and deeply contested relationship between models of the family and models of the state. And it stresses the lack of Renaissance consensus—even within prescriptive writing surrounding companionate marriage—about those models and about their relationships to one another. Amussen adds that, in spite of their disparate formulations, the authors of domestic conduct books did tend to share at least the general conviction that "the family was central to social order; disciplined families were therefore a prerequisite of that order."[22] Sidney's rhetoric of rebellion filters the relationship between an individual woman and her husband through the relationships among private people, public magistrates, and the monarch. In this way, the *Arcadia* offers an idiosyncratic version of the common Renaissance analogy between order within the family and order within the state. That analogy, I argue, sidesteps what many writers of household manuals perceived as a dilemma: how to grant the wife a measure of domestic authority, including an authority over children and servants, without calling into question her subordination to her husband. And it sidesteps what these writers perceived to be a second, related dilemma: how to justify a domestic hierarchy between members of the same social class without in any way calling into question the system of status and authority that defined membership within and the hierarchies among social classes.

I begin to analyze how the *Arcadia* depicts the orderly relationship between husband and wife, on the one hand, and between monarch and subject, on the other, by returning to the narrative's most discredited

22. Amussen, *An Ordered Society*, 37 and 38. For somewhat different analyses of the link between domestic and state politics, see Christopher Martin, "Misdoubting His Estate: Dynastic Anxiety in Sidney's *Arcadia*," *English Literary Renaissance* 18:3 (Autumn 1988): 369–88; Margaret M. Sullivan, "Amazons and Aristocrats: The Function of Pyrocles' Amazon Role in Sidney's Revised *Arcadia*," in *Playing with Gender: A Renaissance Pursuit*, ed. Jean R. Brink, Maryanne C. Horowitz, and Allison P. Coudert (Urbana: University of Illinois Press, 1991), 62–81; and Leonard Tennenhouse, "Arcadian Rhetoric: Sidney and the Politics of Courtship," in Allen, Baker-Smith, and Kinney, *Sir Philip Sidney's Achievements*, 201–13. Martin focuses on the "anxiety over succession" (380) that produces both domestic and dynastic crises. Sullivan focuses on the difficulty, during Elizabeth's rule, "with trying to represent a gender hierarchy within an aristocratic one" (67). And Tennenhouse focuses on the Elizabethan "fantasy that linked power to gender, rather than to the father's bloodline" (206).

spokesperson for refiguring those relationships—Cecropia. Renaissance pro-women writers often noted that contemporary discussions about women who had been raped tended to raise an issue about authority which surfaced more generally in sixteenth- and seventeenth-century definitions of gender relations—how the purportedly weaker woman could be accused of functioning as an aggressor.[23] In a speech, again not endorsed by the *Arcadia*, Cecropia resolves this apparent paradox by celebrating the dynamics of female beauty:

> And see, a fair woman shall not only command without authority but persuade without speaking. She shall not need to procure attention, for their own eyes will chain their ears unto it. Men venture lives to conquer; she conquers lives without venturing. She is served and obeyed, which is the most notable not because the laws so command it, but because they become laws to themselves to obey her; not for her parents' sake, but for her own. She need not dispute whether to govern by fear or love since, without her thinking thereof, their love will bring forth fear, and their fear will fortify their love; and she need not seek offensive or defensive force, since her only lips may stand for ten thousand shields, and ten thousand unevitable shot go from her eyes. Beauty, beauty. (485)

Cecropia's formulation suggests that beautiful women "need not dispute whether to govern by fear or love." Their unparalleled ability to blur the boundaries between force and consent does not produce authority within gender relations. Yet it does produce an illegitimate form of control that might be described as in competition with the authority—the "imperious masterfulness" (534)—typically exercised by men. The *Arcadia* introduces Cecropia's problematic model of the domestic realm in order to discredit it. By dismantling the hierarchy of the husband over his wife, she threatens to create a world where Iberia's Queen Andromana might have "first with the reins of affection, and after with the very use of directing, . . . made herself so absolute a master of her husband's mind that awhile he would not, and after, he could not tell how to govern without being governed by her" (347).

Instead, the *Arcadia* resolves the paradox of women's authority through its idiosyncratic analogy between order within the family and order within the state. The logic of that analogy is clearest when, after Basilius's apparent demise, Euarchus sentences Gynecia to death. Ex-

23. Jordan, *Renaissance Feminism*, 299–300.

plaining that her fate should function "for the everlasting example to all *wives and subjects*" (815, my emphasis), he compares her betrayal of her marriage to that of her country:

> That whereas, both in private and public respects, this woman had most heinously offended—in private (because marriage being the most holy conjunction that falls to mankind, out of which all families and so consequently all societies do proceed, which not only by community of goods but community of children is to knit the minds in a most perfect union; which whoso breaks, dissolves all humanity, no man living free from the danger of so near a neighbour) she had not only broken it, but broken it with death, and the most pretended death that might be: in public respect (the prince's person being in all monarchal governments the very knot of the people's welfare and light of all their doings, to which they are not only in conscience but in necessity bound to be loyal) she had traitorously empoisoned him, neither regarding her country's profit, her own duty, nor the rigour of the laws. (814–15)

Gynecia's crimes are both public and private in several ways. First, not surprisingly, this passage correlates Gynecia's private crimes against her husband with her public crimes against her monarch. Second, again not surprisingly, it demonstrates how all private marital relations are of public concern both to the local community and to the nation. Third, however, the language with which Gynecia's crimes are described and the penalty that she incurs locate her among the *Arcadia*'s rebellious private people. Tried both for her adultery and for the murder caused "by the violence of that ill-answered passion" (816), Gynecia receives a sentence that marshals the language of Renaissance debates about marriage and divorce.[24] Buried alive with her deceased husband, she will be "forced to keep company with the body from which she had made so detestable a severance; and lastly, death might redress their disjoined conjunction of marriage" (815). In short, she must restore Arcadian social order by embracing Parthenia's fate and thus reassembling this severed marital body.

24. Amussen, *An Ordered Society*, 56–57; Catherine Belsey, *The Subject of Tragedy: Identity and Difference in Renaissance Drama* (London: Methuen, 1985), 138–44, 185; Hamilton, *Liberation of Women*, 62–63; Martin Ingram, *Church Courts, Sex, and Marriage in England, 1570–1640* (Cambridge: Cambridge University Press, 1987), 144–50; and Alan Macfarlane, *Marriage and Love in England: Modes of Reproduction, 1300–1840* (Oxford: Basil Blackwell, 1986), 222–31.

In an earlier passage, Sidney had described the apparent beheading of Philoclea as an effort to "divorce the fair marriage of the head and body" (558). He wrote, "Alas, why should they divide such a head from such a body? No other body is worthy of that head; no other head is worthy of that body. . . . Who is there now left that can justify thy tyranny and give reason to thy passion? O cruel divorce of the sweetest marriage that ever was in Nature" (565). Here, as in Euarchus's speech, the *Arcadia* links divorce—the separation of the woman from her rightful "head"—to the tyrannical passions that govern the rebellious private people in the narrative's second and fourth books.

I want to stress that Sidney's rhetoric of rebellion locates Gynecia among the private people *only* when her adulterous passions subvert the hierarchy between her and her husband. In other words, the falling steeple of a disorderly marriage is not altogether like the falling steeple of a disorderly state. According to the *Arcadia*, when a woman rebels against the domestic hierarchy of husbands over their wives, it is not merely the mortar that crumbles but the very parts themselves. Forfeiting her subordinate but equitable role within the marriage, the rebellious wife transforms herself into a private person. Within this analogy, a dutiful wife—like Parthenia—presumably resembles a public magistrate who possesses some authority in relation to, yet never threatens to supersede, the monarch. After all, even those critics who argue that the *Arcadia* does sanction the rebellion of aristocratic magistrates against a tyrannical ruler do not argue that a *single* public magistrate possesses that authority. Thus by redescribing the relationship between an individual man and an individual woman through the relationships among private people, their public magistrates, and the monarch, Sidney's rhetoric of rebellion offers the woman a model of wifely authority in which she nonetheless remains decidedly subordinate to her husband and in which her subordination does not threaten to dissolve the distinctions among social classes.

In the next two chapters, I analyze the rhetoric of concealment in Shakespeare's *The Merry Wives of Windsor* and in Deloney's *Jack of Newbury*. Those analyses retain this chapter's interest in competing models of collective politics yet focus on the particular political identities that Shakespeare's insults and Deloney's proverbs help to promote and to foreclose. I situate those political identities both in relation to feudal and emerging capitalist modes of production and in relation to debates about the proper sphere and nature of Renaissance women's activity.

Chapter Three

"The adoption of abominable terms": Middle Classes, Merry Wives, and the Insults That Shape Windsor

I take the title of this chapter from Francis Ford's first soliloquy in *The Merry Wives of Windsor*.[1] Misconstruing his wife's merriment as unfaithfulness, the distracted Ford laments:

> See the hell of having a false woman! My bed shall be abus'd, my coffers ransack'd, my reputation gnawn at, and I shall not only receive this villainous wrong, but stand under the adoption of abominable terms, and by him that does me this wrong. Terms! names! Amaimon sounds well; Lucifer, well; Barbason, well; yet they are devils' additions, the names of fiends; but Cuckold! Wittol!—Cuckold! the devil himself hath not such a name.
>
> . . . .
>
> I will prevent this, detect my wife, be reveng'd on Falstaff, and laugh at Page. I will about it; better three hours too soon than a minute too late. Fie, fie, fie! cuckold, cuckold, cuckold! (II.ii.291–300, 310–14)

In this passage, Ford tests a series of interchangeable self-designations—Amaimon, Lucifer, Barbason—before settling on the term to which his own particular hell entitles him: cuckold. It is a term that he pre-

---

1. All citations from *The Merry Wives of Windsor* are from the folio edition of the play in *The Riverside Shakespeare*, ed. G. Blakemore Evans (Boston: Houghton Mifflin, 1974). See Leah S. Marcus, "Levelling Shakespeare: Local Customs and Local Texts," *Shakespeare Quarterly* 42:2 (Summer 1991): 168–78, for a discussion about the differences between the folio and quarto editions—especially the ways in which the 1602 quarto depicts Windsor as a less particularized location.

maturely adopts in order to distinguish himself from the "wittol," from the foolish husband who would knowingly endure his wife's infidelity. Ford announces that Alice Ford's adultery would threaten his control over her sexuality, over his wealth, and, most unendurably, over his good name. He emphasizes that she is his property and, more specifically, that she is property with which *she* cannot be entrusted. He does so by marshaling a string of proverbial insults about those who make "fritters of English" (V.v.143). "I will rather trust a Fleming with my butter," he says, "Parson Hugh the Welshman with my cheese, an Irishman with my aquavitae bottle, or a thief to walk my ambling gelding, than my wife with herself" (II.ii.302–5). Ford pledges to diminish the threat of an "abus'd" bed by publicizing his wife's plans. He seals that pledge by reiterating the single, abominable term to which his identity has been reduced: "cuckold, cuckold, cuckold!"

Although Ford's fellow inhabitants of Windsor do not share his disruptive jealousy, they do share his preoccupation with the terms that designate their shifting and uneven relationships to one another. As the play's opening lines indicate, that preoccupation frequently takes the form of a perpetual naming and self-naming:

> SHALLOW: Sir Hugh, persuade me not; I will make a Star Chamber matter of it. If he were twenty Sir John Falstaffs, he shall not abuse Robert Shallow, esquire.
> SLENDER: In the county of Gloucester, Justice of Peace and Coram.
> SHALLOW: Ay, cousin Slender, and *Custa-lorum*.
> SLENDER: Ay, and *Rato-lorum* too; and a gentleman born, Master Parson, who writes himself *Armigero*, in any bill, warrant, quittance, or obligation, *Armigero*.
>
> (I.i.1–11)

I begin my analysis of *The Merry Wives of Windsor* by citing these passages because I am interested in the terms the play's characters adopt and impose on one another. As each passage's emphasis on abuse indicates, insults are central to this process of naming the relationships among Windsor's inhabitants. Accounts of Renaissance slander and defamation cases and accounts of Renaissance shaming rituals, such as the skimmington and the charivari, describe how insults were also central to a larger process of establishing the shifting authority relations among state, local, and ecclesiastical officials and among husbands, wives, and children.[2] I locate the play's network of insults within this larger process and, in so doing, examine those authority relations which Shakespeare's "abominable terms" endorse.

My focus on the play's insults allows me to analyze not only the terms with which Shakespeare locates his characters within Windsor but also the terms with which Shakespeare's critics have located the play within Renaissance struggles over class and over gender. For example, critics generally claim that *The Merry Wives of Windsor* depicts a confrontation between the "bourgeois" or "middle-class" inhabitants of a small town and the nobility who visit from the court. In the first section of this chapter, I demonstrate how this double terminology obscures not only the inhabitants' very different positions within the feudal and emerging capitalist modes of production but also their positions within very different structures of oppression. I then argue that the play's middle class is not a *thing* to be defined but, instead, a *process* of constructing alliances among groups characterized by their multiple and often contradictory

2. S[usan] D[wyer] Amussen, "Gender, Family, and the Social Order, 1560–1725," in *Order and Disorder in Early Modern England*, ed. Anthony Fletcher and John Stevenson (Cambridge: Cambridge University Press, 1985), 196–217, and *An Ordered Society: Gender and Class in Early Modern England* (Oxford: Basil Blackwell, 1988), 50, 95–179; Lynda E. Boose, "Scolding Brides and Bridling Scolds: Taming the Woman's Unruly Member," *Shakespeare Quarterly* 42:2 (Summer 1991): 179–213; Natalie Zemon Davis, *Society and Culture in Early Modern France* (Stanford: Stanford University Press, 1975), 124–51; Anthony Fletcher, "Honour, Reputation, and Local Officeholding in Elizabethan and Stuart England," in Fletcher and Stevenson, *Order and Disorder*, 92–115; R. H. Helmholz, ed., *Select Cases on Defamation to 1600* (London: Seldon Society, 1985); Ralph Houlbrooke, *Church Courts and the People during the English Reformation, 1520–1570* (Oxford: Oxford University Press, 1979), 55–88; Martin Ingram, *Church Courts, Sex, and Marriage in England, 1570–1640* (Cambridge: Cambridge University Press, 1987), 292–319; Andrew J. King, "The Law of Slander in Early Antebellum America," *American Journal of Legal History* 35:1 (January 1991): 1–5; Louis A. Knafla, "'Sin of all sorts swarmeth': Criminal Litigation in an English County in the Early Seventeenth Century," in *Law, Litigants, and the Legal Profession: Papers Presented to the Fourth British Legal History Conference at the University of Birmingham, 10–13 July 1979*, Royal Historical Society Studies in History Series, no. 36, ed. E. W. Ives and A. H. Manchester (Atlantic Highlands, N.J.: Humanities Press, 1983), 50–67; Peter Rushton, "Women, Witchcraft, and Slander in Early Modern England: Cases from the Church Courts of Durham, 1560–1675," *Northern History: A Review of the History of Northern England* 18 (1982): 116–32; D[avid] E. Underdown, "The Taming of the Scold: The Enforcement of Patriarchal Authority in Early Modern England," in Fletcher and Stevenson, *Order and Disorder*, 116–36, and *Revel, Riot, and Rebellion: Popular Politics and Culture in England, 1603–1660* (Oxford: Oxford University Press, 1985; paperback ed., 1987), 39; David Vaisey, "Court Records and the Social History of Seventeenth-Century England," *History Workshop: A Journal of Socialist Historians* 1 (Spring 1976): 185–91; and Carol Z. Wiener, "Sex Roles and Crime in Late Elizabethan Hertfordshire," *Journal of Social History* 8 (Summer 1975): 46–49.

short- and long-term interests. With this argument in mind, I examine
how Shakespeare's insults reinforce categories through which members
of such groups might experience their political identities. By focusing
on Shallow and Sir Hugh Evans—the play's justice of the peace and
parson—and by focusing on the history of Windsor and of its castle, I
locate the play's network of insults within this larger social process. In
this way, I examine how Shakespeare's "abominable terms" promote collective identities—"townsmen" and "gentlemen"—that participate in
Renaissance struggles over absolutism and between commercial and industrial capital precisely by helping to define the range of possible intersections between regional and national affiliations.

Although I locate Alice Ford and Margaret Page's public shaming of
Falstaff within this register, I also analyze that shaming as one instance
of the women's merry response to Falstaff's insults. Critics often claim
that, by resisting Falstaff's advances, the play's title characters contribute
to their husbands' "bourgeois" or "middle-class" status. In the second
section of this chapter, I focus, instead, on the logic of the women's
mirth. It is through that logic, I argue, that the play distinguishes between men's and women's honesty and, in so doing, participates in Renaissance struggles over the sphere and nature of women's activity.

Determining the Middle Class

Critics often describe the townspeople in *The Merry Wives of Windsor* as
alternately "bourgeois" and "middle-class." For example, Camille Wells
Slights describes Windsor as a "robustly middle-class world" that is pop-
ulated by "ordinary bourgeois English men and women." Carol Thomas
Neely describes Windsor as "a thriving bourgeois town" that is popu-
lated by "the middle class." Jan Lawson Hinely analyzes Falstaff's relationship to this "middle class society" and its "bourgeois citizens." Peter
Erickson cautions that any class analysis of the play must consider both
Falstaff's and Fenton's relationship to Windsor's "bourgeois country
folk"—the play's "middle class characters." Anne Barton writes that
George Page, responding to Fenton, "displays the wariness of an English
middle class accustomed . . . to the sexual maneuvers and depredations
of an impoverished aristocracy." And, she explains, by rejecting the aristocratic Falstaff, Margaret Page and Alice Ford—unlike most middle-
class wives in contemporary city comedies—remain loyal to their husbands and to the "bourgeois community to which they belong." Sandra

Clark also notes the wives' imperviousness both to a "gentleman-lover" and to his promises of upward social mobility. She writes that Margaret Page and Alice Ford "participate in the same code of bourgeois social values as their menfolk. . . . [H]e [Falstaff] underestimates both their intelligence and their loyalty to the ethic of the middle-class." Marvin Felheim and Philip Traci describe these women as, alternately, "rich bourgeoisie," "well-to-do middle-class types," and "attractive middle-class housewives."[3]

At first glance, this casual doubling of terminology might seem uncontroversial. As Immanuel Wallerstein explains, critics generally define members of the bourgeoisie either culturally—by their style of life and opportunities for consumption—or economically—by their relations to production and opportunities for investment. Whichever criteria they employ, they identify the bourgeoisie of Renaissance England as that feudal middle class which was neither nobility nor peasantry.[4] In keeping with this definition, Windsor's inhabitants locate themselves below

3. Quotations, in order of presentation, are from Camille Wells Slights, "Pastoral and Parody in *The Merry Wives of Windsor*," *English Studies in Canada* 11:1 (March 1985): 12, 24; Carol Thomas Neely, "Constructing Female Sexuality in the Renaissance: Stratford, London, Windsor, Vienna," in *Feminism and Psychoanalysis*, ed. Richard Feldstein and Judith Roof (Ithaca: Cornell University Press, 1989), 217; Jan Lawson Hinely, "Comic Scapegoats and the Falstaff of *The Merry Wives of Windsor*," *Shakespeare Studies* 15 (1982): 37, 42; Peter Erickson, "The Order of the Garter, the Cult of Elizabeth, and Class-Gender Tension in *The Merry Wives of Windsor*," in *Shakespeare Reproduced: The Text in History and Ideology*, ed. Jean E. Howard and Marion F. O'Connor (New York: Methuen, 1987), 126; Anne Barton, "Falstaff and the Comic Community," in *Shakespeare's "Rough Magic": Renaissance Essays in Honor of C. L. Barber*, ed. Peter Erickson and Coppélia Kahn (Newark: University of Delaware Press, 1985), 138, 139; Sandra Clark, "'Wives may be merry and yet honest too': Women and Wit in *The Merry Wives of Windsor* and Some Other Plays," in *"Fanned and Winnowed Opinions": Shakespearean Essays Presented to Harold Jenkins*, ed. John W. Mahon and Thomas A. Pendleton (London: Methuen, 1987), 254, 263; and Marvin Felheim and Philip Traci, "Realism in *The Merry Wives of Windsor*," *Ball State University Forum* 22:1 (1981): 57, 59. In *Reappraisals in History: New Views on History and Society in Early Modern Europe*, 2d ed. (Chicago: University of Chicago Press, 1979), 71–149, J. H. Hexter argues against historians who describe the Renaissance middle class as possessing a "group consciousness, group pride, or will to power" (99). Hexter's redefinition of the middle class is part of his larger attempt to undermine R. H. Tawney's and Lawrence Stone's claims about the gentry and the English Revolution. Although I find Hexter's work useful because it describes the range of social positions that have been labeled "middle-class," I am not in sympathy with his revisionist project. My chapter argues that the middle class is not a thing to be defined—or redefined—but a process of forming political alliances among groups that occupy a particular range of positions.
4. For a discussion of this definition of the middle class, see Immanuel Wallerstein, "The Bourgeois(ie) as Concept and Reality," *New Left Review* 167 (January/February 1988): 91–106, particularly 91–93.

that "too high a region" (III.ii.73) where the noble Fenton "kept company with the wild prince and Poins" (III.ii.72–73) and where the knightly
Falstaff seems to have contracted his "dissolute disease" (III.iii.191–92).
And, in spite of Falstaff's boasting, those inhabitants do not prove to be
the "peasant[s]" over whom he might "predominate" (II.ii.282). Yet, as
George K. Hunter has pointed out, although *The Merry Wives of Windsor*
is often championed as one of Shakespeare's most "realistic" plays, its
detailed descriptions of Windsor's inhabitants actually offer very little
specific information about their relative material conditions or differing
relations to production.[5] This is a persuasive claim. For example, Shakespeare critics roughly correlate the "bourgeoisie" or "middle class" depicted in the play with those whom members of Renaissance society
increasingly labeled the "middling sort." This latter category generally
designated property owners who might occupy a wide range of positions
within the feudal and emerging capitalist modes of production.[6] The
varied composition of this "middling sort" might account for critics'
disagreement about the enemies against whom Windsor's inhabitants
define themselves: the upper classes (Barton, Hinely), the aristocracy
(Barton, Felheim and Traci, French, Hunter), predatory capitalists
(Freedman), gallants (Clark), the nobility (Hinely, Hunter), courtiers
(Bradbrook, Felheim and Traci, Hinely, Hunter), knights (Felheim and
Traci, Hinely, Hunter), and the gentry (Clark, Hunter)—the latter a
term that, as Bradbrook and Hinely admit, also applies to Windsor's
bourgeois or middle-class inhabitants.[7] In short, as Hunter suggests, the

5. George K. Hunter, "Bourgeois Comedy: Shakespeare and Dekker," in *Shakespeare and His Contemporaries: Essays in Comparison*, ed. E. A. J. Honigmann (Oxford: Manchester University Press, 1986), 1–15.

6. Richard Cust and Ann Hughes discuss the elusiveness of "the middling sort" in historians' analyses of early modern culture ("Introduction: After Revisionism," in *Conflict in Early Stuart England: Studies in Religion and Politics, 1603–1642*, ed. Cust and Hughes [London: Longman, 1989], 33–38). Keith Wrightson argues that the category entered the language of "sorts" at the beginning of the seventeenth century and that it designated an increasingly large range of people ("Estates, Degrees, and Sorts in Tudor and Stuart England," *History Today* 37 [January 1987]: 22).

7. Barton, "Falstaff and the Comic Community," 132–33, 138; M. C. Bradbrook, *Shakespeare the Craftsman* (New York: Barnes and Noble, 1969), 77, 79, 87, 88; Clark, "Women and Wit," 254–55, 263; Felheim and Traci, "Realism," 57–59; Barbara Freedman, "Falstaff's Punishment: Buffoonery as Defensive Posture in *The Merry Wives of Windsor*," *Shakespeare Studies: An Annual Gathering of Research, Criticism, and Reviews* 14 (1981): 172; Marilyn French, *Shakespeare's Division of Experience* (New York: Summit Books, 1981), 107; Hinely, "Comic Scapegoats," 37–38; Hunter, "Bourgeois Comedy," 4–5, 8–14; and Slights, "Pastoral and Parody," 15–17.

play frustrates any consistent definition of its middling sort. In fact, I would argue, its network of insults emphasizes that this middle realm is actually constituted by multiple and often contradictory interests that critics' double terminology has helped to obscure.

My understanding of this contradictory middle realm has been influenced by recent accounts of late-twentieth-century workers who are middle-class not because they are positioned between the aristocracy and the peasantry but because, within the capitalist mode of production, they are neither entirely bourgeois nor entirely proletarian. These accounts are offered by economists and political theorists who locate their work within—or, at least, in dialogue with—a Marxist tradition. These writers generally agree to label "middle-class" those groups whose political alliances are especially uncertain because their economic interests coincide with the interests of both the exploiters and the exploited within any dominant mode of production. In Britain and in the United States, these workers currently include small business owners who do not employ wage laborers and the entire array of white-collar workers. In order to analyze the possible alliances of small business owners, these writers have discussed their contradictory relation to capitalist exploitation: they are neither wage laborers nor employers of wage labor. In order to analyze the possible alliances of white-collar workers, they have examined relations within dominant and nondominant modes of production; the status of manual and nonmanual labor; distinctions between exploitation and domination; positions within authority relations; and opportunities for consumption, investment, mobility, and job autonomy. They ask how those disparate workers' immediate or long-term interests might intersect, how those intersecting middle-class interests also might intersect with proletarian interests, and how these potential affiliations might alter the shape of democracy or of socialism. They stress that the structural position of the middle class makes it difficult to determine which sorts of collective action might be unequivocally in its members' best interests. In other words, they are not discussing groups that are duped into acting against their own best interests; instead, they are addressing those groups whose structural position allows for the construction of multiple and often contradictory interests.[8]

8. Jon Elster, "Three Challenges to Class" in *Analytical Marxism*, ed. John Roemer (Cambridge: Cambridge University Press, 1986), 141–61; Anthony Giddens, *The Class Structure of the Advanced Societies*, 2d ed. (London: Hutchinson, 1981), 99–117, 177–97; Stuart Hall, *The Hard Road to Renewal: Thatcherism and the Crisis of the Left* (London: Verso,

I find this work helpful because the structural location of the middle class prompts each of these writers to consider, more generally, how political identities are produced and to *re*consider the nature of political agency. For example, they ask how class struggle relates to other social struggles; when interests based on perceived common alliances coincide with those based on often unrecognized structural affiliations; under what conditions those affiliations become politically meaningful and thus available for organization into political alliances; how the political realm relates to the economic, to the social, or to the cultural; how we might distinguish not only among different objects of oppression but also among different structures of oppression; and under what conditions any group characterized by multiple and conflicting interests will pursue the more radical of its affiliations. These same sorts of questions have governed recent debates in Britain, France, and the United States about hegemony, about radical democracy, and about the "new social movements." Discussions of the middle class are particularly useful in sorting through these issues because, although they do not accord an inevitable primacy to economic exploitation, they *do* retain the category of exploitation and ask how its structure of oppression might intersect with other oppressive structures. Drawing on these discussions, I argue that Shakespeare's middle class is a process of constructing alliances among groups characterized by their simultaneous participation in very different structures of oppression and thus by their multiple and often contradictory potential short- and long-term interests. Insults are central to that process.

After Falstaff sends identical love letters to Alice Ford and to Margaret Page, sexual slander becomes Windsor's most prevalent form of insult. Recognizing Falstaff's missives as dangerous attacks on their honesty, the women vow to avenge themselves on "this unwholesome humidity, this gross wat'ry pumpion" and to "teach him to know turtles from jays" (III.iii.40–42). Pistol warns Ford that Falstaff plans to seduce his wife and predicts that the cuckolded Ford will be compelled to adopt a particularly abominable term:

1988); Wallerstein, "Bourgeois(ie) as Concept and Reality," 91–106; and Erik Olin Wright, *Class, Crisis, and the State* (London: New Left Books, 1978; London: Verso, 1979), 30–110, "A General Framework for the Analysis of Class Structure," in *The Debate on Classes*, ed. Wright (London: Verso, 1989), 3–43, and "What Is Middle about the Middle Class?" in Roemer, *Analytical Marxism*, 114–40.

PISTOL: Prevent; or go thou
    Like Sir Actaeon he, with Ringwood at thy heels—
    O, odious is the name!
FORD: What name, sir?
PISTOL: The horn, I say. Farewell.

                    (II.i.117–21)

Unlike Page, Ford refuses to trust the honesty of his wife, to let her
actions "lie on my head" (II.i.184). Instead, he searches for Falstaff in
her laundry basket, shouting, "Buck! I would I could wash myself of the
buck! Buck, buck, buck! ay, buck! I warrant you, buck, and of the season
too, it shall appear" (III.iii.157–59). And, posing as Master Brook, he
joins Falstaff in slandering Alice Ford's honesty: "Some say that, though
she appear honest to me, yet in other places she enlargeth her mirth so
far that there is shrewd construction made of her" (II.ii.221–24). Asked
by "Master Brook" whether he knows Ford, the knight responds by
fulfilling Pistol's prediction:

> Hang him, poor cuckoldly knave. I know him not. Yet I wrong him to call
> him poor. They say the jealous wittolly knave hath masses of money, for
> the which his wife seems to me well-favor'd. I will use her as the key of the
> cuckoldly rogue's coffer, and there's my harvest-home. (II.ii.270–75)

Unwilling to be labeled a wittol, Ford vows to make public the activities
that have reduced him to a cuckold.

    Yet he also acknowledges the risk of this course of action: if his wife
actually *is* trustworthy, he will not be labeled a cuckold, yet his very name
will become a proverbial insult:

> Help to search my house this one time. If I find not what I seek, show no
> color for my extremity; let me for ever be your table-sport. Let them say of
> me, "As jealous as Ford, that search'd a hollow walnut for his wive's le-
> man." (IV.ii.160–64)

In the end, of course, the women save Ford from this fate. By costuming
Falstaff with a buck's head and orchestrating his ritual humiliation, they
allow Ford to repudiate his earlier jealousy and to turn Falstaff's slanderous speech on the knight's own head:

Now, sir, who's a cuckold now? Master [Brook], Falstaff's a knave, a cuck-
oldly knave; here are his horns, Master [Brook]; and, Master [Brook], he
hath enjoy'd nothing of Ford's but his buck-basket, his cudgel, and twenty
pounds of money, which must be paid to Master [Brook]. His horses are
arrested for it, Master [Brook]. (V.v.109–15; brackets in source)

Because Ford has not been Falstaff's sole victim, the shaming ritual
concludes with Ford, the Pages, and Evans insulting the knight who has
been to them "as slanderous as Sathan":

FORD: What, a hodge-pudding? A bag of flax?
MRS. PAGE: A puff'd man?
PAGE: Old, cold, wither'd, and of intolerable entrails?
FORD: And one that is as slanderous as Sathan?
PAGE: And as poor as Job?
FORD: And as wicked as his wife?
EVANS: And given to fornications, and to taverns, and sack, and wine, and
    metheglins, and to drinkings and swearings and starings, pribbles and
    prabbles?

(V.v.151–60)

In order to describe the alliances that these insults help promote, I
return to an earlier instance of "pribbles and prabbles" in the play and to
the play's larger network of abuse.

As my earlier summary suggests, critics generally discuss both Fenton's ultimately successful wooing of Anne Page and Falstaff's attempted
seduction of the wives in terms of the relationship between the court and
the townspeople in the play. In assessing this relationship, they often
stress Page's initial suspicion of the noble Fenton, the wives' rejection of
Falstaff's propositions, and the town's collective expulsion of the immoral knight. This stress has deflected attention from Shallow and Evans
and their roles, respectively, as justice of the peace and as parson. My
analysis of the play's insults also addresses the relationship between
Windsor's inhabitants and the court. Yet, by paying attention to Shakespeare's depiction of these two often overlooked inhabitants, I shift the
terms with which that town-court relationship has been described.

In the play's opening lines, Shallow vows to prosecute the abusive
Falstaff in the Star Chamber. This vow compels Evans to suggest alternative methods for keeping the peace:

EVANS: If Sir John Falstaff have committed disparagements unto you, I am of the church, and will be glad to do my benevolence to make atonements and compremises between you.

SHALLOW: The Council shall hear it, it is a riot.

EVANS: It is not meet the Council hear a riot; there is no fear of Got in a riot. The Council, look you, shall desire to hear the fear of Got, and not to hear a riot. Take your vizaments in that.

SHALLOW: Ha! o' my life, if I were young again, the sword should end it.

EVANS: It is petter that friends is the sword, and end it; and there is also another device in my prain, which peradventure prings goot discretions with it. . . .

. . . .

It were a goot motion if we leave our pribbles and prabbles, and desire a marriage between Master Abraham and Mistress Anne Page.

(I.i.30–44, 54–57)

In spite of Evans's misinterpretation, Shallow's "Council" is, of course, a secular body—the Star Chamber, which did try cases of seditious riot.[9] Yet his plan to "make a Star Chamber matter of it" is remarkable in its assumption that committing "disparagements" unto "Robert Shallow, esquire" constitutes "a riot" (I.i.1–2, 31, 3–4, 35). In short, he equates Falstaff's abuse of him as a private individual—not as a public official— with sedition against the state.

Even those who were tried by the county assize courts for seditious speech were generally more direct than Falstaff in their attacks on the crown. For example, a 1592 Essex assize court sentenced Ralph Duckworth, a laborer, to be pilloried for his seditious public complaint that "this is no good government which we now live under, and yt was merrye in Ingland when ther was better government, and yf the Queene dye ther wilbe a change, and all those that be of this religion now used wilbe pulled out." Duckworth punctuated his sentiments by striking John Debanck, a rector, over the head with a cudgel. And a 1590 Surrey assize court jailed Thomas Garner, a baker, for his public claim "that the Quenes Majestie was an arrant whore and his whore, and if he could come to her he wold teare her in peeces, and he wold drink blodd; and

9. Perry Anderson, *Lineages of the Absolutist State* (London: New Left Books, 1974; London: Verso, 1979), 119. The Star Chamber did claim jurisdiction over cases of seditious *libel* that threatened to violently disrupt the national peace—including writing which defamed the monarch and other public officials (if that defamation attacked those officials in their roles as agents of the state) (King, "Law of Slander," 5).

that he wold sett London on fyer and it wolde be a brave sight unto him."[10]

Unlike the justice of the peace, Evans recognizes that Falstaff's greatest injury is not to Shallow or to the state but, instead, to the peace of Windsor: Falstaff is a sower of discord who has created "pribbles and prabbles" (I.i.55) among the town's inhabitants. In the second section of this chapter, I will discuss Evans's plan that Abraham Slender marry Anne Page. For now, I want to focus on the parson's offer to "make atonements and compremises" (I.i.33–34)—a suggestion for restoring the peace which implies that the matter need not extend beyond the town's jurisdiction:

> Peace, I pray you. Now let us understand. There is three umpires in this matter, as I understand: that is, Master Page (*fidelicet* Master Page) and there is myself (*fidelicet* myself) and the three party is (lastly and finally) mine host of the Garter. (I.i.136–41)

The significance of the debate between Shallow and Evans hinges on their positions as justice of the peace and as parson. In order to sort through the terms of this debate, I pause in my reading of *The Merry Wives of Windsor* to discuss the position of justices of the peace in late-sixteenth-century England.

During the Renaissance, justices of the peace held allegiances to both state and local officials and, more generally, to both state and local notions of and methods for maintaining social order. They were members of the gentry who were appointed by the state to keep the peace in their local communities. Their immediate superiors were the judges of the assize courts, their immediate inferiors the town constables. Like the justices, assize judges were state appointees who were commissioned with the task of keeping the peace. Yet, unlike the justices, their jurisdiction was not confined to their native communities. Also known as "circuit judges," these men traveled the English countryside, presiding over semiannual county assize sessions. These sessions were designed to unite the executive and judicial powers of the monarch and to extend those

10. The first quotation is cited in *Calendar of Assize Records*, vol. 3 (Essex Indictments, Elizabeth I), ed. J. S. Cockburn (London: Her Majesty's Stationery Office, 1978), 391 (court case #2364). The second quotation is cited in *Calendar of Assize Records*, vol. 5 (Surrey Indictments, Elizabeth I), ed. J. S. Cockburn (London: Her Majesty's Stationery Office, 1980), 345 (court case #2055).

powers consistently throughout England. "The six circuits of England are like the four rivers of Paradise," Francis Bacon said, "they go to water the whole kingdom." The assize system was well developed by 1597, the year generally suggested as the earliest probable date of the play's composition. In 1595 the Star Chamber resumed regular meetings in which members instructed assize judges about the legislation crucial to Elizabeth and to her governors. Trained in common law, assize judges had already been empowered to hear both crown and common pleas when, in 1590, a royal commission instructed justices of the peace to refer to the assize all cases in which there was any ambiguity or doubt about the common law. In this way, the assize sessions gained control over cases of treason, sedition, embezzlement, forgery, and even, at times, witchcraft and theft. The commission's instructions derived from the central government's more general concern that the justices of the peace, who were usually not legal professionals, were unable or unwilling to enforce the legislation which most concerned Westminster. For this reason, it became mandatory that justices of the peace attend all assize sessions, during which the circuit judges would communicate that legislation to them.

The assize judges were also ordered to carry information both up and down the circuit rivers. Bacon explained this dual role to the judges: "Besides your ordinary administration of justice, you do carry the two glasses or mirrors of the State. For it is your duty in these your visitations to represent to the people the graces and care of the king; and again, upon your return, to present to the king the distastes and griefs of the people." Assize judges reported to the central government the concerns and activities of local communities, the performance of local justices of the peace, and the most desirable candidates for future appointments as local justices. The judges were, in Thomas Coventry's words, the "eyes of the kingdom." This kind of monitoring became increasingly important after Lord Burghley's 1587 injunction that the number of justices—particularly the number of quorum justices—be reduced. Because of their skillful and experienced application of the law, quorum justices were those justices whose presence was necessary to actually constitute a bench that carried legal authority. Elizabeth and her governors had traded coveted appointments to the quorum for the loyalty of the greater gentry families—a loyalty that they hoped would counterbalance the threat of the peerage. Yet, by overpopulating the quorum with justices who were not trained in the law, they also had endangered their own carefully engineered system for promoting absolute rule and a central-ized state.

The effectiveness of this closely regulated judicial system depended, in part, on the willingness of justices to follow the instructions of the assize judges both in the quarter sessions and in their daily decisions about whether to prosecute cases that came to their attention. Quarter sessions were held four times a year in between the assizes, were pre-sided over by the justices, and were attended by the constables. Yet, ideally, the justices would literally earn their titles as gentlemen by medi-ating local disputes without recourse to this legal machinery. The deci-sion to mediate often hinged not only on state-sanctioned criteria—such as the strength of the physical evidence and the reputation of the accused—but also on the justices' less authorized concern that the letter of state law could disrupt the locally defined social order or that, by referring a judgment even to the quarter sessions, they might announce that their local community needed outside assistance in maintaining so-cial order.[11]

Although the justice of the peace retained the final decision about whether to prosecute a case, cases generally came to the attention of the justice only after the community cooperated in identifying and appre-hending the criminal. Private individuals often initiated cases by notic-ing suspicious behavior, spying on the perpetrator, entering residences in an effort to obtain physical evidence, and even, at times, gathering neighbors together in collective pursuit of the accused. Whether sum-

11. For information about the court system and the justices of the peace, see J. S. Cockburn, *A History of the English Assize, 1558–1714* (Cambridge: Cambridge University Press, 1972), 1–11, 153–87, 219–37; T. C. Curtis, "Quarter Sessions Appearances and Their Background: A Seventeenth-Century Regional Study," in *Crime in England, 1550–1800,* ed. J. S. Cockburn (London: Methuen, 1977), 135–54; Cynthia B. Herrup, *The Common Peace: Participation and the Criminal Law in Seventeenth-Century England* (Cambridge: Cambridge University Press, 1987; paperback ed. 1989), 1–92, 193–206; Wallace T. Mac-Caffrey, "Place and Patronage in Elizabethan Politics," in *Elizabethan Government and Society: Essays Presented to Sir John Neale,* ed. S. T. Bindoff, J. Hurstfield, and C. H. Williams (London: University of London, Athlone Press, 1961), 95–126; M. K. McIntosh, "Central Court Supervision of the Ancient Demesne Manor Court of Havering, 1200–1625," in Ives and Manchester, *Law, Litigants, and the Legal Profession,* 87–93; and Keith Wrightson, "Two Concepts of Order: Justices, Constables, and Jurymen in Seventeenth-Century England," in *An Ungovernable People: The English and Their Law in the Seventeenth and Eighteenth Centu-ries,* ed. John Brewer and John Styles (New Brunswick, N.J.: Rutgers University Press, 1980), 21–46. The Bacon quotations are cited in Cockburn, *History of the English Assizes,* 13 and 153; the Coventry quotation is cited in Herrup, *Common Peace,* 52.

moned by this collective "hue and cry" or by verbal and written complaints, the constable became crucial at this stage in the developing case. After leading the chase and capturing the accused, the constable might have been called on to coordinate a local shaming ritual or to bring the captured man to the central government's representative, a local justice of the peace. The justice would then decide whether to prosecute and, if so, whether to settle out of court or to hold the accused for a trial at the next quarter session or the assize court. Unlike the justices, constables were selected from among the yeomen or husbandmen and were selected by the local court leet, county peerage, or town government. Yet, like the justices, they were bound by oath to serve the interests of the monarch and the central government. The position carried a measure of local prestige but, because the constables physically apprehended their fellow townspeople and transported them to local justices, these minor officials were frequently subject to physical and verbal abuse and, as a result, were also frequently the paid substitutes of the elected men of property. Their untenable position was legendary.[12]

The Merry Wives of Windsor depicts this elaborate legal machinery as ludicrously ineffective. In spite of his role as justice, Shallow refuses to keep the peace by settling his differences with Falstaff out of court. Evans, of course, deletes the justice from his list of the "three umpires" (I.i.137) in the case against Falstaff. And, in spite of Nym's fear that Slender will "run the nuthook's humor" (I.i.167–68) on him, both instances of a hue and cry depicted in the play are unsuccessful. In an effort to produce evidence of his own cuckolding, the jealous Ford spies not on a suspicious neighbor but on his own wife and repeatedly calls on his fellow townspeople and "all the officers in Windsor" (III.iii.107) to help him search his own home for Falstaff. When the men pursue the disguised knight, Falstaff eludes all of them, including the constable:

> I was like to be apprehended for the witch of Brainford. But that my admirable dexterity of wit, my counterfeiting the action of an old woman, deliver'd me, the knave constable had set me i' th' stocks, i' th' common stocks, for a witch. (IV.v.116–20)

12. Herrup, *Common Peace*, 42–92; Joan Kent, "The English Village Constable, 1580–1642: The Nature and Dilemmas of the Office," *Journal of British Studies* 20:2 (Spring 1981): 26–49; and Wrightson, "Two Concepts of Order," 21–46.

And the host, robbed of his horses by Evans and Doctor Caius's ruse, shouts to no avail, "Hue and cry, villain, go! Assist me, knight, I am undone! Fly, run, hue and cry, villain! I am undone!" (IV.v.90–92).

Shallow does perform as a proper justice when, attempting to prevent a duel between Evans and Caius, he says, "Master Doctor Caius, I am come to fetch you home. I am sworn of the peace" (II.iii.51–53). Yet, throughout this scene, Shallow oscillates between taunting and soothing the antagonists, and it is not Shallow but the host who ultimately prevents the duel. In so doing, the host actually provokes Evans and Caius to band together in their disorderly behavior. The parson tells the doctor:

> This is well! he [the host] has made us his vlouting-stog. I desire you that we may be friends; and let us knog our prains together to be revenge on this same scall, scurvy, cogging companion, the host of the Garter. (III.i.117–21)

Shakespeare attributes the ineffectiveness of this judicial system, in part, to Shallow's method of resolving the justice of the peace's notorious dual alliance to his local community and to the central government. When Shallow announces that he is an "esquire," his cousin Slender adds, "In the county of Gloucester, Justice of the Peace and Coram" (I.i.4, 5–6). In this way, Slender defines Shallow as a member of the local gentry who has been favored by the state with an appointment as "Coram"—or quorum—justice. The cousins emphasize that Shallow is the county's principal justice—the "*Custa-lorum*" (I.i.7)—and that his three-hundred-year-old title as a local esquire is not merely the temporary designation granted by the state to justices during their tenure. Yet, as I suggested earlier, Shallow's insistence that Falstaff face Star Chamber charges suggests that he also identifies himself with the state and equates slander against a justice with slander against the central government.

In the play's logic, these competing self-definitions are incompatible. Shallow does attempt to make them compatible by redefining the traits that characterize a local esquire. Yet, in order to do so, he must collapse the play's distinction between gentlemanly behavior and courtly affectation. In the play's opening lines, Slender reveals that this "gentleman born . . . writes himself *Armigero*, in any bill, warrant, quittance, or obligation, *Armigero*" (I.i.8–11). With this practice, Shallow stresses that he is a member of the armigerous gentry—a gentleman who, although not a peer, is entitled to bear a coat of arms. Yet, more important, he also stresses that he defines his gentility through the derivation of the term "esquire" from "armiger," an apprentice-knight who bore his master's armor. In short, in a speech designed to defend himself from Falstaff's abuse, Shallow actually locates himself as Falstaff's servant. At the same time, he announces his allegiance to an increasingly anachronistic, martial form of status that Elizabethans often associated with the affectations of those courtiers who feebly mimicked a much earlier incarnation of the aristocracy.

The host of the Garter reinforces this association and claims that gentlemanly behavior and courtly affectation are incommensurate when, in one breath, he greets Page, "How now, bully-rook? thou'rt a gentleman," and summons Shallow, "Cavaleiro Justice, I say!" (II.i.193–94). The host's conjunction of "Cavaleiro" and "Justice" and Shallow's writing "himself *Armigero*, in any bill, warrant, quittance, or obligation" suggest that the play's justice of the peace performs his official duties by asserting his markedly ungentlemanly status. This behavior makes him an ineffective keeper of local peace and thus an ineffective agent of the state. For example, Evans suggests that Shallow settle his differences with Falstaff out of court. Instead, in spite of his role as justice, Shallow responds to the knight's insulting behavior by shouting, "Ha! o' my life, if I were young again, the sword should end it" (I.i.40–41). The gentler Evans reminds him that "it is petter that friends is the sword, and end it" (I.i.42–43). Later, Page attempts to cast Shallow's affection for the sword as a youthful predilection that could only predate his serving as justice of the peace. "You have yourself *been* a great fighter," he says, "though *now* a man of peace" (II.iii.42–43, my emphases). Shallow responds that his affection for fighting has not diminished: "Bodykins, Master Page, though I now be old and of the peace, if I see a sword out, my finger itches to make one" (II.iii.44–46).

Shakespeare's depiction of Shallow is part of the play's more general emphasis on royal efforts to use the resources of a centralized state in order to establish absolute rule in England. Shakespeare sets *The Merry Wives of Windsor* in the shadow of Windsor castle. Mistress Quickly reminisces about a time "when the court lay at Windsor" (II.ii.61–62), and when Page, Shallow, and Slender observe Falstaff's ritual humiliation, they "couch i' th' castle-ditch" (V.ii.1) into which royal officials famously cast the possessions of one treacherous Knight of the Garter, the earl of Northumberland. This setting accentuates both England's centralization and the nation's conflicted relationship to absolutism. Windsor castle is one of several English castles constructed by William the Conqueror both as military strongholds and as royal reminders of the power and pervasiveness of the monarchy. Almost three centuries later, Edward III continued this effort to unite England under royal control by founding the Order of the Garter at Windsor castle. Selecting the warrior St. George as the order's patron, the king hoped to install as Garter knights nobility who would then support the French wars through which he intended to expand England's territory. Elizabeth I attempted to buttress England's increasingly centralized state and its always tenuous absolute rule by personally controlling and often withholding from the aristocracy their installation into the Order of the Garter, by increasing the public pageantry of Garter celebrations, and by relocating from Windsor to her residence in London the order's annual feast of St. George.[13] As we have seen, Elizabeth and her governors also fostered an elaborate legal system which was designed to promote absolute rule and a centralized state. That system depended, in part, on justices who derived their authority and their status both from state and from local structures. Yet Shakespeare discredits Shallow's effort to resolve this dual alliance with the central government and with his local community. In attempting to maintain both of these alliances, the ungentlemanly Shallow retreats into anachronism and courtly affectation and, as a result, presides over the disintegration of Elizabeth's legal machinery.

By setting his play in Windsor, Shakespeare also stresses how royal efforts to use the resources of a centralized state in order to reinforce absolute rule often inflected tensions surrounding town demands for limited autonomy from the crown. In fact, the castle ditch from which

13. W. H. St. John Hope, *Windsor Castle: An Architectural History*, Part I (London: Published at the Offices of Country Life, 1913), 4–7; Roy Strong, *The Cult of Elizabeth: Elizabethan Portraiture and Pageantry* (London: Thames and Hudson, 1977), 164–85; *The Transition from Feudalism to Capitalism* (London: New Left Books, 1976; London: Verso, 1978), chapters by Maurice Dobb, Christopher Hill, Rodney Hilton, Eric Hobsbawm, and John Merrington; and *The Victoria History of the Counties of England: Berkshire*, vol. 3 (London: St. Catherine Press, 1924; reprint, Folkestone: Dawsons of Pall Mall for the University of London Institute of Historical Research, 1972), 8–9, 29, 31. See Anderson, *Lineages*, 113–42, and Ellen Meiksins Wood, *The Pristine Culture of Capitalism: A Historical Essay on Old Regimes and Modern States* (London: Verso, 1991), 22–28, 60–62, for discussions about the relationship between absolutism and centralization in England. Although Wood disagrees with Anderson's claims (elsewhere) about the development of English capitalism, both writers stress England's relatively early centralization and the relatively brief and limited character of English absolutism. Erickson, "Order of the Garter," describes how *The Merry Wives of Windsor* is able to celebrate an aristocratic national identity by drawing on the popular and public drama of the Elizabethan Garter installation (126–27).

Page, Shallow, and Slender observe Falstaff's shaming also marked the boundary between royal property and that of the town. Windsor is remarkable among English towns because it was formed as a royal borough that owed neither rent nor loyalty to any overlord except the king. As a result of this relatively direct relationship between Windsor and the monarch, the authority relations that underpinned absolute rule were visibly feudal and visibly associated with royal prerogative. These authority relations were particularly clear at the time of the play's composition, as Windsor's governing burgesses pleaded futilely for Elizabeth to renegotiate their town charter. Town charters were one forum in which the alliances and the tensions between town governors and their monarch were played out. When Elizabeth visited Windsor in 1586, the mayor, giving her his mace, stressed that he was "offering up not only this small peece of government which we sustaine and exercise under your Majestie, but ourselves also and all that we have freely, not co-arctedly, joyfullie not grudgingly, to be for ever at your gratious disposing." At Elizabeth's "gratious disposing," the corporation waited until James's succession before receiving their new charter. A series of town charters, beginning in 1277, and the town's charter of incorporation in 1467 had gradually extended the powers of the mayor, the bailiffs, and the burgesses and had made possible the eventual near merging of the town's Trinity Guild with its governing burgesses or corporation. For example, the charter of 1439 assured the governing burgesses that they, rather than the justices of the peace, would have jurisdiction over all nonfelonious cases involving laborers or artisans; the burgesses would try these cases in the borough courts over which they presided in the guild halls. Although the membership of the town corporation and the Trinity Guild had long overlapped and although guild membership had long been the accepted route to town leadership, by the time of the play's composition, these two bodies actually shared one record book. The long awaited charter, awarded in the first year of James I's reign, would outline in detail the corporation's internal structure and would further extend its legislative and economic privileges. In so doing, the charter would promote the governing burgesses' increasing autonomy from the crown and would make formal their inseparability from the guild. In this respect, Windsor followed a pattern common to many English towns in the late sixteenth century.[14]

14. Peter Clark and Paul Slack, *English Towns in Transition, 1500–1700* (London: Oxford University Press, 1976), 126–40; *The History and Antiquities of Windsor Castle and the Royal College, and Chapel of St. George* (Eton: Printed by Joseph Pote, 1749), 1–30; Robert Richard Tighe and James Edward Davis, *Annals of Windsor, Being a History of the Castle and Town; with*

Although *The Merry Wives of Windsor* does not depict the intricacies of town charters, it does suggest that Shallow's effort to maintain his dual alliance actually threatens the limited autonomy from the crown which Windsor's corporation sought to extend and which town charters generally guaranteed. For example, if Shallow had made a "Star Chamber matter" of Falstaff's abuse, he would have announced that Windsor's magistrates were incapable of controlling disorder and thus required the direct intervention of the crown in their local affairs. Governing burgesses were particularly wary of this sort of intervention during the 1590s, when Elizabeth often responded to local unrest by infringing on rights that had been guaranteed to towns in their charters. It was precisely this sort of intervention that corporation directives, local shaming rituals, and justices' efforts at mediation often helped to prevent.[15]

In addition, rather than keeping the peace, Shallow actually contributes to one common form of local disorder—verbal abuse. In the play's opening scene, Evans describes Falstaff's abuses not only as property crimes against Shallow but also as insults that threaten the community's peace: Falstaff has "committed disparagements unto" Shallow and has sown "pribbles and prabbles" among Windsor's inhabitants (I.i.31–32, 55). Yet, ignoring Evans's plea that he make peace with Falstaff, the justice confronts the knight:

SHALLOW: Knight, you have beaten my men, kill'd my deer, and broke open my lodge.
FALSTAFF: But not kiss'd your keeper's daughter?

(I.i.111–13)

In spite of this warning that Falstaff's abusive behavior might readily extend into sexual abuse, the pugnacious Shallow refuses to back down. The terms of the dispute escalate as Falstaff and his servants utter or provoke a barrage of insulting appellations that are not restricted to Shallow—"good cabbage," "cony-catching rascals," "Banbury cheese," "Mephostophilus," "Slice," "mountain-foreigner," "latten bilbo," "Froth

some Account of Eton and Places Adjacent (London: Longman, Brown, Green, Longmans and Roberts, 1858), vol. 1, 104–5, and vol. 2, 53–56; and *Victoria History: Berkshire*, 21, 57–61. The quotation is from *Victoria History: Berkshire*, 61.

15. Amussen, "Gender, Family, and the Social Order," 205–17, and *An Ordered Society*, 159–79; Clark and Slack, *English Towns in Transition*, 134–36; Underdown, "Taming of the Scold," 132–35.

and scum," "Scarlet," and "drunken knaves" (I.i.121, 124–25, 128, 130, 132, 161, 162, 164, 173, 184)—and as Falstaff exits by kissing Mistress Ford. Shallow allows Falstaff to become an uncontrollable threat to Windsor's peace. In so doing, the ungentlemanly justice also allows the knight to propel Ford into becoming yet one more sower of community discord. The jealous Ford slanders not only himself and his wife but also George Page and his wife. He labels Page a wittol, a "secure fool" who "stands so firmly on his wive's frailty" (II.i.233–34) and plans to "take him [Falstaff], then torture my wife, pluck the borrow'd veil of modesty from the so-seeming Mistress Page, divulge Page himself for a secure and willful Actaeon; and to these violent proceedings all my neighbors shall cry aim" (III.ii.40–44).[16]

In this way, Shallow's ungentlemanly behavior provokes a series of offenses that are increasingly situated within the jurisdiction of another Elizabethan keeper of local peace—the church. Evans's redescription of Falstaff's property crimes as "disparagements" (I.i.31), Evans's confusion between the secular and the ecclesiastical "Council," and Falstaff's remark about the keeper's daughter all signal that the knight's abuses are bordering on ecclesiastical jurisdiction. As Shallow persists in antagonizing Falstaff, the knight combines nonsexual with sexual offenses and, eventually, focuses almost exclusively on the latter—particularly the sexual slander with which he attacks the Fords and the Pages. His servants and the jealous Ford follow his lead. In the 1590s church courts, in spite of attempts by secular courts and by Puritans to restrict their power, remained primarily responsible for trying cases concerning fornication, adultery, incest, disputed matrimonial promises, scolding, theft of church property, and, perhaps most frequently, defamation. In ecclesiastical courts, the latter category designated cases in which defendants had accused plaintiffs of crimes that the church was empowered to prosecute. For example, when, earlier in the century, Elizabeth Johnson brought an ecclesiastical defamation charge against Alice Roper because Roper had purportedly accused Johnson of the "crimes of adultery and theft," the presiding church officer agreed to try Roper for defaming

---

16. In this way, Ford would also have violated the regulations of the Trinity Guild, which announced its interest in keeping the peace and protecting social hierarchies by forbidding fighting and scolding on the part of its members—the "substauncylest and wysest men of the towne"—and by reserving its strongest punishments for those who would "stryke, myssuse, revyle, rayle or mocke" a fellow member of the guild (*Victoria History: Berkshire*, 60).

Johnson's sexual honesty. Yet he dismissed the charge that Roper had called Johnson a thief because theft was a secular crime. Church defamation cases overwhelmingly involved sexual slander—particularly accusations of adultery, whoredom, and cuckoldry. By trying these cases and by gradually broadening the definition of "defamation" to include disruptive verbal abuse and rumors that actually alleged neither secular nor religious offenses, church courts were one key instrument for quelling local disorder. Like the justices, church officials were encouraged, if possible, to settle these cases locally and peacefully by "compromise and arbitration" rather than forwarding them to the higher ecclesiastical courts. And, like the justices, these local ministers often relied on community consensus that the accused had threatened the common peace.[17] Participating in this structure, Evans determines that Falstaff's disparagements are a threat to Windsor's peace yet judges those abuses an inappropriate topic for a higher ecclesiastical court.

Evans then offers his services as local mediator precisely as an agent of the church. "I am of the church," he reminds Shallow, "and will be glad to do my benevolence to make atonements and compremises between you" (I.i.32–34). It is also as a man "of the church" that Evans lauds Page's offer to mediate between Falstaff and the recalcitrant justice of the peace:

SHALLOW: Is Sir John Falstaff here?
PAGE: Sir, he is within; and I would I could do a good office between you.
EVANS: It is spoke as a Christians ought to speak.

(I.i.97–101)

Yet the parson is unable stop the characters' stream of insults—including the purely sexual slander that is squarely within his jurisdiction—and thus is unable to restore Windsor's peace and protect the limited autonomy of its governing burgesses from the crown. In fact, when Evans rebukes the "slanderous" (V.v.155) Falstaff, the knight seizes upon the parson's words, "*Pauca verba*; Sir John, good worts" (I.i.120), as an opportunity to insult him by drawing attention to his Welsh accent: "Good worts? good cabbage" (I.i.121). And, attempting to check Ford's inces-

---

17. Helmholz, *Select Cases on Defamation*, xiv–cxi; Houlbrooke, *Church Courts and the People*, 7–20, 55–88; Ingram, *Church Courts, Sex, and Marriage*, 1–24, 27–69, 292–319; and Wiener, "Sex Roles and Crime," 46–47. The Roper case is in Helmholz, *Select Cases on Defamation*, 24.

sant sexual slander, Evans advises ineffectually: "Master Ford, you must pray, and not follow the imaginations of your own heart. This is jealousies" (IV.ii.155–57). Ford compels Evans to bear witness both of the times that, searching his own home, he slanders his wife's honesty. The parson joins with Caius, Page, and Shallow in reprimanding Ford and in defending the honesty of his wife. During the first search, Evans warns Ford that his suspicions are merely "fery fantastical humors and jealousies" (III.iii.170–71) and insists that Alice Ford "is as honest a omans as I will desires among five thousand, and five hundred too" (III.iii.220–21). And when, during the second search, Ford demands to search his wife's dirty laundry, Evans draws attention to his inversion of the proper gender order: "Why, this is lunatics! this is mad as a mad dog! . . . 'Tis unreasonable! Will you take up your wive's clothes? Come away" (IV.ii.124–25, 141–42). The parson's words have no effect.

What is the significance of Shakespeare's depiction of Shallow and of Evans? Not surprisingly, keeping the peace in Renaissance England was very much a matter of constructing and imposing the terms of that peace. By depicting Shallow's and Evans's failed attempts to keep the peace, *The Merry Wives of Windsor* perpetuates a generalized fear of local disorder. That fear often united otherwise disparate property owners— small traders, master craftsmen, and local gentry—against the apprentices, peasants, and poor immigrants whose rebelliousness they feared. The fear of disorder was particularly well developed in the 1590s after more than a decade of crop failures, inflation, and sporadic food and apprentice riots, and helped to prevent alliances between, for example, peasants and the lesser craftsmen.[18]

The play's depictions of Shallow and Evans also suggest that the justice and parson are unable to maintain local order precisely because they do not share the collective identities of "townsmen" and "gentlemen." When Shallow attempts to make sense of the justice's dual alliance with the central government and with his local community, he defines the local community from which he derives his status not as the town of Windsor but as the "county of Gloucester" (I.i.5). In order to maintain

18. Peter Clark, "A Crisis Contained? The Condition of English Towns in the 1590s," in *The European Crisis of the 1590s: Essays in Comparative History*, ed. Peter Clark (London: George Allen and Unwin, 1985), 44–66, and *English Provincial Society from the Reformation to the Revolution: Religion, Politics, and Society in Kent, 1500–1640* (Hassocks, Sussex: Harvester Press, 1977), 221–68; Clark and Slack, *English Towns in Transition*, 56–57, 82–96, 133; and R. B. Outhwaite, "Dearth, the English Crown, and the 'Crisis of the 1590s,'" in Clark, *European Crisis*, 23–43.

both his status as county esquire and his status as an agent of the central government, Shallow describes himself not as a town gentleman but as the aristocratic servant of a knight and, as a result, fosters local disorder. As a parson, Evans's social status would have been notoriously ambiguous and determined solely by his position within an ecclesiastical system that many contemporaries associated not with local English communities but with an absolute monarch and with "popery." Although it was not inevitable that parsons would further the interests of the religious hierarchy or the central government, those who disseminated the church's morality uncritically were fairly likely to do so. The play designates Evans as a parson whose status is determined by his role as an agent of the state church. Both Shallow and the host refer to him as "Sir Hugh"— a title that would have been conferred on the parson solely because he was a church official.[19]

The play then attributes this church official's inability to control his neighbors' slander, in part, to the Welsh origins that override his identity as an inhabitant of Windsor. Several of the play's insults—"base Hungarian wight" (I.iii.20), "Base Phrygian Turk" (I.iii.88), "Flemish drunkard" (II.i.23), "Cataian" (II.i.144), "Ethiopian" (II.iii.27), "Francisco" (II.iii.28), "Castalion-King-Urinal" (II.iii.33), "Anthropophaginian" (IV.v.9), and "Bohemian-Tartar" (IV.v.20)—suggest how race, ethnicity, and nationality help to define "Englishness" for the play's characters. And, although Evans and Caius are generally respected by their fellow inhabitants of Windsor, their regional and national origins expose them to a variety of insults. Even when those origins are not being insulted, they are insistently remarked upon as a source of curiosity and as a defining trait that is at least as crucial as their professions. Shallow tries to tempt Page into attending a duel by saying, "Sir, there is a fray to be fought between Sir Hugh the Welsh priest and Caius the French doctor" (II.i.200–202). And, in his eventual effort to stop that fray, the host calls out: "Peace, I say, Gallia and Gaul, French and Welsh, soul-curer and body-curer!" (III.i.97–98). In fact, in spite of Evans's belief that "it is petter that friends is the sword," he and the doctor are apparently susceptible to becoming martial, and anachronistic, threats to the local peace precisely because of their origins. Page has "heard that the Frenchman hath good skill in his rapier" (II.i.222–23), and Shallow asks Evans,

19. Amussen, *An Ordered Society*, 147–51; Ingram, *Church Courts, Sex, and Marriage*, 84–124; and Underdown, *Revel, Riot, and Rebellion*, 29.

"What? the sword and the word? Do you study them both, Master Parson?" (III.i.44–45).

Shallow's taunt refers, of course, both to Evans's occupation and to perhaps the most remarked upon feature of Evans's and Caius's regional and national origins—the pronunciation that leads them to "hack our English" (III.i.77–78) and make "fritters of English" (V.v.143). Ford stresses that the parson will never entirely become an Englishman when he assures Evans, "I will never mistrust my wife again, till thou art able to woo her in good English" (V.v.133–34). Even when the disguised Evans speaks in unaccountably "good English" during the shaming ritual, the otherwise bewildered Falstaff shouts, "Heavens defend me from that Welsh fairy, lest he transform me to a piece of cheese!" (V.v.81–82). And, finally, Quickly stresses that Caius's pronunciation is actually an insult against the nation when she describes her employer's verbal insults with the same terms that describe his frittered English. Explaining to John Rugby why he must watch at the window for Caius's approach, she predicts that if the doctor were to "find any body in the house, here will be an old abusing of God's patience and the King's English" (I.iv.4–6). In short, the parson is unable to keep the local peace because, in the host's words, he combines "proverbs" with "no-verbs" (III.i.105).[20] As this discussion about constructing "Englishness" indicates, the play does not diminish its fervid nationalism when it promotes the collective identities of "gentlemen" and "townsmen." *The Merry Wives of Windsor* does suggest, however, that justices and churchmen whose local loyalties are not *town* loyalties will serve neither the central government nor the town well. And it suggests that town gentlemen are best equipped to define and protect local and national order.

Yet, in spite of the play's emphasis on gentle*men* and towns*men*, it is Alice Ford and Margaret Page who publicly shame Falstaff and, thus, restore Windsor's peace. In the next section of this chapter, I analyze this

20. For a different interpretation of Evans's role in the play, see Joan Rees, "Shakespeare's Welshmen," in *Literature and Nationalism*, ed. Vincent Newey and Ann Thompson (Liverpool: Liverpool University Press, 1991), 22–40. Rees acknowledges that Shakespeare's Welsh characters are presented as distinctly "un-English" yet emphasizes the benevolence of this depiction. Assessing the role of Welshmen in the English imagination several decades after the Act of Union, she argues that "Shakespeare could genuinely have hoped that honour of both Welsh and English might be preserved and both subsumed in a common pride" (38–39). Patricia Parker, "*The Merry Wives of Windsor* and Shakespearean Translation," *Modern Language Quarterly* 52:3 (September 1991): 225–61, locates the pronunciation of Evans and Caius within the play's more general interest in translation.

public shaming as one instance of the wives' merry response to Falstaff's insults. For the moment, however, I am interested in how it helps create alliances within Windsor. The play attributes Evans's failure to restore the peace, in part, to his initial tendency to settle offenses privately. For example, he pledges to Shallow that he, Page, and the host "will afterwards ork upon the cause with as great discreetly as we can" (I.i.145–46). Shallow complains to Page that he will not be satisfied by discretion—by a confession "in some sort":

> SHALLOW: He hath wrong'd me, Master Page.
> PAGE: Sir, he doth in some sort confess it.
> SHALLOW: If it be confess'd, it is not redress'd. Is not that so, Master Page? He hath wrong'd me, indeed he hath, at a word he hath. Believe me, Robert Shallow, esquire, saith he is wrong'd.
>
> (I.i.102–7)

Shallow's seemingly excessive repetition—"He hath wrong'd me," "He hath wrong'd me," "Robert Shallow, esquire, saith he is wrong'd"— suggests that the justice would prefer that Falstaff receive a public and lengthy shaming. Here Shallow concurs with the officials who meted out punishments for secular and ecclesiastical offenses—including verbal abuse—and with contemporaries who complained when the county assize courts condemned criminals to a disappointingly speedy hanging.[21] Page echoes Shallow's sentiments. Ford invites Page, Evans, and Caius to dinner after admitting that his jealousy and slander are "my fault, Master Page," and after begging Alice Ford, "I pray you pardon me; pray heartly pardon me" (III.iii.218, 226–27). Page accepts the invitation yet promises the parson and doctor that they will soon receive from Ford more than a simple "pardon me": "Let's go in, gentlemen, but (trust me) we'll mock him" (III.iii.228–29). This preference for a lengthy shaming is also echoed by the play's plotting and deferred conclusions—the "fine-baited delay" (II.i.95–96) with which the wives cure Falstaff. Yet the shaming rituals depicted throughout the play are generally meted out not by secular or ecclesiastical officials but by the women, and resemble not the public punishments sanctioned by the courts or the public shamings initiated by governing burgesses but, instead, popular Renaissance charivari and skimmington rituals.

In practice, these popular rituals often helped to maintain a social

---

21. Herrup, *Common Peace*, 5, 165–82.

order—particularly a gender order—that the governing burgesses and the central government endorsed. Yet they were frequently instigated by men who did not occupy official positions of authority and were associated with unsanctioned peasant rituals and the threat of class subversion. For this reason, those who engaged in the rituals often risked appearing before Elizabeth's secular or ecclesiastical courts on charges of disturbing the peace and defamation.[22] In *The Merry Wives of Windsor*, it is the wives who assume that risk during their various shamings of Falstaff. Those shamings then culminate in a well-monitored reappropriation and staging by the town gentry of a tale that the "superstitious idle-headed eld / Receiv'd and did deliver to our age / . . . for a truth" (IV.iv.36–38). The town wives plan this shaming ritual after predicting that their husbands will "have him publicly sham'd, and methinks there would be no period to the jest, should he not be publicly sham'd" (IV.ii.220–22). In consultation with their husbands, they stage the public shaming not in the town but in the forest, which was under royal jurisdiction.[23] And they cast this potential usurpation of royal authority as the patriotic poaching of a self-proclaimed "Windsor stag" in honor of that "radiant Queen" who "hates sluts and sluttery" (V.v.12–13, 46). In short, the wives' response to Falstaff's "abominable terms" actually restores social order by reinforcing the play's more general sense that town gentlemen are the ideal custodians of both the town and the nation.

By assigning to town gentlemen the task of defining and protecting local and national order, Shakespeare promotes, more precisely, the regional and national authority of the towns' official representatives— their governing burgesses. Throughout the sixteenth century, those burgesses feared incursions on corporation rights not only from peasants, apprentices, and poor immigrants from below but also from the county peerage and, at times, the country gentry from above. Neither the peerage nor the country gentry were necessarily hostile to those burgesses, and, in fact, the gentry were often strong allies. Yet the play's endorsement of town identities implies that the national patriotism of peerage and gentry is demonstrated by their willingness to support these town authorities. By promoting the national authority of the governing burgesses, Shakespeare further endorses the limited autonomy of town corporations from the crown. That limited autonomy was generally a form

22. Amussen, "Gender, Family, and the Social Order," 196–217, and *An Ordered Society*, 95–133; and Underdown, "Taming of the Scold," and *Revel, Riot, and Rebellion*, 39.

23. *Victoria History: Berkshire*, 25.

of self-regulation which was not necessarily hostile to absolutism. In fact, local corporations, their members benefiting from Elizabeth's policies, often furthered not only the economic interests of the absolutist state but also those cultural and political practices which supported absolutism and its feudal authority relations. Yet, at the same time, this limited autonomy did sever the central government's direct control over the burgesses and often marked the corporations' growing dissatisfaction with both the crown's economic policies and its dedication to absolute rule.[24]

Finally, Shakespeare does not offer information about Ford's and Page's relations to production or their roles within town government. In this way his collective identities of "townsmen" and "gentlemen" support the regional and national authority of town corporations and yet obscure the role of those corporations and of the crown within struggles between commercial and industrial capital. Increasingly unable to obtain revenue from the feudal rents of her landed aristocracy, Elizabeth generally supported the commercial interests of merchants over the industrial interests of master craftsmen and the interests of both merchants and master craftsmen over the interests of the laborers whom they employed. When she legislated that towns' governing burgesses must rise to office primarily through prominent merchant guilds, she helped to consolidate the merchants' control over the town. In fact, Windsor's Trinity Guild probably emerged from an earlier medieval merchant guild, and the town's successive charters granted the corporation legislative and economic privileges often explicitly linked to its monopoly over trade on the Thames and within the town. For example, in 1560, 1576, and 1588 the corporation enacted legislation restricting the trading rights of foreigners and of nonburgesses. Yet this fairly straightforward relationship between the crown and commercial capital was complicated, in part, by tensions surrounding London merchants. By the late sixteenth century, particularly in clothing towns, retail traders began to join with master craftsmen in order to restrict industry to the town and thereby prevent

---

24. Clark and Slack, *English Towns in Transition*, 97–140, and Underdown, *Revel, Riot, and Rebellion*, 107–45. Tensions between Windsor and the monarchy would grow in the decades immediately following the town's receipt of a charter during the first year of James I's rule. During the early seventeenth century, its inhabitants were frequently cited for Puritan activity, and, during the revolution, their sentiments were predominantly antiroyalist (*Victoria History: Berkshire*, 61–62). Absolutism is not central to Clark and Slack's analysis of English towns; drawing on my earlier comments about absolutism, I locate their claims in relation to this category.

larger London merchants from purchasing products from country manufacturers. These retail traders and master craftsmen often articulated
this alliance between town commercial and industrial interests as a patriotic support for town privileges in opposition to country manufacture
and to the prosperous London merchants who, with Elizabeth's support,
specialized in foreign and export trade. Those London merchants, they
claimed, were plundering the coffers of both the town and the nation.[25]

Falstaff depicts himself as one of those merchants whose prosperity
depends on raiding the town's coffers—describing his attempt to obtain
Ford's and Page's wealth directly from their wives as a violation of the
town gentlemen's monopoly over trade. "I am about thrift" (I.iii.43), he
tells his servants. "Briefly—I do mean to make love to Ford's wife. . . .
Now, the report goes she has all the rule of her husband's purse"
(I.iii.43–44, 52–53). He adds that Margaret Page "bears the purse too;
she is a region in Guiana, all gold and bounty" (I.iii.68–69). After determining that Alice Ford and Margaret Page are in charge of their husbands' wealth, Falstaff casts himself as the prosperous merchant whose
trade with them will plunder the town's wealth: "I will be cheaters to
them both, and they shall be exchequers to me. They shall be my East
and West Indies, and I will trade to them both" (I.iii.69–72). In these
metaphors, the plundering of the women, like that of Guiana, is cast as
an inherently uneven exchange whose primary victims, nonetheless, will
be the purses of the town gentry.

In this section of the chapter, I have analyzed how the play's "abominable terms" promote political alliances among groups whose united
resistance to the crown's economic policies and whose ability to secure
town monopoly over trade and industry would have been predicated on
obscuring both the town gentlemen's varying relations to absolutism and
their varying positions within the struggle between commercial and industrial capital. In the next section, I focus on Alice Ford and Margaret
Page's merry response to Falstaff's abominable terms in order to analyze
how men and women are situated quite differently within the play's
network of insults.

25. Clark and Slack, *English Towns in Transition*, 97–110; Karl Marx, "Intercourse and
Productive Forces," in *The German Ideology*, Part I, orig. pub. 1932, trans. S. Ryazanskaya
(Moscow: Foreign Languages Publishing House, 1963), reprinted in *The Marx-Engels Read-
er*, 2d ed., ed. Robert C. Tucker (New York: Norton, 1978), 176–86; and George Unwin,
Industrial Organization in the Sixteenth and Seventeenth Centuries (Oxford: Clarendon Press,
1904; reprint, New York: Augustus M. Kelley, 1963), 70–125.

Coming to Terms with the Women's Mirth

Shakespeare critics often address the surprising degree of autonomy that the playwright grants to his female characters, particularly in the comedies. Feminist debates about Shakespeare's role within Renaissance struggles over gender, about the role of feminism within Renaissance studies, and about the cultural role of feminist literary criticism and pedagogy often turn on competing assessments of that autonomy.[26] Discussions of *The Merry Wives of Windsor* also emphasize its title characters' remarkable autonomy and the gendered nature of their activity, focusing, for example, on the ways in which their merry—and moral—rejection of Falstaff preserves the middle-class or bourgeois status of both the women and their husbands.[27] I want to shift the terms of these discussions by analyzing how the logic of the merry wives' mirth participates in Renaissance struggles over the sphere and nature of women's activity precisely by distinguishing between men's and women's honest behavior. By restricting women's honesty to sexual propriety, the wives' merry response to Falstaff's insults helps to restrict the proper sphere of women's activity to the conservation of that honesty and, thus, of their husbands' wealth.

In a play that is otherwise marked by perpetual naming and self-naming, Alice Ford, Margaret Page, and Anne Page are insulted by men who have too *few* terms for describing the differences among women.

26. For discussions, and instances, of this phenomenon see Lynda E. Boose, "The Family in Shakespeare Studies; or—Studies in the Family of Shakespeareans; or—The Politics of Politics," *Renaissance Quarterly* 40:4 (Winter 1987): 707–42, and Ann Thompson, "'The warrant of womanhood': Shakespeare and Feminist Criticism," *The Shakespeare Myth*, ed. Graham Holderness (Manchester: Manchester University Press, 1988), 74–88.

27. See Barton, "Falstaff and the Comic Community"; Bradbrook, *Shakespeare the Craftsman*; Sandra Clark, "Women and Wit"; Felheim and Traci, "Realism"; French, *Shakespeare's Division of Experience*, 106–10; Hinely, "Comic Scapegoats"; Neely, "Constructing Female Sexuality," 217–24; Jeanne Addison Roberts, *Shakespeare's English Comedy: "The Merry Wives of Windsor" in Context* (Lincoln: University of Nebraska Press, 1979), 75; and Anne Parten, "Falstaff's Horns: Masculine Inadequacy and Feminine Mirth in *The Merry Wives of Windsor*," *Studies in Philology* 82:2 (Spring 1985): 184–99. Erickson's article, "Order of the Garter," is one interesting exception; he locates the wives' autonomy at the vexed intersection between class and gender order during the reign of Elizabeth. Parker, "Shakespearean Translation," stresses not the scenes that bring together Falstaff, Alice Ford, and Margaret Page but, instead, the less frequently analyzed scene which brings together Quickly, Evans, and William Page. When she does discuss the wives, she examines their mirth in terms of the play's more general tendency to exploit a contemporary link between women and translation and thus to make visible the Renaissance production of a binary logic in which women are cast as secondary and defective. Because the translation of words was often associated with the transfer of property, including women, Parker also argues that translation would have been a particularly appropriate figure for a play depicting "bourgeois" characters who are dependent on the "mercantile world of trade."

For example, when Margaret Page and Alice Ford discover that Falstaff has sent them identical love letters, they respond:

> MRS. PAGE: Letter for letter; but that the name of Page and Ford differs! To thy great comfort in this mystery of ill opinions, here's thy twin-brother of thy letter. . . . I warrant he hath a thousand of these letters, writ with blank space for different names (sure, more!); and these are of the second edition.
>
> . . . .
>
> MRS. FORD: Why, this is the very same: the very hand; the very words. What doth he think of us?
>
> (II.i.70–77, 82–83)

Pistol explains Falstaff's philosophy to Ford: "He woos both high and low, both rich and poor, / Both young and old, one with another, Ford. / He loves the gallimaufry, Ford. Perpend" (II.i.113–15). Ford and Slender share Falstaff's notion that women are interchangeable. Ford curses "all Eve's daughters, of what complexion soever" (IV.ii.24–25). And, after Shallow tells Anne Page that "my cousin loves you," the bumbling Slender confirms, "Ay, that I do—as well as I love any woman in Gloucestershire" (III.iv.42–44).[28]

The play associates the notion that women are interchangeable with the sort of generalizing which characterized the sixteenth-century tradition of misogynist writing in England. Margaret Page warns Alice Ford:

> Why, woman, your husband is in his old lines again. He so takes on yonder with my husband; so rails against all married mankind; so curses all Eve's daughters, of what complexion soever; and so buffets himself on the forehead, crying, "Peer out, peer out!", that any madness I ever yet beheld seem'd but tameness, civility, and patience to this his distemper he is in now. (IV.ii.21–28)

As the reference to Ford's "old lines" suggests, this genre of writing had dwindled in popularity by the time of the play's composition. Yet in this

28. See Parker's discussion of twinning in "Shakespearean Translation," 246–48, for another account of these identical love letters. In addition, see Elizabeth Pittenger, "Dispatch Quickly: The Mechanical Reproduction of Pages," *Shakespeare Quarterly* 42:4 (Winter 1991): 389–408. Pittenger analyzes the relationship between the play's sexual and textual economies. Within this framework, she stresses that the wives respond to their interchangeability by "expressing contempt for the mechanically reproduced letters, as though they would prefer the sincerity and singularity of a love letter written by hand. . . . The printing press stands in for the duplicity and duplication of Falstaff's desire" (394).

genre's heyday, its attacks against women had existed in dialogue with a series of defenses of women; those defenses customarily lamented the misogynists' strategy of extrapolating from a single woman's behavior to that of all womankind. Writing in 1617, within a new market for these attacks and defenses, Rachel Speght and Ester Sowernam argue that the tendency to generalize still figured prominently in Joseph Swetnam's 1615 *The Araignment Of Lewde, idle, froward, and unconstant women: Or the vanitie of them, choose you whether. With a Commendacion of wise, vertuous, and honest Women.* In her response to Swetnam, Speght notes that his title page deceptively claims to discriminate among women: "In your title leaf you arraign none but lewd, idle, froward and unconstant women, but in the sequel (through defect of memory as it seemeth), forgetting that you had made a distinction of good from bad, condemning all in general you advise men to beware of, and not to match with, any of these six sorts of women, viz. Good and Bad, Fair and Foul, Rich and Poor." Sowernam concurs. "I found the discourse as far off from performing what the title promised as I found it scandalous and blasphemous," she writes. "For where the author pretended to write against lewd, idle and unconstant women, he doth most impudently rage and rail generally against all the whole sex of women." Sowernam counteracts this "scandalous and blasphemous" tendency to generalize. She addresses her work "to all right honorable, noble and worthy ladies, gentlewomen and others virtuously disposed of the feminine sex" and then immediately emphasizes that not all noble, worthy, and gentle women are honorably or "virtuously disposed." Her essay's first sentence abbreviates that address to "right honorable, and all others of our sex."[29]

29. For discussions of misogynist writing and pro-women responses to that writing, see Katherine Usher Henderson and Barbara F. McManus, *Half Humankind: Contexts and Texts of the Controversy about Women in England, 1540–1640* (Urbana: University of Illinois Press, 1985), 3–46; Constance Jordan, *Renaissance Feminism: Literary Texts and Political Models* (Ithaca: Cornell University Press, 1990), 116–33, 297–307; Joan Kelly, "Early Feminist Theory and the *Querelle des Femmes*, 1400–1789," in *Women, History, and Theory: The Essays of Joan Kelly* (Chicago: University of Chicago Press, 1984; paperback ed., 1986), 65–109; Paula Louise Scalingi, "The Scepter or the Distaff: The Question of Female Sovereignty, 1516–1607," *Historian* 41:1 (November 1978): 59–75; Betty Travitsky, "The Lady Doth Protest: Protest in the Popular Writings of Renaissance Englishwomen," *English Literary Renaissance* 14:3 (Autumn 1984): 255–83; and Linda Woodbridge, *Women and the English Renaissance: Literature and the Nature of Womankind, 1540–1620* (Urbana: University of Illinois Press, 1984), 13–136. Woodbridge suggests that the sixteenth-century tradition of misogynist writing culminates in 1592.

The quotations are from Rachel Speght, *A Mouzell for Melastomus, The Cynical Bayter of, and foul mouthed Barker against Evahs Sex*, orig. pub. 1617, and Ester Sowernam, *Ester hath hang'd Haman: Or An Answere To a lewd Pamphlet, entituled "The Arraignment of Women,"* orig.

By labeling Ford's habitual misogyny his "old lines" and by casting that misogyny as a railing "against all married mankind" (IV.ii.22–23), Margaret Page links Ford's generalized cursing of women to the old line in Catholic England that celibacy was preferable to marriage. Although marriage was a sacrament in the Catholic church, the church favored celibacy because marriage necessarily entailed the lust that accompanied sexual intercourse. Ford reinforces the necessary connection between marriage and lust when he cries:

> This 'tis to be married! This 'tis to have linen and buck-baskets! Well, I will proclaim myself what I am. I will now take the lecher; he is at my house.
> . . . .
> But lest the devil that guides him should aid him, I will search impossible places. Though what I am I cannot avoid, yet to be what I would not shall not make me tame. If I have horns to make one mad, let the proverb go with me: I'll be horn-mad. (III.v.142–45, 147–52)

Ford associates his wife's household labors—the "linen and buck-baskets"—with his being cuckolded and, following sixteenth-century custom, equates being cuckolded with being lecherous. Conflating himself with Falstaff, Ford says, "I will now take the lecher; he is at my house."

Slender shares Ford's assessment of marriage. After debating with Evans and Shallow whether marriage is a "marring," Slender reluctantly consents to court Anne Page: "But if you say, 'Marry her,' I will marry her; that I am freely dissolv'd, and dissolutely" (I.i.250–52). Evans responds, "It is a fery discretion answer, save the fall is in the ord 'dissolutely.' The ort is (according to our meaning) 'resolutely.' His meaning is good" (I.i.253–56). Slender's fault or, in Evans's appropriate blunder, his "fall" is in using Adam and Eve as a paradigm for marital relations and thus in considering women an impediment to salvation and marriage an inherently lustful state.

As I suggested in the previous chapter, Protestant marriage doctrines in Renaissance England borrowed the language of mutual affection with which Catholic doctrines had defined marital relations yet mobilized the language of mutuality in a way that focused attention more firmly on the

---

pub. 1617, both reprinted in *The Women's Sharp Revenge: Five Women's Pamphlets from the Renaissance*, ed. Simon Shepherd (New York: St. Martin's Press, 1985), 62, 87. Sowernam is generally agreed to be a pseudonym (devised in response to Swetnam).

woman's role as companion and helpmate within the nuclear family. In 1598, Robert Cleaver wrote:

> So that a wife is called by God Himselfe, an Helper and not an impedi-
> ment, or a necessaire evil as some advisedly doe say, as other some say: It is
> better to burie a wife, then to marrie one. Againe if wee could be without
> women, we could be without great troubles. . . . These and such like say-
> ings, tending to the dispraise of women, some maliciously and indiscreetly
> doe vomitte out, contrary to the mind of the Holy Ghost.[30]

The Merry Wives of Windsor endorses this view of wives as companions and
helpmates by discrediting the tendency of Falstaff, Ford, and Slender to
"vomitte out" generalizations about women. Shakespeare suggests that
these men are retreating to the "old lines" (IV.ii.22) of a misogynist
tradition and links that tradition to the Catholic church's teachings on
marriage. Yet when the wives design their elaborate plot to teach Falstaff
that women are not interchangeable, they, like Sowernam, are interested in
distinguishing women according to only one term. "We'll teach him to know
turtles from jays" (III.iii.42), they vow—to know "Right Honorable" wom-
en from "all others of our Sex" who would be receptive to his invitations.

   In order to make sense of this lesson within the rubric of companionate marriages, I turn to the ways in which women's mirth functions as a
response to insults in *The Merry Wives of Windsor*. After receiving Falstaff's "love-letter," a horrified Margaret Page reads his words aloud:

> You are not young, no more am I; go to then, there's sympathy. You are
> merry, so am I: ha, ha! then there's more sympathy. You love sack, and so
> do I; would you desire better sympathy? (II.i.6–10)

Insulted, she asks herself how she might have provoked Falstaff's sexual
advances:

> What an unweigh'd behavior hath this Flemish drunkard pick'd (with the
> devil's name!) out of my conversation, that he dares in this manner assay
> me? Why, he hath not been thrice in my company! What should I say to
> him? I was then frugal of my mirth. Heaven forgive me! (II.i.22–28)

---

30. For a lengthier discussion of companionate marriages and for appropriate citations,
see 67–68 in chapter 2 of this book. Cleaver is quoted by Roberta Hamilton, *The Liberation
of Women: A Study of Patriarchy and Capitalism* (London: George Allen and Unwin, 1978), 65.

Focusing on Falstaff's observation that both he and she are "merry," Margaret Page associates female mirth with entwined verbal and sexual excess—with conversations in which, in spite of her attempt to be "frugal of my mirth," she unwittingly communicated some "unweigh'd behavior" to the knight. As a result, Falstaff believes that she would be receptive to his wooing. By labeling her behavior "unweigh'd," she signals the gendered nature of that behavior. The sixteenth-century woman whose verbal excesses disrupted the peace of her local community was often placed in cucking stool. Until the beginning of the fifteenth century, the stool had been used to punish both men and women who cheated in the marketplace with their weights and measures: neither the crime nor the punishment had been gendered.[31] Margaret Page reinforces the sixteenth-century gendered association between a woman's "unweigh'd" behavior and her entwined verbal and sexual excess when she insists that she is "(I hope) . . . an unmeasurable distance" (II.i.104–5) from giving her husband cause for jealousy. In short, the wives suggest that women's behavior is constantly being weighed and measured primarily in terms of its sexual propriety and that this monitoring is performed not only by the women themselves but also by their husbands and the other members of their local communities.

Yet Margaret Page's use of "mirth" in this passage complicates this fairly straightforward reading. "I was then frugal of my mirth," she says. "Heaven forgive me!" Here she either laments the excess mirth that she dispensed in spite of her effort to be frugal or, in an alternate reading, she laments that she was *too* frugal of her mirth. In that second reading, she disentangles merry behavior from excessive or "unweigh'd" verbal and sexual behavior and suggests that mirth might have actually prevented Falstaff's unwarranted attentions. Instead, her reticence allowed him to translate "her will, out of honesty":

FALSTAFF: Briefly—I do mean to make love to Ford's wife. I spy entertainment in her. She discourses, she carves, she gives the leer of invitation. I can construe the action of her familiar style, and the hardest voice of her behavior (to be English'd rightly) is, "I am Sir John Falstaff's."
PISTOL: He hath studied her [well], and translated her will, out of honesty into English.

(I.iii.43–50)

31. Boose, "Scolding Brides and Bridling Scolds," 185.

In 1589 Jane Anger, responding to the sixteenth-century tradition of misogynist writing, advocated that women abandon culturally sanctioned notions of silence in order to put an end to the slanders that emerge not from women's "unweigh'd" behavior but from men's "vile minds." Women cannot, as the minister Richard Brathwait would advise in 1631, "be as one that vnderstandeth, and yet hold thy tongue." Anger writes: "Fie on the falshoode of men, whose minds goe oft a madding, & whose tongues can not so soone bee wagging, but straight they fal a railing. Was there ever any so abused, so slaundered, so railed upon, or so wickedly handeled undeservedly, as are we women? . . . Shal surfeiters raile on our kindnes, you stand stil & say nought." As I have argued, although Falstaff does not rail against women, he shares with the railers a tendency to believe that all women are interchangeable. Anger adds that there is little distance between lovers' excessive claims and misogynists' slander.

In fact Falstaff resembles the "late Surfeiting Lover" who is Anger's ostensible occasion for writing *Her Protection for Women*. Like Falstaff, the aging lover praises women's virtues, curses sexual immorality, and then, "our backes once turned," slanders women with his vile construings. After receiving Falstaff's love letter, a bewildered Alice Ford remembers Falstaff's previous behavior:

> And yet he would not swear; [prais'd] women's modesty; and gave such orderly and well-behav'd reproof to all uncomeliness, that I would have sworn his disposition would have gone to the truth of his words; but they do no more adhere and keep place together than the hundred Psalms to the tune of "Green-sleeves." (II.i.57–63)

Alice Ford and Margaret Page set out to cure the knight of his lust—his "dissolute disease" (III.iii.191–92)—by orchestrating a series of small shamings and then a larger, public ritual in which "till he tell the truth, / Let the supposed fairies pinch him sound, / And burn him with their tapers" (IV.iv.61–63). Here they echo Anger's response to the misogynist lover: "You must beare with the olde Lover his surfeit, because hee was diseased when he did write it, and peradventure hereafter when he shal be well amended, he wil repent himselfe of his slanderous speaches against our sex, and curse the dead man which was the cause of it, and make a publique recantation." Page sanctions Anger's advice and his wife's scolding of Falstaff. When Ford worries that Falstaff might be pursuing their wives, Page responds, "If he should intend this voyage toward my wife, I would turn her loose to him; and what he gets more of her than sharp words, let it lie on my head" (II.i.181–84). In short, Page trusts that his wife's mirth will actually prevent his being cuckolded.[32]

I do not mean to suggest that the wives relinquish their association of mirth with entwined verbal and sexual excess and, instead, celebrate the mirth that can protect their reputations from men's "vile minds" and viler words. The tensions surrounding the term "mirth" are not resolved in that earlier passage and, in fact, are reinforced when Margaret Page vows:

> We'll leave a proof, by that which we will do,
> Wives may be merry, and yet honest too:
> We do not act that often jest and laugh;
> 'Tis old, but true, still swine eats all the draff.
>
> (IV.ii.104–7)

Here Margaret Page claims that through mirth—"by that which we will do"—the wives will prove that "we do not act." And she contrasts jests and laughter both with action and with stillness—with the silence and *in*activity of the unrewarded swine. In short, the tensions that surround the term "mirth" in the play are tensions, more generally, about the nature and contexts of women's activity.

I suggested in the previous chapter that writing about and the practices surrounding Renaissance companionate marriage were deeply contested and that they provided one site where women's subordination to men threatened to become recognizable as a form of oppression. In this way, they participated in a larger struggle over defining the sphere and nature of women's activity. As historians and literary critics have noted, that struggle was evident in claims that men need not absolutely control the actions of their wives because, in couples who experienced mutual

32. Jane Anger, *Jane Anger her protection for Women To defend them against the Scandalous Reportes Of a late Surfeiting Lover, and all other like Venerians that complaine so to bee overcloyed with women's kindness,* orig. pub. 1589, in *First Feminists: British Women Writers, 1578–1799,* ed. Moira Ferguson (Bloomington: Indiana University Press, 1985; Old Westbury, N.Y.: Feminist Press, 1985), 58–73. For quotations, see 59, 71. Anger is generally agreed to be a pseudonym. For the Brathwait quotation, see Jan de Bruyn, "The Ideal Lady and the Rise of Feminism in Seventeenth-Century England," *Mosaic* 17:1 (Winter 1984): 21. Parten, "Falstaff's Horns," 195, also cites Anger in connection with the play; she emphasizes the connection between adulterer and cuckold in the *Protection for Women* in order to explain how mirth and chastity are "brought into equipoise by the play's end" (190).

affection, wives would already be irrevocably yoked to their husbands' wills. It was evident in the sanctioning of wifely actions that violated a husband's ungodly will without offering women the authority to make a judgment about his godliness, particularly as domestic, ecclesiastical, and state authority became increasingly embodied in the father of the nuclear family. It was evident in the notion that women were subordinated to their husbands yet shared with those husbands an equal authority over their servants and an equal responsibility for their children. It was evident in the legal status of women who participated in food and enclosure riots. It was evident in the contradictory position of wives who shared equally with their husbands economic responsibility for maintaining their families yet found their authority increasingly restricted to the management of the household. It was evident in the business activities of those widowed wives of guild members who retained their husbands' guild privileges until they remarried. It was evident in the practices of women who, turning to local customs and wills, were able to mitigate their husbands' control over family property. It was evident in the dilemma of merchants' wives whose relocation to cities often stripped them of their traditional, if unofficial, economic responsibilities. And it was evident in the practice of monitoring the credit and honesty of both men and women but in assessing women's credit and honesty primarily on the basis of their sexual behavior.[33] As even this abbreviated list indicates, neither the doctrine surrounding nor the practices within Protestant marriages produced a monolithic blueprint for Renaissance gender relations.

By depicting women as active partners, or helpmates, in their marriages, Shakespeare reinforces the Protestant notion of a companionate marriage. By defining the terms of the marital partnership, he participates in the larger struggle over the sphere and nature of women's activity. In their merry responses to insults, Alice Ford and Margaret Page suggest that an individual term often has several meanings and that its meaning, at any one time, depends on its context—on whether it is

33. Amussen, "Gender, Family, and the Social Order," 196–205, and *An Ordered Society*, 34–66, 91–93, 98–104; Boose, "Scolding Brides and Bridling Scolds," 179–213; Davis, *Society and Culture*, 124–51; Hamilton, *Liberation of Women*, 23–75; Pearl Hogrefe, "Legal Rights of Tudor Women and the Circumvention by Men and Women," *Sixteenth Century Journal* 3:1 (April 1972): 97–105; Jordan, *Renaissance Feminism*, 11–64, 248–50, 286–307; Mary Prior, "Women and the Urban Economy: Oxford, 1500–1800," in *Women in English Society, 1500–1800*, ed. Prior (London: Methuen, 1985), 93–117; and Keith Wrightson, *English Society, 1580–1680* (New Brunswick, N.J.: Rutgers University Press, 1982), 66–118.

describing men's or women's behavior. The importance of scrutinizing a term's context is reinforced by the shifting contexts that, more generally, govern wordplay in *The Merry Wives of Windsor*. For example, Peter Simple is the name of Slender's servant who shares Caius's closet with the "simples" (I.iv.63), or medicinal herbs, which, in turn, give the midsummer its name, "simple time" (III.iii.73). And Margaret Page speculates that the wives' medicine will have cured Falstaff unless he was entirely possessed by the devil—"in fee-simple" (IV.ii.210–11). Finally, the exasperated Evans accuses Quickly of being "very simplicity" (IV.i.30), or a complete fool, and Page threatens that if Anne marries Fenton she will do so "simply" (III.ii.76), or without a dowry and thus foolishly; instead, he wishes her to marry the foolish Slender because of Slender's self-declared "simple" (I.i.219), or humble, status. The merry wives help to distinguish the sphere and nature of women's activity from that of men by bringing this same sort of scrutiny to bear on the gendered implications of terms such as "honesty," "truth," and "reputation."[34]

I return now to the significance of the wives' pledge that they will teach Falstaff "to know turtles from jays" (III.iii.42). After receiving Falstaff's letter, Alice Ford confers with Margaret Page:

> MRS. FORD: If I would but go to hell for an eternal moment or so, I could be knighted.
> MRS. PAGE: What? thou liest! Sir Alice Ford! These knights will hack, and so thou shouldst not alter the article of thy gentry.
>
> (II.i.49–53)

Margaret Page's exclamation—"Sir Alice Ford!"—signals that, by accepting Falstaff's advances, Alice Ford would forfeit her membership among the town gentry whom the play celebrates. In so doing, she would disrupt the gender order on which her marriage is based and according to which the sphere and nature of women's activity has been determined. She would become not only a knight but a *female* knight whose social

---

34. The wives' strategy is in keeping with the secular courts' *mitior sensus* criterion for defamation cases. By the late 1590s, the criterion of *mitior sensus* demanded that the court consider the *context* of the defendant's statements and then interpret the defendant's words as generously as possible. Thus a statement's context determined whether the supposed insults constituted defamation and, if so, whether the words used implied an ecclesiastical or a secular offense. In this way, the court system drew attention to the ways in which individual words could signal both ecclesiastical and secular offenses (Helmholz, *Select Cases on Defamation*, xcii–xcv).

status would not be dependent on and, in fact, would supersede, that of her husband and, presumably, that of her father.

Margaret Page's punning exclamation—"thou liest!"—associates female falsehood with this disruptive sexual impropriety. After realizing that Falstaff has sent them identical letters, the women add that female "honesty" inevitably denotes unimpeachable sexual behavior:

> MRS. FORD: What doth he think of us?
> MRS. PAGE: Nay, I know not; it makes me almost ready to wrangle with mine own honesty.
>
> (II.i.83–85)

When Margaret Page proposes to "be revenged on him," Alice Ford agrees to "consent to act any villainy against him, that may not sully the chariness of our honesty" (II.i.93, 98–100). And during their villainous revenge, the women define their reputations solely in terms of their sexual honesty and locate that honesty in the interstices between "that which we will do" (IV.ii.104) and being "undone for ever" (III.iii.95–96). As her husband and "half Windsor" (III.iii.114) approach, Alice Ford announces that she must hide her lover. Margaret Page responds, for Falstaff's benefit, "O Mistress Ford, what have you done? . . . [Y]' are undone for ever! . . . [D]efend your reputation. . . . O, how have you deceiv'd me!" (III.iii.94–96, 119, 128–29).

These exchanges between Alice Ford and Margaret Page are part of the play's larger attempt to restrict the terms of women's honesty to their sexual behavior and, thus, to distinguish women primarily as turtles or as jays. For example, by trading on Quickly's verbal blunders and imprecision, Falstaff implies that her mother gave birth to her without marrying and that Quickly herself is an unmarried maid who is not a virgin:

> QUICKLY: Give your worship good morrow.
> FALSTAFF: Good morrow, goodwife.
> QUICKLY: Not so, and't please your worship.
> FALSTAFF: Good maid then.
> QUICKLY: I'll be sworn,
>   As my mother was the first hour I was born.
> FALSTAFF: I do believe the swearer.
>
> (II.ii.33–39)

By believing "the swearer," Falstaff attacks the sexual honesty of both

Quickly and her mother. And as Ford describes the threatening powers of deception possessed by his wife's aunt from Brainford, he insistently conjoins the elderly woman's dishonesty with her promiscuity. She is "a witch, a quean, an old cozening quean!"—a "runnion" who works by "daub'ry . . . beyond our element; we know nothing" (IV.ii.172, 185, 177–78). Evans associates this sexual deceptiveness with a betrayal of proper womanliness when, remarking unwittingly on Falstaff's slipshod disguise, he says, "I think the oman is a witch indeed. I like not when a oman has a great peard. I spy a great peard under his muffler" (IV.ii.192–94).

For the play's men, however, "honesty" signals a much wider array of possible behavior—including, but not restricted to, sexual propriety. In the play's first scene, for example, the parson announces himself as an arbiter of true and false men:

> SHALLOW: Well, let us see honest Master Page. Is Falstaff there?
> EVANS: Shall I tell you a lie? I do despise a liar as I do despise one that is false, or as I despise one that is not true.
>
> (I.i.66–70)

When Slender accuses Pistol of having picked his pocket, Falstaff asks, "Is this true, Pistol?" Evans responds, "No, it is false, if it is a pick-purse" (I.i.159–60). And, when Nym and Pistol tell Ford and Page of Falstaff's plan to seduce their wives, the husbands debate whether to believe the news:

> FORD: Do you think there is truth in them?
> PAGE: Hang 'em, slaves! I do not think the knight would offer it; but these that accuse him in his intent towards our wives are a yoke of his discarded men—very rogues, now they be out of service.
>
> (II.i.172–76)

Unlike the jealous Ford, Page trusts his marriage yoke, in part, because it has been impugned by a yoke of men whose dismissal from service makes their truth—their business credit—questionable.

In this way, the play helps support other Renaissance social practices which viewed women's activities primarily through the lens of their sexual honesty and which cast that honesty as a community concern. As historians have noted, during the second half of England's sixteenth century, there was a dramatic increase in the perception that women were disorderly, in the equation between women's disorderliness—including their verbal excess—and sexual impropriety, and in the public prosecution of women's sexual offenses primarily through church courts and through local shaming rituals. Not surprisingly, a disproportionate number of the women who were prosecuted lived outside the protection of an economically stable, male-dominated family. These women included the overlapping categories of poor women, widows, elderly "spinsters," unmarried mothers, and women who had moved to towns where they had no relatives. For example, when Mary Stracke was charged in a Norfolk ecclesiastical court in 1597 for being a "sower of discord betweene neighboures & a breaker of the Christian Charity," she replied "that she have three children and is verie poore, and when she spoke for her reelefe they say she skoldethe."[35]

The queen did not escape the logic by which women's disruptive behavior was cast as sexual dishonesty. During the final years of Elizabeth's reign, for example, a general anxiety about the effectiveness of a female ruler, about her unwillingness to marry and, by then, about her inability to produce an heir took the specific shape of elaborate narratives about her sexual impropriety. A 1590 Essex assize court ordered that Denise Deryck be pilloried during market time with a paper on her head for having uttered the "scandalous words" that the queen "hath had alredye as manye childerne as I, and that too of them were yet alyve, thone beinge a man childe and thother a mayden childe. And furder that the other were burned. And beinge demanded by whome she had them, she said by my Lord of Leycester who was father to them and wrapped them upp in the embers in the chymney which was in the Chamber wher they were borne." The unlucky Deryck apparently repeated a tale that enjoyed some popularity. Later that same year, the Essex assize court ordered the same punishment for Robert Gardner, who said "that my lord of Leycester had foure childerne by the Queens Majestie whereof thre of them were dawghters and alyve and the fourthe a sonne that was burnte." And both Deryck's and Gardner's "scandalous words" were amplified versions of rumors which circulated as early as 1585, before

35. See Amussen, "Gender, Family, and the Social Order," 205–17, and *An Ordered Society*, 95–133; Boose, "Scolding Brides and Bridling Scolds," 179–213; Houlbrooke, *Church Courts and the People*, 55–88; Ingram, *Church Courts, Sex, and Marriage*, 238–81, 292–319; and Underdown, "The Taming of the Scold," 116–36, and *Revel, Riot, and Rebellion*, 39. Stracke is quoted by Paul Hair, ed., *Before the Bawdy Court: Selections from Church Court and Other Records Relating to the Correction of Moral Offenses in England, Scotland, and New England, 1300–1800* (London: Paul Elek Books, 1972), 147 (case #356).

Leicester's death, when the Surrey assize court convicted Alice Austen for saying that "the Queene is no mayd and she hath had thre sunnes by the Earle of Leicester, and that they shold have bene made Earles" and Thomas Lee Ballewe, a foreign yeoman residing in Southwark, for having said that "the papists in oure countrey saye that your Queene is an hore and that she hath had two children."[36]

The importance for women of maintaining their sexual honesty might be measured not only by the assize courts' diligent prosecution of these "scandalous words" about the queen, but also by the number of women who filed defamation charges in ecclesiastical courts. These plaintiffs were generally married women who were protecting their reputations from slanderous rumors of adultery, gossiping, scolding, and quarreling with their husbands; the plaintiffs and the defendants, who were often women, generally occupied roughly equivalent social positions in their communities. Men outnumbered women, on the other hand, in initiating defamation cases in secular courts after they had been accused of property crimes such as theft. Historians usually interpret the disproportionately large number of women who appear as plaintiffs in church defamation cases as an indication both that women were more vulnerable to sexual slander than men and that, unlike men, their reputations were dependent primarily on their sexual behavior.[37]

In order to describe one way in which this gendering of honesty and reputation helped to designate the nature and sphere of men's and women's activity, I turn to the late-sixteenth-century secular courts that tentatively began to accept *non*criminal defamation cases. In these cases, the defendant's words threatened the credit and thus the livelihood of the plaintiff. In a well-publicized 1594 secular court case, for example, Robert Brook, a merchant, charged John Watson with defamation because Watson, claiming that Brook "keeps a false debt-book," had caused the merchant to lose his good reputation and thus a great deal of trade.[38] In a less publicized secular court case in 1591, William Blunt, a citizen and clothworker of London, charged Thomas Robertes, esquire, with defaming his good name and thus bringing him to financial ruin. I

36. Quotations are from Cockburn, *Calendar of Assize Records* 3:355 (case #2128 and #2129), and Cockburn, *Calendar of Assize Records* 5:276, 290 (case #1602 and #1700).

37. Amussen, *An Ordered Society*, 101–4; Houlbrooke, *Church Courts and the People*, 79–83; Ingram, *Church Courts, Sex, and Marriage*, 292–319; and Wiener, "Sex Roles and Crime," 46–49.

38. Helmholz, *Select Cases on Defamation*, lxxxix.

cite at length from this case in order to stress how the language of
litigation helped determine the meaning of men's reputations and of
their good credit:

> Although the same William Blunt is a good, true and faithful subject and
> liegeman of this realm of England, and has borne himself during all the
> time of his life as a good, true and faithful subject and liegeman of the
> lady the present queen, and has remained of good name, fame and repu-
> tation among all his neighbours during all that time, and has been one of
> the leading merchants of this realm of England for the space of the six
> years now just past, and still is, and has been daily accustomed, and still is
> accustomed, to receive and take into his hands many substantial goods and
> merchandise on his credit and trustworthiness, as well from many mer-
> chants and other subjects of this realm of England as from many foreign
> merchants, and also the same William Blunt has been and remained of the
> greatest repute, credit and esteem among many magnates and nobles of
> this realm of England; . . . nevertheless the aforesaid Thomas, not igno-
> rant of the foregoing, but seduced and stirred up by the most wicked
> malice and diabolical inspiration, scheming and intending not only to strip
> and deprive the same William Blunt of his good name, fame, credit and
> esteem aforesaid, but also to bring the selfsame William into public scan-
> dal and ignominy on the fourteenth day of January in the thirty-third year
> of the reign of the lady Elizabeth, now Queen of England, at Lambeth in
> the county of Surrey, in the presence and hearing of divers faithful sub-
> jects of the said lady the present queen, then and there present and
> hearing, did speak, announce and utter in a loud voice these false,
> feigned, disgraceful and slanderous English words to a certain Anne
> Blunt, then and there present, the wife of the selfsame William namely,
> "Thy husband (meaning the same William the present plaintiff) was but a
> bankrupt."

Blunt's attorney claimed that these "false and slanderous English words"
had cost Blunt "his credit and esteem" and, as a result, had also cost him,
first, "various gains, earnings and profits which he could have had and
earned in buying, selling and lawfully bargaining" and, second, the business of "liegemen subjects of the said lady the present queen, and all
other foreign merchants" who "have on this account refused to deal
further with him, and have withdrawn themselves, and still do withdraw

themselves, from the company of the selfsame William, to the selfsame William's great ruin and manifest impoverishment."[39]

Although it was rare for secular courts to hear noncriminal defamation charges brought by a woman, in 1600 Mary Holwood did persuade secular officials to hear her case. Holwood claimed that Roland Hopkins told her servants, "Thy mistress is an arrant whore and would have lain with me seven years ago. And I would not unless she would go to the hedge." Although the secular officials initially maintained that this was "slander in the spiritual law," she insisted that "whereas she was of good name and fame and whereas there was a communication of a certain marriage between her and one J. S., that by these words spoken by the defendant she had lost her good name and fame, by which the marriage did not take place." On the basis of this argument, the court agreed to try the case because, although the slander might have been spiritual, the damage it caused was temporal. In the language of the case, Holwood's reputation hinges upon her sexual honesty, and the cost of Hopkins's slander is the loss of her opportunity to marry. In this way the case reinforces the equation between a woman's reputation and her sexual honesty. By admitting the parallel between Holwood's case and that of men like Blunt—between the withdrawing of J. S. and the withdrawing of liegemen and other merchants—the court officials make visible how a single-minded focus on the "spiritual" distinction between moral and immoral women helps to limit women's proper "gains, earnings and profits" to their domestic relations.[40]

As the vanishing of Holwood's suitor suggests and a brief return to Blunt's case will demonstrate, these court cases also suggest that men cannot divorce their business credit from the verbal and sexual behavior of their domestic companions. Blunt does not contradict Robertes's claim that Anne Blunt's unruly speech actually prompted the slander which supposedly destroyed the clothworker's business. She "spoke these English words following to the said Thomas, namely, 'Burchett? What was Burchett's father but a butcher?' Upon which the aforesaid Thomas replied to the same Anne Blunt, then and there, in these English words

---

39. Blunt's case is in Helmholz, *Select Cases on Defamation*, 68–71; the quotations are from 69, 70.

40. Holwood's case is in Helmholz, *Select Cases on Defamation*, 89–92; the quotation is from 89.

following, 'Then what was Blunt but a bankrupt?'"[41] Unable to control his wife's speech, the discredited Blunt loses his case and pays Robertes's court fees. Accounts of Renaissance court cases and shaming rituals make clear that husbands and even neighbors were often held responsible for allowing women to become disorderly; for example, charivari rituals often targeted not only an abusive wife but also her husband and the couple's nearest neighbor. Yet *The Merry Wives of Windsor* shames and reforms those men whose misogyny not only threatens to invert the gender hierarchy on which marital relations are predicated but, more specifically, threatens to deny the distinction between turtles and jays. It is through that distinction that the play helps restrict women's honesty to sexual propriety and, in so doing, helps restrict the proper sphere of women's activity to the conservation of that honesty and, thus, of their husbands' wealth.

When the jealous Ford fears that Page "pieces out his wive's inclination; he gives her folly motion and advantage" (III.ii.34–35), he fears that women's activity or, more specifically, their merry plotting, inclines toward their fallen natures. Yet he registers his anxiety about women's activity as an anxiety about female idleness. And he figures that idleness as a threat to heterosexual marriage:

> FORD: Ay, and as idle as she may hang together, for want of company. I think if your husbands were dead, you two would marry.
> MRS. PAGE: Be sure of that—two other husbands.
>
> (III.ii.13–17)

Ford's terminology is compatible with late-sixteenth- and early-seventeenth-century writing that associated female idleness not with *in*activity but with the morally unproductive activity—including unregulated verbal and sexual excess—which inevitably accompanied women's excessive and unregulated spending. Domestic conduct books assigned to women responsibility for managing their households; within this sanctioned realm of female authority, women were entrusted not with the acquisition but with the conservation of the family's wealth.[42] Charges of immoral idleness, increasingly leveled against the urban wives of up-

---

41. Helmholz, *Select Cases on Defamation,* 70.

42. Amussen, *An Ordered Society,* 41–47, 49, and Jordan, *Renaissance Feminism,* 11–21. Hamilton, *Liberation of Women,* 41–45, discusses the increasing importance of women's "idleness" in the seventeenth century.

wardly mobile merchants and master craftsmen, both reinforced the assumption that these women inevitably spent much more of the family wealth than they acquired and reinforced the notion that they would only exacerbate their drain on that wealth should they abandon their assigned posts as thrifty household managers. As Ford's anxiety about the wives' marriage to one another suggests, women who governed the transfer of family wealth would render their husbands superfluous.

Quickly reminisces to Falstaff about the supposed suitors whose property and "alligant terms" the thrifty Alice Ford acquired without spending even "an eye-wink" on them:

> There has been knights, and lords, and gentlemen, with their coaches; I warrant you, coach after coach, letter after letter, gift after gift; smelling so sweetly, all musk; and so rushling, I warrant you, in silk and gold; and in such alligant terms, and in such wine and sugar of the best, and the fairest, that would have won any woman's heart; and I warrant you, they could never get an eye-wink of her. (II.ii.63–71)

Those suitors, she explains, were indistinguishable to Alice Ford—"all is one with her" (II.ii.78). Yet, coached by the wives, Quickly assures Falstaff that he has distinguished himself in Alice Ford's eyes and thus that she will trade in "the way of honesty" (II.ii.74) for the objects and "alligant terms" which demonstrate his affection. By trading in her honesty, Alice Ford, like Margaret Page, would transfer to Falstaff the contents of her husband's coffers. Falstaff tells his servants:

> I will be cheaters to them both, and they shall be exchequers to me. They shall be my East and West Indies, and I will trade to them both. Go, bear thou this letter to Mistress Page; and thou this to Mistress Ford. We will thrive, lads, we will thrive.
>
> . . . .
>
> Hold, sirrah, bear you these letters tightly;
> Sail like my pinnace to these golden shores.
> Rogues, hence, avaunt, vanish like hailstones; go!
> Trudge! Plod away i' th' hoof! Seek shelter, pack!
> (I.iii.69–74, 79–82)

Yet, in spite of Ford's fears, through their merry "motions" the wives are inclined to make visible their sexual honesty and thus to conserve their husbands' wealth.

That inclination falters, however, when the women find a "double excellency" in the fact that both Ford and Falstaff are "deceiv'd" (III.iii.176, 179), when Margaret Page comments, "My husband will not rejoice so much at the abuse of Falstaff as he will chafe at the doctor's marrying my daughter" (V.iii.6–9), and when they resolve to "still be the ministers" (IV.ii.218–19) of Falstaff's final shaming. Margaret Page reminds Alice Ford of the association between mocking and dishonesty: "If he [Falstaff] be not amaz'd, he will be mock'd; if he be amaz'd, he will every way be mock'd" (V.iii.18–19). In so doing, she reinforces the tension, surrounding the term "mirth," between "that which we will do" and "being undone forever." Page also emphasizes that tension by warning Ford not to be so "extreme in submission" as to tell his wife that, "do what thou wilt," he will worship her honesty (IV.iv.11, 6). And he emphasizes that tension by inviting Falstaff to dinner where, after the announcement of Anne's marriage to Slender, "I will desire thee to laugh at my wife, that now laughs at thee" (V.v.171–72). In other words, by assuming the moral authority to minister to their marriages—in order to conserve their honesty and their husbands' wealth—the women risk assuming the moral authority that sanctions their husbands' rule over the family. In this way, the tension surrounding the term "mirth" registers the anxiety that, even in the sphere of activity to which the rubric of sexual honesty restricted women, women's subordination might become recognizable as oppression and that the notion of moral equality might offer women a language—however problematic—with which to voice their demands for social change.

The Merry Wives of Windsor relocates this tension between men's authority and that of their wives to a tension between parents' authority and that of their children. By extending to its logical extreme the rhetoric surrounding companionate marriages, the play depicts a couple who reduce all of the criteria that determined an equal match to the single criterion of mutual affection—the "proportion held in love" (V.v.222)—and who extend the children's participation in selecting a spouse to Fenton's advice that Anne "must be thyself" (III.iv.3) and select her own marriage partner. Fenton links this exclusive emphasis on love with the notion of Anne's autonomy from her parents when he vows that he loves the "very riches of thyself" (III.iv.17) and then tells the host that she "mutually hath answer'd my affection / (So far forth as herself might be her chooser) / Even to my wish" (IV.vi.10–12). This logical extreme is made possible, in part, because of the extremity of the other characters' opposition to the tenets of companionate marriages. Like Evans, these characters focus entirely on economic criteria and believe the "meaning is good" (I.i.255–56) when children abdicate all voice in the selection of marriage partners. Thus, in order to enter into a companionate marriage, Anne must be "seemingly obedient" to her father and to her mother and thus must "consent" to matches with both Slender and Caius in spite of her having "long since contracted" (V.v.223) with Fenton. When the baffled host asks, "Which means she to deceive, father or mother?" Fenton replies, "Both, my good host, to go along with me" (IV.vi.46–47). And in deceiving Anne's parents, the couple must "cozen" Slender and Caius into marrying boys. As this summary suggests, in spite of the couple's careful plans that they "in the lawful name of marrying" give their "hearts united ceremony" in a church (IV.vi.50–51), and in spite of Fenton's protestations to the contrary, "th' offense is holy that she [Anne] hath committed" (V.v.225) and would have fallen under the jurisdiction of the ecclesiastical courts.

By relocating this tension over the authority relations between husband and wife to a tension over the authority relations between parents and their children, *The Merry Wives of Windsor* recasts the central issue of moral equality.[43] Here Anne's deceptions threaten equally the husband's and wife's control over their child and do so in order to assert the moral authority of companionate marriages. The tenuousness of this solution, however, is signaled by the words with which Margaret Page sanctions the match: "Master Fenton, / Heaven give you many, many merry days!" (V.v.239–40).

43. For a discussion of how domestic conduct books described the authority relations between husband and wife, on the one hand, and parents and children, on the other, see Amussen, *An Ordered Society*, 38–47.

Chapter Four

"Euery Gentlemans companion": Middle-Class Hegemony, Marital Harmony, and the Making of Proverbs in *Jack of Newbury*

As he begins his first volume of *The History of the Worthies of England*, Thomas Fuller laments the dearth of proverbs in Berkshire. "I meet with but one in this county," he complains. Elaborating on this incredible state of affairs, Fuller admits that the county's inhabitants do trade wise sayings, yet he dismisses those sayings as "either so narrow that they stretch not beyond the bonds thereof, or else so broad, that all other counties equally share in the cause and usage of them." He ignores the county's overly particular wisdom and promises to turn, for lack of better local material, to the "proverbs general of England" after he parses the sole proverb of Berkshire: "The Vicar of Bray will be Vicar of Bray still." This proverb, he explains, refers to a "vivacious vicar" who avoided the martyr's fire, "too hot for his tender temper," by living under Henry VIII, Edward VI, Mary I, and Elizabeth I as, in turn, a Catholic, a Protestant, a Catholic, and a Protestant once again. When accused of inconstancy, the vicar defended himself by saying, "Not so . . . for I always kept my principle, which is this, to live and die the vicar of Bray." "Such many now-a-days," Fuller moralizes, "who though they cannot turn the wind will turn their mills, and set them so, that wheresoever it bloweth their grist shall certainly be grinded."[1]

I begin my discussion about Thomas Deloney by turning my mill toward Fuller's comments, published over sixty years after Deloney com-

---

1. Thomas Fuller, *The History of the Worthies of England*, vol. 1 (1662; reprint, London: Printed by Nuttall and Hodgson for Thomas Tegg, 1840), 112, 113. All subsequent citations will refer to this edition.

posed *Jack of Newbury*, because I am interested in how both authors construct proverbs whose commonsense wisdom, not surprisingly, is not so common after all. *Jack of Newbury* is Deloney's 1597 tale of Berkshire's legendary broadcloth weaver and his rise from apprentice to burgher in the earlier part of the century. In my analysis of this tale, I return to Fuller and link his remarks about proverbs with his more frequently cited account of that "most considerable clothier" (137), variously known as John Smallwood, John Winchcombe, and—in honor of the Berkshire town in which he prospered—Jack of Newbury.

In a discussion about *Jack of Newbury*, a return to Fuller is also a return to Deloney criticism. Fuller has occupied a prominent position within that criticism, where his account of Deloney's title character is often cited in order to confirm that Deloney derived his tale in part from popular legend. This use of Fuller has been involved in a more general critical effort to explain *Jack of Newbury*'s formal contradictions. On its title page, the book announces itself as "The Pleasant History of Iohn Winchcomb, in his younger yeares *called* Iack *of* Newberie, *the famous* and worthy Clothier of England: declaring *his life and loue, together with his charitable* deeds and great hospitality; And how hee set continually fiue *hundred poore people at worke*, to the great benefit of the Common-wealth: *worthy to be read and regarded.*"[2] Deloney does narrate Jack's elevation from apprentice to burgher, yet he interrupts the narrative of that elevation with chapters which focus on isolated, often grotesquely humorous incidents that are only tangentially related to Jack's tale. For example, episodes focusing on Jack's complex status negotiations alternate with Will Sommers's bath in dog droppings and with Master Bennedicke's bedtime embrace of a sow. In addition, between and within those chapters which *do* further the book's announced narrative, there are abrupt shifts in pacing, in genre, in style, in focus, and in forms of humor.

Although critics debate whether *Jack of Newbury* is more or less "novelistic" than *Thomas of Reading* and the two parts of *The Gentle Craft*, they generally agree that the book's formal contradictions place it on some sort of middle ground: between tales transmitted orally and the English novels which begin to emerge in the late seventeenth century, between romance and realism, or between collections of euphuistic wisdom and collections of popular proverbs, riddles, or jests.[3] Discussions about the

2. All citations are from *The Novels of Thomas Deloney*, ed. Merritt E. Lawlis (Bloomington: Indiana University Press, 1961).

3. Ernest A. Baker, *The History of the English Novel: The Elizabethan Age and After* (London: H. F. and G. Witherby, 1929), 170–78; Frank Wadleigh Chandler, *The Literature of*

book's form open into discussions about its potential audience, about literacy, about the changing reading tastes of England's middle class, and about that class's construction of its tastes in tension with those of the aristocracy, on the one hand, and a variously defined "lower class," on the other.[4] These disparate readings share a conviction that *Jack of Newbury*'s formal middle ground roughly corresponds with the middling social positions inhabited by Deloney, his audience, or his characters.[5]

Roguery, vol. 1 (Boston: Houghton, Mifflin and Company, 1907), 71–72; Walter R. Davis, *Idea and Act in Elizabethan Fiction* (Princeton: Princeton University Press, 1969), 238–52; Paul Devine, "Unity and Meaning in Thomas Deloney's *Thomas of Reading*," *Neuphilologische Mitteilungen* 87:4 (1986): 578–93; Max Dorsinville, "Design in Deloney's *Jack of Newbury*," *PMLA* 88:2 (March 1973): 233–39; Constance Jordan, "The 'Art of Clothing': Role-Playing in Deloney's Fiction," *English Literary Renaissance* 11:2 (Spring 1981): 183–93; E. D. Mackerness, "Thomas Deloney and the Virtuous Proletariat," *Cambridge Journal* 5:1 (October 1951): 34–50; David Margolies, *Novel and Society in Elizabethan England* (London: Croom Helm, 1985), 5, 144, 146–47; Edwin Haviland Miller, *The Professional Writer in Elizabethan England: A Study of Nondramatic Literature* (Cambridge: Harvard University Press, 1959), 203–44; S. Diana Neill, *A Short History of the English Novel* (New York: Macmillan, 1952), 25–26; David Parker, "*Jack of Newbury*: A New Source," *English Language Notes* 10:3 (March 1973): 172–80; Kurt-Michael Pätzold, "Thomas Deloney and the English Jest-Book Tradition," *English Studies* 53 (1972): 313–28; Ole Reuter, "Some Aspects of Thomas Deloney's Prose Style," *Neuphilologische Mitteilungen* 40 (1939): 23–72; Hyder E. Rollins, "Thomas Deloney's Euphuistic Learning and *The Forest*," *PMLA* 50:3 (September 1935): 679–86; John Simons, *Realistic Romance: The Prose Fiction of Thomas Deloney* (Winchester: King Alfred's College, 1983), 1–12; Laura Caroline Stevenson, *Praise and Paradox: Merchants and Craftsmen in Elizabethan Popular Literature* (Cambridge: Cambridge University Press, 1984), 16–17, 89–91; Edward Wagenknecht, *Cavalcade of the English Novel: From Elizabeth to George VI* (New York: Henry Holt, 1943), 12–14; Eugene P. Wright, *Thomas Deloney* (Boston: Twayne Publishers, 1981), 15–19, 51–74; and Louis B. Wright, *Middle-Class Culture in Elizabethan England* (Ithaca: Cornell University Press, 1935), 413. Michael McKeon, *The Origins of the English Novel, 1600–1740* (Baltimore: Johns Hopkins University Press, 1987; paperback ed., 1988), 223–26, argues that *Jack of Newbury* is one instance of the "transition between stories of assimilation and stories of supersession" (222).

4. Baker, *History of the English Novel*, 170; Devine, "Unity and Meaning," 591; Dorsinville, "Design in *Jack of Newbury*," 238; Margolies, *Novel and Society*, 9–45, 144–49; McKeon, *Origins of the English Novel*, 212–18; Miller, *Professional Writer*, 27–93; Parker, "A New Source," 179–80; Pätzold, "English Jest-Book Tradition," 313–28; Reuter, "Thomas Deloney's Prose Style," 28–32; Rollins, "Euphuistic Learning," 679; Simons, *Realistic Romance*, 1–7; Stevenson, *Praise and Paradox*, 40–74; Eugene P. Wright, *Thomas Deloney*, 55–58; and Louis B. Wright, *Middle-Class Culture*, 3, 413–17.

5. This middling social position is generally described as "middle-class" or, at times, "bourgeois." Within this rubric, three critics do analyze how *Jack of Newbury* is situated with respect to Renaissance relations of production. Mackerness, "Virtuous Proletariat," and Margolies, *Novel and Society*, demonstrate how this tale obscures the distinction between employers and their laborers and, in so doing, operates in favor of the former and at the expense of the latter. McKeon, *Origins of the English Novel*, argues that the instability of generic and social categories (such as "the novel" and "the middle class") is symptomatic of changing attitudes about how to signify truth and virtue; the novel mediates this change in

My reading of *Jack of Newbury* challenges such descriptions of a formal middle ground or of a middling social position. Yet I am indebted to these critics and, in particular, to their conviction that a discussion about sixteenth-century social relations is crucial to any analysis of the book's formal properties. I have been especially influenced by critics who focus on sixteenth-century jestbooks, because they often link the form of individual passages with the larger construction of the book. For example, some argue that jestbooks provide material for and one method of structuring particular episodes in *Jack of Newbury*. Others add that whenever Deloney abandons his narrative of Jack's life, he borrows the organizing logic of jestbook collections—treating his book as a string of discrete and not necessarily related episodes. Drawing on these attempts to connect the book's local with its more general formal traits, my analysis of Deloney's proverbs addresses individual moralizing passages, the proverbial nature of Jack's life, and the coexistence of disparate sorts of commonsense wisdom within a single book.

In "Proverbial Wisdom and Popular Errors," Natalie Zemon Davis investigates the impulses that motivated both the collection of proverbial wisdom and the use of proverb collections in sixteenth-century France.[6] Davis's analysis cannot be transported directly to England, of course, yet her attention to the ways in which supposedly popular wisdom is selected, revised, and appropriated suggests another resemblance between English jestbooks and *Jack of Newbury*. Like the jests in *A C. Mery Talys, Tales and quicke answeres*, and a 1583 translation of *The Mirrour of Mirth* that is often attributed to Deloney,[7] the proverbs in *Jack of Newbury* create

---

attitudes. For example, he argues that *Jack of Newbury* acknowledges the distinction between employers and their laborers and yet suggests that both groups are united, as clothiers, "in virtuous service to the public interest" (225). In this way, Deloney defines the clothiers against corrupt courtiers who receive the hostility that otherwise might have been directed against the upwardly mobile employers. Like these critics, I argue that *Jack of Newbury* operates in favor of employers and at the expense of laborers. And, like McKeon, I analyze the formal mediation through which this occurs. Yet, unlike these critics, I analyze the middle class as a process of constructing political identities among groups characterized by their multiple and often contradictory interests. In so doing, I analyze how proverbs help to mediate the relationship between struggles over commercial and industrial capital, on the one hand, and national, regional, town, and guild structures, on the other.

6. Natalie Zemon Davis, *Society and Culture in Early Modern France* (Stanford: Stanford University Press, 1975), 227–67.

7. These jestbooks are included in *A Hundred Merry Tales, and Other English Jestbooks of the Fifteenth and Sixteenth Centuries*, ed. P. M. Zall (Lincoln: University of Nebraska Press, 1963).

the impression that they emerge from some common group of people. In the first section of this chapter, I analyze how each proverb participates in sixteenth-century class struggle precisely by identifying its common constituency. This analysis redefines the terms that generally govern discussions about *Jack of Newbury* and England's sixteenth-century middle class. David Margolies, Michael McKeon, and John Simons have pointed out that this middle class—whether defined by Deloney or by his critics—is a notoriously ambiguous category, often encompassing cultural positions with which neither Deloney nor Jack is aligned.[8] In other words, in most Deloney criticism—as in most criticism of *The Merry Wives of Windsor*—the middle class correlates roughly with those whom members of Renaissance society increasingly labeled the "middling sort." As I explained in the previous chapter, this category included groups that occupied very different positions within the feudal and emerging capitalist modes of production.[9] Yet Deloney's proverbs stress that although Jack may not be a friend to all of the people who occupy those positions, he is frequently their companion. Like the vicar who inhabits Berkshire's sole proverb, Jack of Newbury operates within a system whose range of possible affiliations—and their consequences—is always in flux. I examine the logic of Jack's companionableness and the collective identities it promotes.

My analysis assumes that Deloney's proverb making is a hegemonic process that constructs alliances among groups characterized by their simultaneous participation in very different structures of oppression and thus by their multiple and often contradictory potential interests. Deloney's commonsense wisdom—like Shakespeare's network of insults—reinforces categories through which members of such groups might experience their political identities. I examine how Deloney's proverbs and Jack's "good fellowship" (5) promote the collective identities of "craftsmen" and "clothiers." And I analyze how the process of proverb making exploits the tensions between commercial and industrial capital and the tensions among national, regional, town, and guild structures.

Although *Jack of Newbury* has prompted a great deal of discussion about class, it has inspired remarkably little feminist commentary. In the chapter's second section, I examine the metaphor of yarn and web

8. Margolies, *Novel and Society*, 145–46; McKeon, *Origins of the English Novel*, 15, 19, 22, 161–68, 174–75; Simons, *Realistic Romance*, 5–6.

9. For a lengthier discussion of the "middling sort" and for appropriate citations, see 81–84 in chapter 3 of this book.

through which Deloney links the clothier's trade to the proverbial process of establishing and maintaining marital harmony. By focusing on the *trading* of proverbs between Jack and the widow, I analyze an irresolvable tension in the narrative. That tension, I argue, marks *Jack of Newbury*'s location within two very different sites of struggle over the sphere and nature of Renaissance women's activity: Deloney's model of marital harmony promotes the sexual division of skilled and unskilled labor, and, at the same time, it attempts to sidestep the direct threat that propertied widows posed to Renaissance gender relations.

A Jack of All Trades

Deloney begins *Jack of Newbury* by describing his title character:

> In the daies of King *Henery* the eight that most noble and victorious Prince, in the beginning of his reigne, *Iohn Winchcomb*, a broad cloth Weauer, dwelt in *Newberie*, a towne in *Barkshire*: who for that he was a man of a merry disposition, and honest conuersation, was wondrous welbeloued of Rich and Poore, especiallie because in euery place where hee came, hee would spend his money with the best, and was not at any time found a churle of his purse. Wherefore beeing so good a companion, he was called of old and young *Iack* of *Newbery*: a man so generally well knowne in all his countrey for his good fellowship, that hee could goe in no place but hee found acquaintance; by meanes whereof *Iack* could no sooner get a Crowne, but straight hee found meanes to spend it: yet had hee euer this care, that hee would alwaies keepe himselfe in comely and decent apparell, neither at any time would hee bee ouercome in drinke, but so discreetly behaue himselfe with honest mirth, and pleasant conceits, that hee was euery Gentlemans companion.
>
> After that *Iacke* had long led this pleasant life, beeing (though hee were but poore) in good estimation; it was his Masters chance to die, and his Dame to bee a Widow, who was a very comely auncient Woman, and of reasonable Wealth. (5)

In this passage, John Smallwood earns the epithet "*Iack* of *Newbery*" because he is "so good a companion" to all—to rich and poor and to young and old. According to the first sentence, Jack's "good fellowship" hinges on the apprentice's "merry disposition, and honest conuersation" but, even more importantly, on his tendency to "spend his money with the best." According to the syntax of the second sentence, however, that spending is actually an unfortunate by-product of Jack's wide network of acquaintances; its potentially disastrous effects are now mitigated only by Jack's care to substitute "honest mirth, and pleasant conceits" for improper dress and excess drink. By adopting this sanctioned mirth, Jack becomes "euery Gentlemans companion." A few paragraphs later, Deloney represents Jack's companionship—his "merry disposition, and honest conuersation"—as a string of proverbs encased in tetrameter couplets. Realizing that his Sunday and holy day companions would "euer be borrowing of him, but neuer could hee get pennie of it againe" (6), Jack resolves that he

> would neuer after carry aboue twelue pence at once in his purse, and that being spent, hee would streight returne home merily, taking his leaue of the company in this sort.

> My Masters I thank you, its time to pack home,
> For he that wants money is counted a Mome:
> And twelue pence a Sunday being spent in good cheare,
> To fifty two shillings amounts in the yeare;
> Enough for a crafts man that liues by his hands,
> And he that exceedes it shall purchase no lands.
> For that I spend this day, Ile work hard to morrow,
> For woe is that party that seeketh to borrow.
> My money doth make me full merry to be,
> And without my money none careth for mee:
> Therefore wanting money what should I do heere?
> But haste home, and thanke you for all my good cheer.
>
> (6–7)

Once again, Deloney substitutes Jack's merry proverbial wisdom for his excess spending and associates proverb making with Jack's companionship.

What is the significance of this substitution? First, Deloney emphasizes its prudence. Although Jack's thrift demands that he take "his leaue of the company," his departure actually guarantees that Jack's companions will remain devoted to him: "My money doth make me full merry to be, / And without my money none careth for mee." The merry terms of this companionship announce that Jack is an apprentice who poses no threat to society. Deloney published *Jack of Newbury* in 1597 amid a flurry of apprentice rebellions. Between 1581 and 1602, there were thirty-five such outbreaks in London alone.[10] An eighteenth-century edition of John Stow's *Survey of the Cities of London and Westminster*, sifting through Renaissance accounts of these rebellions, describes the sorts of apprentices who did threaten the social order:

> The Apprentices of London are so considerable a Body, that they have sometimes made themselves formidable by Insurrections and Mutinies in the City, getting some Thousands of them together, and pulling down Houses, breaking open the Gates of Newgate, and other Prisons, and setting the Prisoners free. . . . But they have been commonly assisted, and often egged on and headed by Apprentices of the Dreggs of the Vulgar, Fellows void of worthy Blood, and worthy Breeding; *yea, perhaps not apprentices at all, but forlorn Companions*, masterless Men, and Tradeless, and the like.[11] (My emphasis)

The merry Jack, beloved of all, is neither forlorn nor lacking in companionship. Having substituted proverbial mirth for excess spending, he is, in contemporaries' terms, neither the unruly rebel whose Sunday and holy day festivities spill into riot nor the apprenticed son of a gentleman whose riotous spending promotes that rebellious atmosphere.[12]

In addition, by restricting himself to the "comely and decent apparell" (5) that is appropriate for an apprentice, Jack avoids the conflict and confusion among classes which contemporary accounts of apprentice rebellions find particularly threatening. In 1584 W. Fletewood reported to Lord Burghley that when he returned to London on a Tuesday evening he

> found all the wardes full of watches. The cause thereof was for that neere the theatre or curten, at the tyme of the playes, there laye a prentice sleeping upon the grasse; and one Challes alias Grostock did turne upon the toe upon the belly of the same prentice; whereupon this apprentice start up, and after words they fell to playne blowes. The companie in-

10. Roger B. Manning, *Village Revolts: Social Protest and Popular Disturbances in England, 1509–1640* (Oxford: Clarendon Press, 1988), 187.

11. John Strype's 1720 edition of John Stow's *Survey of the Cities of London and Westminster* is quoted in Manning, *Village Revolts*, 192.

12. Manning, *Village Revolts*, 187–219. John Stow, *A Svrvay of London, Contayning the Originall, Antiquity, Increase, Moderne Estate, and Description of that Citie, written in the year 1598*, ed. Henry Morley (London: George Routledge and Sons, 1890), cites "an insurrection of youths against aliens on May-day, 1517" as the reason that London's "great mayings, and May-games" are not "so freely used as afore" (124).

creased of bothe sides to the number of 500, at the least. This Challes exclaimed and said, that he was a gentleman, and that the apprentice was but a rascal, and some there were littel better than roogs, that tooke upon them the name of gentelmen, and saide the prentizes were but the skumme of the worlde. Upon these troubles, the prentizes began the next daye, being Tuesdaye, to make mutinies and assemblies, and did conspyre to have broken the prisones, and to have taken forth the prentizes that were imprisoned. But my Lord and I having intelligence thereof, apprehended four or fyve of the chief conspirators, who are in Newgate, and stand indicted of their lewd demeanours.[13]

And in 1597 Bartholomew Steere, a Hampton-Gay carpenter, testified that—when informed by James Bradshaw that "between 40 and 60 men had been to Lord Norris, at Rycott, and had threatened to pull down the hedges and knock down gentlemen, if they could not have remedy," such as "some corn to relieve their distress"—he had advised that "after they had risen, if they found themselves weak, they should go towards London, as he thought the apprentices there would take their part" and "was induced to think so by the late intended insurrection in London, when certain apprentices were hanged."

Roger Symonds, one of the men under investigation, explained that he

> met Bartholomew Steere, who asked him how he did this hard year, and how he maintained his wife and children, having seven sons; told him he did so by hard work, and could hardly find them bread and water. Steere replied, "care not for work, for we shall have a merrier world shortly; there be lusty fellows abroad, and I will get more, and I will work one day and play the other," adding, that there was once a rising at Enslow Hill, when they were entreated to go down, and after were hanged like dogs, but now they would never yield, but go through with it; that he knew where there was harness for 100 men; that servants were so held in and kept like dogs, that they would be ready to cut their master's throats.

Symonds maintained that he discounted Steere's threats since "he commonly heard the poor people say that they were ready to famish for want

13. Fletewood is quoted in *Queen Elizabeth and Her Times: A Series of Original Letters, Selected from the Inedited Private Correspondence of Lord Treasurer Burghley, the Earl of Leicester, the Secretaries Walsingham and Smith, Sir Christopher Hatton, and Most of the Distinguished Persons of the Period*, vol. 2, ed. Thomas Wright (London: Henry Colburn, 1838), 227.

of corn, and thought they should be forced by hunger to take it out of men's houses." He did admit, however, that Steere outlined a fairly precise course of action: "Steere said that when they were up, the London apprentices would join them; that they would murder Mr. Power, as also Mr. Berry and his daughter, and spoil Rabone, the yeoman, Geo. Whilton, Sir Hen. Lee, Sir Wm. Spencer, Mr. Frere, and Lord Norris, and then go to London, and that it would only be a month's work to overrun the realm; and that the poor once rose in Spain and cut down the gentry, since which they had lived merrily."[14]

Deloney also suggests that Jack's thrift is a form of cultural capital that, to his credit, readily will be transformed into property. Jack's pleasant conceits promise that thrifty and diligent craftsmen will, as one proverb's rhyming end words predict, be able to transform "hands" into "lands." This transformation of manual labor into landed wealth conventionally marked the Renaissance craftsman's acquisition of gentility.[15] The reaction of Newbury's inhabitants to Jack's departure verifies the wisdom of these rhyming end words. Deloney assures us that Jack's "good gouernment and discretion" has been "noted of the best and substantiallest men of the Towne, so that it wrought his great commendations" and that the widow "thought herselfe not a little blest to haue such a seruant, that was so obedient vnto her, and so carefull for her profit . . . [that] shee began to cast very good countenance to her man *Iohn*, and to vse very much talk with him in priuate" (7). Jack's commendable behavior fuels the widow's love for him so that, after their impending marriage, her profit, for which he so diligently cared, becomes his own. Jack's control over that profit is briefly threatened when the widow's servants protest his elevation from apprentice to master. In the end, however, "knowing his good gouernment before time," they agree to pass "their yeares with him in dutifull manner" (22).

Yet Jack's "good gouernment and discretion" (7) consist as much in the

14. For the testimony of Steere and Symonds, see *Calendar of State Papers, Domestic Series, of the Reign of Elizabeth, 1595–1597*, ed. Mary Anne Everett Green (London: Her Majesty's Stationers Office, 1869; reprint, Nendeln, Liechtenstein: Kraus Reprint, 1967), 342–45.

15. Peter Clark and Paul Slack, *English Towns in Transition, 1500–1700* (London: Oxford University Press, 1976), 117–20, and Keith Wrightson, *English Society, 1580–1680* (New Brunswick, N.J.: Rutgers University Press, 1982), 23–31. Lawrence Stone, *The Causes of the English Revolution, 1529–1642* (New York: Harper and Row, 1972), 72–76, discusses the more general shift in landholding patterns during the late sixteenth and early seventeenth centuries. Christopher Hill, *Change and Continuity in Seventeenth-Century England* (London: Weidenfeld and Nicolson, 1974), 219–24, discusses the low status accorded to manual labor.

form of his departure as in its explicit endorsement of thrift. Introducing Jack's string of proverbial wisdom, Deloney stresses that Jack's merry departure is successful because he takes "his leaue of the company *in this sort*" (6, my emphasis). In other words, Jack's departing speech is valuable not only for the lesson that it teaches but also for the *proverbial form* of its instruction. Why is this form so crucial? In order to answer this question, I pause in my reading of *Jack of Newbury* and turn to the characteristics that, over sixty years after the book's composition, secure Jack a position among Berkshire's "Memorable Persons" in Fuller's *The History of the Worthies of England*. As I explained earlier, Fuller provides one lens through which historians and literary critics frequently have viewed Deloney as the great chronicler of England's sixteenth-century middle class. In his preface to the *Worthies*, Fuller discusses the categories through which he describes each county's history. The category "Memorable Persons" follows a series of professional categories: princes, saints, martyrs, confessors, cardinals, prelates, statesmen, soldiers, writers, and benefactors. Fuller explains that these

> former heads were like *private houses*, in which persons accordingly qualified have their several habitations. But this last topic is like a public *inn*, admitting all comers and goers, having any extraordinary, not vicious, remark upon them, and which are not clearly reducible to any of the former titles. Such, therefore, who are over, under, or beside the standard of common persons, for strength, stature, fruitfulness, vivacity, or any other observable eminence, are *lodged* here under the notion of memorable persons. . . .
>   Under this title we also repose all such mechanics, who in any manual trade have reached a clear note above others in their vocation. (55)

Within this passage, the "notion of memorable persons" is a public inn that Fuller distinguishes from private houses not because its guests are too common but, in fact, because they are observably *un*common. These guests are "over, under, or beside the standard of common persons" precisely because they are irreducible to a single professional identity.

In this way, each memorable person becomes a public inn who cannot be assigned to one of several dwellings because that individual embodies the traits not of one but of several professions. These memorable persons achieve an "observable eminence" only by relinquishing their former membership within a single "ingenius profession." According to this passage, manual trade is a special instance because, by definition, any excellence within that single endeavor automatically guarantees its transcendence. That transcendence depends, in part, on a seventeenth-century slippage between "ingenious" and "ingenuous."[16] When Fuller's phantom interlocutor objects that these "handy craftsmen blended with eminencies in ingenius professions" are an "uncouth sight," Fuller replies that "such a motley colour" encourages the sort of competition that can only improve those of "honest industry and ingenuous diligence" (55). In his narrative of Berkshire history, Fuller describes Jack of Newbury as a "Memorable Person" whose professional ingenuity is actually inseparable from the ingenuous diligence of the self-improved handy craftsman. Emphasizing the importance of the clothing industry within Berkshire's economy, Fuller writes: "*Broad Cloth* (wherein the wealth of our nation is folded up) made with broad looms, two men attending each of them, began here in the reign of king Henry the Eighth. And I have been informed that Jack of Newberry was the first that introduced it into this county. Well may the poets feign Minerva the goddess of wit and the foundress of weaving, so great is the ingenuity thereof" (112). By condensing a feigned goddess into a foundress and by alliteratively linking wit with weaving, Fuller emphasizes the ingenuity that characterizes both poet and clothier. Fuller contrasts Jack's ingenious broad cloth with "*Fine Cloth* (though narrow)." Unlike Jack's ingenious product, fine cloth has a restricted constituency of "persons of worth at home," on the one hand, and foreigners, on the other (112). In Fuller's terms, "the wealth of our nation is folded up" in broad cloth's ingenious weave, whereas fine cloth's contribution to the nation, like its weave, is "narrow."

This use of the word "narrow" links Fuller's description of "Memorable Persons" with his description of proverbial wisdom. Fuller begins his prefatory comments about "Local Proverbs" by distinguishing proverbs from orations, riddles, secrets, sentences, upstarts, and libels; unlike these, he writes, a "perfect proverb" is short, plain, common, figurative, ancient, and true (7). Yet he concludes his comments by admitting that he lists among local proverbs several wise sayings that deviate from these criteria yet "afford us a fit occasion to sally forth into such discourse as may conduce to the history of our nation" (8). In the intervening para-

16. Here Fuller's use of the word "ingenuous" conveys both its current meanings—noble, freeborn, candid, natural—and an additional meaning that was current in the seventeenth century—ingenious. The *O.E.D.* entry for "ingenuous" explains this seventeenth-century slippage between "ingenuous" and "ingenious."

graphs, Fuller explains which sorts of common wisdom allow him to construct that single national history:

> Herein I have neglected such narrow and restrictive Proverbs as never travelled beyond the smoke of the chimneys of that town wherein they were made, and, though perchance significant in themselves, are unknown to the neighbouring counties, so far they are from acquiring a national reception. Besides, I have declined all such which are frivolous, scurrilous, scandalous, confining ourselves only to such whose expounding may contribute to the understanding of those shires wherein they are in fashion. (7)

Within this logic, our "understanding of those shires" depends on the nation's receptiveness to their proverbial wisdom. Each proverb is figured as an individual who must shun provinciality, frivolity, scurrility, and scandal in order to receive an audience within the nation. Although "perchance significant in themselves," these proverbs—and the counties in which they reside—are incomprehensibly narrow unless they are conducive to Fuller's narrative of English history. Not surprisingly, the royalist Fuller figures the proverb's national readership as an audience with England's ruler. As Fuller's discussion of Berkshire's sole proverb taught us, no proverb will be received at the end of its pilgrimage if it exchanges provinciality for a complete lack of regional specificity. In fact, the proverb most conducive to local, and thus national, history is one "wherein some proper place or person is mentioned; such as suggest unto us some historical hint, and the interpretation thereof afford some considerable information" (7).

Although Fuller counsels that we read proverbs which mention "some proper place or person," he cautions against becoming the person who inhabits those proverbs. Fuller's phantom interlocutor criticizes his interest in proverbs by demanding to know why he is "busied in what may be pleasant, not profitable; yea, what may inform the fleshly, not edify the inward man" (7). Fuller replies by invoking a Christly precedent for the recreative and yet edifying use of "natural or native proverbs" (8). Then he adds: "Lastly, besides information much good may redound to the reader hereby. It was the counsel which a wise gave to a great man; 'Read histories, that thou dost not become a history.' So may we say, 'Read Proverbs, that thou beest not made a proverb'" (8). If, in Fuller's hands, Jack of Newbury is not quite "made a proverb," this "Memorable Person" does, at the very least, "become a history." Fuller summarizes Deloney's account of the memorable clothier in order to contrast the prosperous Newbury which Jack inhabited with the Newbury which Fuller visited in the summer of 1654. "He feasted king Henry the Eighth and his first queen Katharine at his own house," Fuller writes, "extant at Newberry at this day, but divided into many tenements. Well may his house now make sixteen clothiers' houses, whose wealth would amount to six hundred of their estates" (137). The subdivision of Jack's home parallels the decline of England's clothing industry and of his town's good fortune. At the beginning of the sixteenth century, Jack of Newbury helped to revive the clothing industry, which transformed Newbury from an agricultural town into a large manufacturing town that benefited from its strategic location on major routes to London and to Winchester. When Deloney wrote his tale at the end of that century, the clothing industry and Newbury were still relatively healthy.[17] In the intervening years before Fuller's visit, the clothing industry decayed, poor relief became insufficient, and the town was torn by revolutionary battles. Later, fearing that it would be censured by Charles II for having abandoned his father during the war, Newbury would relinquish its old charter and assent to one which required all town officials to take an oath of allegiance to the state.[18] In Fuller's narrative, the decline of the clothing industry transforms Jack's home—which admitted all comers and goers—into private tenements. Those tenements are inhabited by clothiers whose historical circumstances render them unmemorable. Unlike Jack, they are not "over, under, or beside the standard of common persons"; instead, they reinforce the uncommonness of a man whose life they can only approximate.

In other words, Fuller's account of Jack of Newbury suggests that the clothier's memorable ability to exceed a single professional identity is inextricable from his proverbial ability to negotiate between past and

17. Walter Money, *A History of Newbury* (orig. pub. by W. J. Blackett as *The Popular History of Newbury* in 1905; reprint, Newbury: Newbury Bookshop, 1972; Maidenhead: Thames Valley Press, 1972), 25. My chapter draws on a number of antiquarians—Thomas Fuller, E. W. Gray, Walter Money, and John Stow. For a brief history of this sort of work, see W[illiam] G[eorge] Hoskins, *Local History in England*, 2d ed. (London: Longman, 1972), 17–27. See Clark and Slack, *English Towns in Transition*, 97–110, for a more general discussion of the sixteenth- and seventeenth-century economies of English towns.

18. Money, *History of Newbury*, 70–73, 118, and *The Victoria History of the Counties of England: Berkshire*, vol. 4 (London: St. Catherine Press, 1924; reprint, Folkestone: Dawsons of Pall Mall for the University of London Institute of Historical Research, 1972), 141–42, 144.

present and between regional and national identities. In short, a memorable life shares the structure of a proverb: both are peculiarly irreducible to a single identity and peculiarly adamant that their multiplicity signals social difference without signaling social conflict. This lengthy digression from Deloney's *Jack of Newbury* to Fuller's *Worthies* is particularly apt for two reasons. First, Fuller derives his account of Jack and of Newbury primarily from Deloney's own attempt to raise "out of the dust of forgetfulnesse a most famous and worthie man, whose name was John Winchcombe." In this way, Deloney's tale helped to influence Fuller's formulations about proverbial wisdom and political identities. Second, the role of proverbs both in obscuring social conflict and in forging together regional and national identities is in keeping with my own understanding of how *Jack of Newbury* participates in Renaissance struggles over class.

My analysis of *Jack of Newbury*, like my analysis of *The Merry Wives of Windsor*, is indebted to historians sometimes associated with revisionist history because they focus on the importance of local and regional political identities. The most controversial forms of revisionist history argue that sixteenth- and seventeenth-century England produced neither a coherent nor a collective oppositional politics. For example, many revisionists suggest that, particularly prior to the revolution, the government maintained a rough social consensus—a consensus interrupted only occasionally by conflict which was, at best, local and coincidental. Others suggest that the revolution and interregnum produced no lasting changes in English society. As I explain in this book's introduction, I find these accounts of local and regional alliances unconvincing as a challenge to Marxist narratives about social struggle—particularly class struggle—before, during, and after the revolution. They are, however, one valuable resource for a Marxist analysis of the complicated relationships among political identities, economic structures, and social change in Renaissance England.[19] For instance, in my readings of *The Merry Wives of Windsor* and *Jack of Newbury*, I assume that Shakespeare's insults and Deloney's proverbs participate in sixteenth-century class struggle precisely by promoting collective identities which help define the range of possible intersections between local and national affiliations.

With Fuller's definition of proverbs and professional identities in

19. For a lengthier discussion of revisionist history and for appropriate citations, see 5–6 in this book's introduction.

mind, I return to *Jack of Newbury* and to the question that prompted this analysis of the *Worthies of England*: why is Jack's use of *proverbs* an appropriate substitute for his excess spending? In the book's introductory passage, Deloney describes Jack's financial excess by noting that "in euery place where hee came, hee would spend his money with the best, and was not at any time found a churle of his purse" (5). As the multiple meanings of "churle" suggest, this spending guarantees Jack a wide network of companionship that is as destructive in its indiscriminateness as in its excess: "hee could goe in no place but hee found acquaintance; by meanes whereof *Iack* could no sooner get a Crowne, but straight hee found meanes to spend it" (5). Deloney substitutes for this indiscriminateness and excess the "honest mirth, and pleasant conceits" (5) that are capable of fashioning collective identities.

As I explained earlier, Jack addresses his initial proverbs to fellow craftsmen who live by their hands. He figures social mobility as the acquisition of wealth and land and assures his common constituency that gentility is within the grasp of every handicraftsman. Later, describing his portrait gallery to the same constituency, Jack promises that diligent craftsmen will "spend their dayes in credit" (55). He moralizes, "The idle hand shall euer goe in a ragged garment, and the slothfull liue in reproach" (55). His portraits depict the socially mobile sons of shepherds, potters, cobblers, rope makers, cloth weavers, shoemakers, mariners, ploughmen, and tailors who "have been aduanced to high estate and Princely dignities by wisedome, learning, and diligence" (55). As I discussed in my analysis of *The Arte of English Poesie*, manual labor actually brought neither high wages nor social mobility to most workers. In spite of Jack's good fortune, those laboring craftsmen who were not master artisans and shop owners had little opportunity to advance their social positions. Finally, wage laborers were increasingly unlikely to control the means of production or to have access to any means of subsistence other than the sale of their labor power. And, particularly within the clothing industry, apprentices were increasingly likely to become wage laborers.[20] In this way, Jack's commonsense appeal to all craftsmen who live by their hands acknowledges the difference between employers and their laborers without acknowledging that this difference is conflictual. The

---

20. For a lengthier discussion of craftsmen's social mobility and for appropriate citations, see 36–37 in chapter 1 of this book.

same logic governs Jack's refusal to be knighted by Henry VIII: "O my drad Soueraigne said *Iacke*, honour and worship may be compared to the Lake of *Laethe*, which makes men forget themselues that taste thereof: and to the end I may still keepe in minde from whence I came, and what I am, I beseech your Grace let mee rest in my russet coat a poore Clothier to my dying day" (49). Here Jack acknowledges the difference between the apprentice and the employer who, in the words of the title page, "set continually fiue *hundred poore people at worke*." Yet his memorable life encompasses that difference as continuity rather than as conflict.

This reading might imply that Jack's proverbs create a collective identity—craftsmen—that, by denying conflict, operates in the interests of employers and at the expense of laborers. But this is only part of the story. *Jack of Newbury* also suggests that particular employers and laborers share an interest in the prominence of the textile industry within town government. Deloney's proverbs create this common constituency by exploiting the overlapping authority structures of the nation, the region, the town, and the guild.

In order to tell this part of the story, I turn to Newbury's town charter and to the position of clothing towns within struggles between commercial and industrial capital. Queen Elizabeth granted Newbury its charter of incorporation in 1596, one year before Deloney published *Jack of Newbury*. Town charters dictated the extent of the town's autonomy from the crown by distributing authority among local officials who were appointed by the state, by county peerage and gentry, by the town oligarchy, and by the guilds. In addition, during the last half of the sixteenth century, in clothing towns such as Newbury, these charters generally helped to reinforce the prominence of master clothiers—and the industrial and commercial interests of these employers—in town government. Their municipal authority would often entail, more generally, uniting the disparate crafts that comprised the town's textile industry against the threat posed by manufacturers in the countryside. And it would entail creating alliances between this larger group of town manufacturers and town merchants, such as the drapers; the latter increasingly sought such alliances when London merchants, generally supported by Elizabeth's policies, threatened both local industrial and local commercial interests. For almost 150 years prior to Elizabeth's charter, Newbury had been owned by royalty who retained their right to appoint local officials. During Jack's life, for example, possession of Newbury passed from Henry

VII's wife to Anne Boleyn and, upon her demise, to Jane Seymour. In
1551 the town passed into Elizabeth's hands.[21]

Although Newbury's early records were destroyed during the revolution, town historians speculate that Newbury's 1596 charter reshaped its
governing body—the commonality—by strengthening the autonomy of
the town's government from the crown, the inseparability of that government from the guilds, and thus the relative strength of guild members
over county peerage in determining municipal policy. The 1596 charter
dictates that the town be governed by an oligarchic body called the
corporation, which would consist of thirty-one capital burgesses, including the town's six aldermen and its mayor. With the exception of the
mayor, these men would hold office for life. The mayor would be elected
annually by the corporation, which, in practice, routinely elevated one
of its own members to that office. The full corporation and its smaller
governing councils wielded a great deal of power—awarding lifetime
appointments to attorneys, trying all vagabonds and laborers charged
with disorder, and supervising all property claims, trade and industry
regulations, and treason charges. The powerful governing burgesses
most likely were drawn from among guild officers. Elizabeth's charter
also determined which guilds might yield those officers by licensing only
five companies and by dictating that all freemen who pursued a trade be
affiliated with one of those five. Jack's clothier company was one of those
five powerful companies. Thus Newbury's scriveners and schoolmasters
were, oddly enough, members of Jack's clothier company. The five companies forbid freemen to open shops, operate crafts, or employ labor
without their approval.[22]

Jack calls for the unity of *all* who participate in the textile industry
when he rallies all clothworkers against the royal wars that have closed

21. Clark and Slack, *English Towns in Transition*, 97–110, 126–40; Karl Marx, "Inter-
course and Productive Forces," in *The German Ideology*, Part I, orig. pub. 1932, trans.
S. Ryazanskaya (Moscow: Foreign Languages Publishing House, 1963), reprinted in *The
Marx-Engels Reader*, 2d ed., ed. Robert C. Tucker (New York: Norton, 1978), 176–86; and
George Unwin, *Industrial Organization in the Sixteenth and Seventeenth Centuries* (Oxford:
Clarendon Press, 1904; reprint, New York: Augustus M. Kelley, 1963), 39–40, 70–125. For
information about Newbury, see Money, *History of Newbury*, 117, and *Victoria History: Berk-
shire*, 136, 139.

22. E. W. Gray, *The History and Antiquities of Newbury and its Environs, Including Twenty-
eight Parishes, Situate in the County of Berks: also a Catalogue of Plants, found in the Neighborhood*
(Speenhamland: Hall and Marsh, 1839), 129–30; Walter Money, *The History of the Ancient
Town and Borough of Newbury, in the County of Berks.* (London: Parker and Co., 1887), 227–
29, and *A History of Newbury*, 117; and *Victoria History: Berkshire*, 140.

off clothing trade with France and the Low Countries and, thus, impoverished employer and employee alike:

> When I had well thought thereon, I found that nothing was more neede-full herein then a faithfull vnity among our selues. This sore of necessity can no way be cured but by concord: for like as the flame consumes the candle, so men through discorde waste themselues. The poore hate the rich, because they will not set them on worke: and the rich hate the poore, because they seeme burdenous: so both are offended for want of gaine. . . . [S]o let our Art of Clothing, which like a kinde mother hath cherished vs with the excellency of her secrets, perswade vs to an vnity. (56–57)

Jack addresses his back-to-back proverbs to all clothworkers—rich and poor. And, although Henry VIII quickly selects Jack to serve as the group's representative, the members of the textile industry initially do present their petition to the king in the first person singular, "as it were one man" (57). Jack's letter unites the disparate crafts within that industry—speaking, at once, for "Weauers, Shearemen, Spinners and Carders" (56). And it denies any distinction between the "Clothiers, and those they maintained" (57). The clothworkers present this unified front in order to obtain royal favor. Yet, given the late-sixteenth-century terms of Newbury's charter and given the late-sixteenth-century threat of country manufacturers and London merchants, this passage and its proverbs also suggest that all who participate in Newbury's textile industry should share an interest in strengthening the role of that industry in setting town policy. Finally, in *Jack of Newbury* the municipal prominence of the textile industry is secured, in part, because the well-being of the nation actually turns on the "Art of Clothing." For example, in his prefatory comments, Deloney writes that "among all manuall Arts vsed in this Land, none is more famous for desert, or more beneficiall to the Commonwealth, than is the most necessarie Art of Cloathing" (3).

In this way, Deloney's proverbs create collective identities—craftsmen and clothiers—that turn on the uneven relationship between struggles over commercial and industrial capital, on the one hand, and tensions among national, regional, town, and guild structures, on the other. These identities promote the ability of employers to exploit their laborers, and they support the prominence of the textile industry and, in particular, one segment of its clothworkers, the clothiers, within town government. During the late sixteenth century, these clothiers and their fellow members of town oligarchies often feared incursions on their corporation rights both from above and from below.[23] *Jack of Newbury* suggests that Jack's ability to "perswade" these groups "to an vnity" (57) helps to guarantee social order. In turn, that social order, often reinforced with charity, protects the town government from direct crown intervention. In his letter to the clothworkers, Jack promises relief to the poor, and in his role as burgess he donates to town charities at "no small charges vnto him" (70). "Emptie platters make greedy stomackes," he warns his second wife, "and where scarcitie is kept, hunger is nourished" (73).

This proverbial emphasis on social order makes even more crucial Deloney's insistence that the young Jack is a model apprentice. Late-sixteenth-century accounts of apprentice riots emphasize the threat those riots posed to the autonomy of local officials. Although contemporary commentators attributed most of the riots to the perception, on the part of apprentices, that French and Dutch immigrants were responsible for the economic hardships endured by English workers, those same commentators emphasized the threat such riots posed to local officials. For example, in 1592, the Privy Council, "informed that certaine apprentyces and other idle people theire adherentes that were authors and partakers of the late mutynous and foule disorder in Southwarke in moste outrageous and tumultuous sorte, have a further purpose and meaninge on Midsommer eveninge or Midsommer nighte or about that tyme to renewe theire lewd assemblye togeather by cullour of the tyme for some bad and mischeivous intencion, to the disturbance and breache of her Majesty's Peace, and comyttinge some outrage," ordered London's mayor to instruct his constables to enforce curfews on all servants and apprentices and to prevent their unlawful assembly.[24] And, in 1595, Attorney General Edward Coke charged that rioting London apprentices had intended to "take the sworde of Auchthoryte from the magistrates and governours Lawfully Aucthorised and there unto appointed."

These accounts often were haunted by the specter of the 1517 May Day uprising after which Cardinal Wolsey ordered that the captured rebels be paraded through the streets of London in harnesses. By staging a shaming ritual, the cardinal emphasized that he had been forced to

23. Clark and Slack, *English Towns in Transition*, 122, 132–36.
24. *Acts of the Privy Council of England*, ed. John Roche Dasent, new series, vol. 22 (London: Mackie and Co., 1901), 549–50.

intervene in an incident which should have been contained locally by officials or by popular forms of abuse and shaming. For example, in Edward Hall's 1542 account, one of the rebellion's organizers, Jhon Lyncoln, persuaded Doctor Bele to incite his congregation "too move the Mayre and Aldermen to take parte with the comminaltie agaynste the straungers." Bele agreed, preaching a sermon in which he read from a "pitifull byll":

> To all you, the worshypfull lordes and masters of the cytie, that will take compassion over the pore people your neighbours, and also of the greate importable hurtes, losses and hynderaunces, whereof proceadeth the extreme povertie too all the kynges subjectes that inhabite within this cytie and suburbes of the same, for so it is that alyens and straungers eate the bread from the poore fatherles chyldren, and take the livynge from all the artificers, and the entercourse from all merchauntes, wherby povertie is so muche encreased that every man bewaileth the misery of other, for craftes men be brought to beggery and merchauntes to nedynes. Wherefore the premisses considered, the redresse muste be of the commons, knyt and unite to one parte, and as the hurt and dammage greveth all men, so muste all men set to their willyng power for remedy, and not to suffre the sayed alyens so highly in their wealth, and the naturall borne men of his region to come to confusion.

Bele then glossed "*Coelum coeli domino, terram autem dedit filiis hominum*" and "*pugna pro patria*" in order to justify as divinely authorized and patriotic a rebellion that would surely "breke the kynges peace." In spite of Bele's sermon and the "commen secret rumour . . . that on May daye next the citie would rebell and slaye all Aliens," the local authorities remained unprepared. In fact, the mayor assured a concerned cardinal that "I trust so to governe them that the kynges peace shalbe observed." The cardinal responded that the mayor might "go home and wisely forsee this matter, for and yf any suche thing be, you may shortly prevent it." In Hall's account, the mayor, the aldermen, and the sheriffs were unable either to prevent or to subdue the uprising. In fact, the rebellion began when one ineffectual alderman attempted to enforce a newly issued curfew: "Then all the young men resisted the Alderman . . . and cryed prentyses and clubbes. Then out at every doore came clubbes and weapons, and the Alderman fled, and was in great daungier. The more people arose out of every quarter . . . and by a xi.

of the clocke there were in Chepe vi. or vii. hundreth. . . . The Mayre and Shrifes were there present, and made Proclamacion in the kynges name, but nothynge was obeyed."²⁵ In other words, even when local magistrates and governors were not the rebels' explicit targets, any rebellion challenged their ability to maintain order. In this way, rebellion would threaten the town's tenuous autonomy from the crown, on the one hand, and the burgesses' tenuous control over their laborers, on the other. For example, in 1597, the year in which Deloney published *Jack of Newbury*, Newbury's corporation issued a list of ordinances in an effort to ensure that it would be able to maintain town order without direct interference from the crown. After successfully increasing the jurisdiction of its mayor and aldermen, the corporation made illegal any unauthorized assembly of "all persons of an inferior sort, freemen, journeymen and apprentices." Members of the corporation orchestrated, instead, mandatory assemblies in the guildhall in order to demonstrate popular endorsement of their authority—attempting, in Jack's words, to "perswade vs to an vnity" that actually might prevent the sort of knitting and uniting provoked by Bele's sermon.²⁶

I close with a biographical note. When the young Jack announces, with his proverbial wisdom, that he is an apprentice who poses no threat to local authority, "it wrought his great commendations" among the "best and substantiallest" of Newbury's citizens (7). Many years later, Jack's future father-in-law endorses his daughter's marriage to the clothier "because che heare very good condemnation of you in euery place" (28). This malapropism invokes Deloney's own inadvertent threat to local authority only two years before *Jack of Newbury*'s publication. In 1595, Deloney and fourteen other weavers attempted to restrict French and Dutch immigrants' opportunities for apprenticeship. Surprised that local authorities had imprisoned him rather than support his protests, Deloney petitioned to the high chief justice who overruled the local mayor and alderman and released Deloney "with good Commendacions."²⁷ Like Jack's father-in-law, the book's proverbs actually condemn Deloney's error.

25. Edward Hall, *Hall's Chronicle, in Henry VIII*, in *Tudor Economic Documents, Being Select Documents Illustrating the Economic and Social History of Tudor England*, ed. R. H. Tawney and Eileen Power, vol. 3 (London: Longmans, Green and Co., 1924), 82–90.
26. *Victoria History: Berkshire*, 140.
27. Lawlis, introduction to *The Novels of Thomas Deloney*, xxvii–xxviii.

Trading Proverbs with Women

I organize my analysis of marital harmony in *Jack of Newbury* around the widows with whom Deloney introduces and concludes his tale—the "very comely auncient Woman" (5) who becomes Jack's first wife and the "leud paltrie thing" (82) who, disguised as a widow, becomes the wife of Sir George. The courtship and marriage of Jack and the widow occupy most of *Jack of Newbury*'s first chapter and almost one quarter of the entire book. Noting Jack's "singular vertue" as an apprentice, the widow

> began to cast very good countenance to her man *Iohn,* and to vse very much talk with him in priuate: and first by way of communication, shee would tell vnto him what suters shee had, and the great offers they made her, what gifts they sent her, and the great affection they bare her, crauing his opinion in the matter.
>
> When *Iacke* found the fauour to bee his dames Secretarie, he thought it an extraordinary kindnesse: and ghessing by the yarne it would prooue a good Web, began to question with his dame in this sort. (7)

When Jack begins "to question with his dame *in this sort*" (my emphasis), he employs a very different form of proverbial wisdom than the sort with which he takes leave of his Sunday and holy day companions. That sort of leave-taking stresses how each proverb helps to shape regional and national alliances. This sort of questioning stresses the very process of *trading* proverbs through which, in Deloney's terms, Jack and the widow weave the fabric of their marital harmony.[28]

For example, Jack asks the widow whether he might know the names and professions of her suitors. Rather than respond directly, she addresses Jack's concern about his status as her servant by suggesting that he sit on a cushion beside her. When he protests that he is undeserving, she responds that

> faint souldiers neuer find fauour.
>
> *Iohn* replied, that makes mee indeed to want fauour: for I durst not trie

---

28. The *O.E.D.*'s first definition of "web" is "A woven fabric; *spec.* a whole piece of cloth in process of being woven or after it comes from the loom. . . . Something likened to a woven fabric; something of complicated structure or workmanship. Also, the texture of such a fabric."

Maydens because they seeme coy, nor Wiues for feare of their Husbands, nor Widowes, doubting their disdainfullnesse.

Tush *Iohn* (quoth shee) hee that feares and doubts Womankind, cannot bee counted Mankind: and take this for a principle, all things are not as they seeme. (7)

After this exchange, the widow evaluates, in turn, the tanner, the tailor, and the parson as potential husbands. In each case, she concludes her evaluation with a proverbial reference to the suitor's most disturbing marital flaw. The tanner "being ouerworne in yeares makes mee ouerloth to loue him" (8). The tailor "being so long a ranger, he would at home be a stranger" (8). And the parson "will bee so bent to his books, that he will haue little minde of his bed" (9). The widow adds that each flawed suitor compares unfavorably with another "one nearer hand" (8–9). When she first offers that comparison, Jack replies with a proverb: "I perceiue store is no sore, and profered ware is worse by ten in the hundred than that which is sought" (8). When she repeats the formula for a third time, he asks the name of that "fortunate man that is so highly placed in your fauour" (9). She replies that "they are worthy to knowe nothing, that cannot keepe something: that man (I tell thee) must goe namelesse" (9). Deloney casts this trading of proverbs in professional terms: in initiating their courtship, the widow provides the yarn with which the well-trained clothworker guesses that a good web might be woven. Yet, as I will demonstrate, the metaphor of yarn and web locates this proverbial process of establishing and maintaining marital harmony in two not entirely compatible registers. I would argue that *Jack of Newbury* participates in struggles over the conditions that shaped Renaissance women's lives precisely by *emphasizing* this incompatibility. In order to analyze the significance of Deloney's metaphor of yarn and web, I want to outline briefly the role of women's skilled and unskilled labor within the textile industries.

Because textiles occupied a central role in the economy of Renaissance England, because they were among the earliest crafts to capitalize, and because, throughout Europe, they were the site of explicit struggles over the nature of women's labor, these industries, especially the woolen trade, are particularly well-documented examples of what some historians have characterized as Renaissance women's fall from feudalism into capitalism. I offer this formulation—"Renaissance women's fall"—to emphasize the tone of this work, a tone that I read not as a celebration of feudalism but as a polemical response both to twentieth-century celebrations of capitalism and to twentieth-century celebrations of a cultural Renaissance which was, these historians insist, less available to women than to men. Within one version of this "fall," a shift away from household production reinforced a sexual division of labor. Women were increasingly circumscribed within a newly defined and undervalued private sphere. And those women who worked in the public sphere were relegated to the less skilled and lower paid segments of the work force. For example, throughout Europe, in the woolen trade, men took over the task of weaving the yarn that women were expected to spin.[29]

Other historians have made explicit what was implicit in this narrative of a "fall"—that capitalism alone cannot explain why women's labor should have been so consistently undervalued. By bringing together shifting economic structures with shifting structures of patriarchy, these historians analyze how the value of women's labor power—the socially agreed upon cost of reproducing a woman—came to be so low. In so doing, they caution that portions of earlier arguments regarding women's labor—particularly discussions about the family wage and about labor within and outside of the home—turn on a conflation of capitalism and industrialization. And they point out that those earlier arguments were most attentive to forms of women's oppression which resembled the oppression of women under twentieth-century capitalism. Finally, they study women's experiences within a range of crafts across England and the Continent in order to reexamine the various ways in which the shift from a feudal to an early-capitalist economy might have affected women's labor.[30]

29. For example, Joan Kelly, "Did Women Have a Renaissance?" *Women, History, and Theory: The Essays of Joan Kelly* (Chicago: University of Chicago Press, 1984; paperback ed., 1986), 19–50, offers an influential account of this "fall" that focuses on Renaissance noblewomen in Italy. And Alice Clark, *Working Life of Women in the Seventeenth Century* (New York: E. P. Dutton and Co., 1919), 93–235, offers another influential account that focuses on England's female laborers, including women working in the textile industries.

30. Judith C. Brown, "A Woman's Place Was in the Home: Women's Work in Renaissance Tuscany," in *Rewriting the Renaissance: The Discourses of Sexual Difference in Early Modern Europe*, ed. Margaret W. Ferguson, Maureen Quilligan, and Nancy J. Vickers (Chicago: University of Chicago Press, 1986), 206–24; Roberta Hamilton, *The Liberation of Women: A Study of Patriarchy and Capitalism* (London: George Allen and Unwin, 1978), 23–75; Margaret L. King, *Women of the Renaissance* (Chicago: University of Chicago Press, 1991), 64–72; Chris Middleton, "Women's Labour and the Transition to Pre-Industrial Capitalism," in

Within this framework, the distinction between labor which was thought to be skilled and that which was thought to be unskilled is significant in part because these forms of labor were differently valued and entailed very different access to cultural, economic, and political authority. In addition, within the textile industry of the late sixteenth century, this distinction would affect who would be most likely to obtain—and retain—control over the means of production and how its male and female laborers would be unevenly exploited. Historians argue that, within medieval and Renaissance England, a married woman often helped to organize her family's household production and to direct its finances and the trading of its goods, but she less frequently helped her husband in the skilled labor of his craft; that many women joined guilds if, as apprentices, daughters, or wives, they had learned a skilled trade; that, through the end of the sixteenth century, English craft guilds granted membership to women primarily on the basis of their fathers' and husbands' occupations; that these guilds usually restricted women to the social and religious aspects of their activity and denied them any voice in shaping economic policy; that these early craft guilds were organized around skilled labor, while the majority of women performed unskilled labor that was protected neither by nor from the guilds; and that, in England, women in all-female skilled occupations, such as the silk workers, did organize to protect their trade yet did not organize into women's guilds.[31]

These historians tend to agree that some medieval and Renaissance Englishwomen had an active role in the productive and commercial enterprises of their families yet that relatively few of these women were allowed access to skilled labor and thus to the relative privileges such

Women and Work in Pre-Industrial England, ed. Lindsey Charles and Lorna Duffin (London: Croom Helm, 1985), 181–206; Mary Prior, "Women and the Urban Economy: Oxford, 1500–1800," in *Women in English Society, 1500–1800*, ed. Prior (London: Methuen, 1985), 93–117; and Merry E. Wiesner, "Spinsters and Seamstresses: Women in Cloth and Clothing Production," in Ferguson, Quilligan, and Vickers, *Rewriting the Renaissance*, 191–205.

31. Dianne Hutton, "Women in Fourteenth-Century Shrewsbury," in Charles and Duffin, *Women and Work*, 83–99; Maryanne Kowaleski and Judith M. Bennett, "Crafts, Gilds, and Women in the Middle Ages: Fifty Years after Marian K. Dale," *Signs* 14:2 (Winter 1989): 474–88; Kay E. Lacey, "Women and Work in Fourteenth- and Fifteenth-Century London," in Charles and Duffin, *Women and Work*, 24–82; Prior, "Women and the Urban Economy," 96–98; and Sue Wright, "'Churmaids, Huswyfes and Hucksters': The Employment of Women in Tudor and Stuart Salisbury," in Charles and Duffin, *Women and Work*, 100–121.

labor entailed. They also tend to agree that, with the capitalization and professionalization of crafts, women were increasingly excluded from skilled work such as the weaving of wool. Not surprisingly, the nature of women's labor also had been and continued to be susceptible to guild members' fluctuating sense of their craft's economic well-being. For example, Sue Wright explains that when Bristol weavers perceived a decline in their trade and employment in 1461, "men were ordered not to set their wives, daughters or maids to work, either for themselves or for any other men. Two years later, however, conditions had evidently improved for women were specifically advised to 'help and labour with hir housband for thair boothe sustynaunce and thair childryn thair encrease.'"[32] In 1595, a petition by the Yeoman Weavers against foreign immigrant weavers charged that, among other crimes, these immigrants were willing to share with women the secrets of their crafts.[33] Finally, during the late sixteenth century, women in the textile industry usually performed unskilled labor, such as spinning, within their homes. These women generally were not paid a regular wage—the merchant or master craftsman purchased not their labor power but their dead labor in the form of piecework.[34]

Although their labor was certainly undervalued, these women were more likely to earn a subsistence income from this piecework when they were able to retain control over the means of production. When poverty increasingly forced them—or their families—into debt, they tended not only to lose control over the means of production but also to lose access to an alternate means of subsistence. Thus they depended more fully on individual employers and the raw materials and tools that these employers provided. For example, according to Renaissance commentators, this situation was exacerbated by clothiers who attempted to control cloth production outside of the town limits "by engrossing of looms into their hands and possession and letting them out at such unreasonable rents as the poor artificers are not able to maintain themselves, much less their wives, family and children, some also by giving much less wages and hire for the weaving and workmanship of cloth than in times past they did."[35]

32. Sue Wright, "Employment of Women," 106.
33. Kowaleski and Bennett, "Crafts, Gilds, and Women," 468 n. 34.
34. Middleton, "Women's Labour," 192–94.
35. "Act . . . 1555," discussed by W. Cunningham, *The Growth of English Industry and Commerce during the Early and Middle Ages*, 3d ed. (Cambridge: Cambridge University Press, 1896), 523–24. Cunningham refers to John Winchcombe (523); the quotation is cited on 524.

In short, the practices of the increasingly capitalized and increasingly professionalized clothing industry often contributed to the dependence of both male and female wage laborers on their employers and to the sexual division of skilled and unskilled labor through which women within that system were unevenly exploited and unevenly oppressed.

As Joan Pong Linton has noted, the "factory" that Jack later displays to his future in-laws is organized according to this division of labor: men weave, shear, row and dye; women card and spin (*Jack of Newbury*, 26–27). And, as she also notes, both men and women delight in their respective labors:

> Within one roome being large and long,
> There stood two hundred Loomes full strong:
> Two hundred men, the truth is so,
> Wrought in theese Loomes all in a rowe,
> By euery one a prety boy,
> Sate making quils with mickle ioie.
> And in another place hard by,
> An hundred women merrily,
> Were carding hard with ioyfull cheere,
> Who singing sate with voices cleare.
> And in a chamber close beside,
> Two hundred maidens did abide,
>
> . . . .
>
> These prety maides did neuer lin,
> But in that place all day did spin:
> And spinning so with voices meete,
> Like Nightingales they sung full sweet.
>
> (26–27)

Linton argues that this reference to the nightingale as a joyous spinster registers—and naturalizes—the economic displacement of women from skilled labor.[36] I would agree that the nightingale's song does aestheticize and conventionalize whatever sorrow the "prety maides" might feel. Yet I would also argue that this process is part of a more general pattern

36. Joan Pong Linton, "*Jack of Newbery* and Drake in California: Domestic and Colonial Narratives of English Cloth and Manhood," *ELH* 59:1 (Spring 1992): 23–51. Unlike Linton, I argue that the depiction of spinning and weaving demonstrates an irresolvable tension in the narrative—a tension that marks two very different ways in which *Jack of Newbury* promotes what she calls the "domesticating" of women (37).

in *Jack of Newbury*: although this narrative is often cited for its attention to details about everyday life, its descriptions of women's labor are curiously indistinct and casually contradictory. In fact, these descriptions are consistent *only* in their insistence on the necessity of a sexual division of skilled and unskilled labor.

For example, another section of the ballad quoted above does suggest that some of the laborers—the children who sit picking wool "in poore aray" (27)—obtain one penny each day for their work. During a subsequent visit from the king and queen, Jack places these children in a pageant, explaining to his appreciative audience that "these are the children of poore people: that do get their liuing by picking of woll, hauing scant a good meale once in a weeke" (49). Prompted by the king and queen, the visiting nobility acknowledge that, unlike Jack, whose trade is "the life of the poor" (47), they have been shirking their responsibility for poor relief.[37] They become the children's patrons "so that (in the end) not one was left to picke wool, but were all so prouided for, that their Parents neuer needed to care for them: and God so blessed them, that each of them came to be men of great account and authority in the land, whose posterities remaine to this day worshipfull and famous" (49). Not surprisingly, charity is the only economic solution which *Jack of Newbury* can envision—a charity, moreover, that the children deserve precisely because they possess noble traits which have been masked by their "poore aray" (27). And, again not surprisingly, the tale attributes their poverty to an unproductive and uncharitable nobility. In fact, the clothier is remarkably unconcerned about losing the children as one particularly cheap source of labor. Yet, more important for the purposes of my argument, this narrative about the exploitation of laborers is cast solely in terms of children and, ultimately, in terms of male social mobility.

In another passage, Deloney hints that, unlike children, the women in Jack's "factory" who card and spin actually might produce piecework rather than earn a daily wage. He explains that, "among other, two were appointed to keepe the beames and waights, to waighe out wooll to the

37. In this way, *Jack of Newbury* echoes the language of Elizabeth's demands that clothiers provide relief by "setting of the poore," and unemployed, textile workers "on worke." Jack both fulfills this responsibility and notes that it is the aristocracy who shirk the relief of the poor. Quotations are from a 1586 letter to the Sommerset sheriffs and justices of the peace. See *Acts of the Privy Council of England*, new series, vol. 14, ed. John Roche Dasent (London: Eyre and Spottiswoode, 1897), 93–94.

Carders and Spinners, and to receiue it in againe by waight: one of them was a comely mayden, fayre and louely, borne of wealthy parents, and brought vp in good qualities" (60–61). Although it is possible to reconcile this passage with the earlier description of Jack's "factory," *Jack of Newbury* is not particularly interested in that reconciliation or in making vivid or consistent its depiction of women's unskilled labor. In fact, this second passage is an almost parenthetical introduction to Joan, the servant whose beauty, good birth, and good upbringing outweigh the fate of the carders and spinners and will, in the tale's xenophobic logic, make her a predictably reluctant object of the foreign Master Bennedicke's affection.

With this in mind, I return to the trading of proverbs between the widow and Jack and to the metaphor of yarn and web with which Deloney describes that process. If the conditions of women's labor are curiously indistinct in Deloney's tale, that tale makes remarkably explicit that a sexual division of skilled and unskilled labor is both necessary and inseparable from marital harmony. For example, one ballad describes Penelope at her spinning and the men at their looms and adds:

> Had *Helen* then sate carding wooll
>   (whose beautious face did breed such strife)
> Shee had not been sir *Paris* trull,
>   nor caused so many lose their life.
>
> (41)

Thus when Jack recognizes that the widow is offering him "yarne" that "would prooue a good Web" (7), the tale suggests that, although she initiates the courtship and its trading of proverbs, her behavior might not challenge the Renaissance authority of men over women. In other words, it suggests that, while her role in the courtship temporally precedes Jack's, she actually behaves as a spinner whose task is not incompatible with male authority and domestic harmony. In fact, this is in keeping with the widow's earlier behavior. Even before initiating the courtship, she demonstrates that she would be an effective partner in their future household. For example, after her first husband's death, the widow, "hauing a good opinion of her man *Iohn*, committed vnto his gouerment the guiding of all hir Workefolkes, for the space of three yeares together: In which time shee found him so carefull and diligent, that all things came forward and prospered wondrous well" (5). Jack's care and diligence prove that he is a desirable match, yet her decision to award him a central role in operating her shop also proves that she can effectively manage a household.

Deloney emphasizes the desirability of this trait when he describes the courtship of Jack and his second wife, Joan:

> Now *Iacke* of *Newberie* beeing a widower, had the choise of many Wiues, mens daughters of good credit and widowes of great wealth. Notwithstanding he bent his onely like to one of his owne seruants, whom hee had tried in the guiding of his house a yeere or two: and knowing her carefull in her businesse, faithfull in her dealing, and an excellent good huswife, thought it better to haue her with nothing, than some other with much treasure. (26)

Later, when Joan succumbs temporarily to the poor advice of a gossip, she explains that she feels herself to be "but a greene housewife, and one that hath but small tryall in the world" who therefore "should bee verie glad to learne any thing that were for my husbands profite, and my commoditie" (71). And, when Jack criticizes Joan's new efforts to economize by reducing the quality and quantity of their servants' meals, she warns her husband that, based on the gossip's report, her former beneficence "hath bred me no small discredit for looking no better to it" (73). In short, the metaphor of yarn and web makes the widow's role in initiating the courtship consistent with the tale's more general claim that a wife's ability to effectively manage a household is much to her husband's credit. Finally, the metaphorical reference to "yarne" also suggests that the widow's behavior is morally proper. As Helen's carding indicates, a wife's moral propriety also helps ensure domestic harmony. In fact, when Jack later receives only a modest dowry from Joan's impoverished father, he will be "content, making more reckning of the womans modestie, than her Fathers money" (28). In *Jack of Newbury*, as in *The Merry Wives of Windsor*, a wife's moral credit is inseparable from her husband's business credit.

Yet the metaphor of yarn and web also suggests that the widow's behavior does not fall comfortably into that necessarily sexual division of skilled and unskilled labor which, in the tale's logic, promotes harmonious marriages and reinforces male authority. The "yarne" portion of that metaphor might help to make socially acceptable the widow's role in initiating the courtship. But the widow and Jack subsequently *continue* to share the task of weaving the "good Web" (7) of their courtship and marriage. The threat of this sort of mutual authority—made vivid in the trading of proverbs—cannot entirely be explained away by the chapter's concluding passage, where an exasperated Jack tells his new wife:

> From henceforth I will leaue you to your own wilfulnes, and neither vexe my minde nor trouble my selfe to restraine you. . . .
>
> Husband (quoth shee) thinke that women are like Starlings, that will burst their gall before they will yeelde to the Fowler: or like the fish *Scolopendra*, that cannot be touched without danger. Notwithstanding, as the hard steele doth yeelde to the hammers stroke, being vsed to his kinde, so will women to their husbands, where they are not too much crost. And seeing yee haue sworne to giue mee my will, I vowe likewise that my wilfulnesse shall not offend you. . . .
>
> Her husband curteously consented: and after this time, they liued long together, in most godly, louing and kind sort, till, in the end she died, leauing her husband wondrous wealthie. (25)

This harmonious portrait depicts the equitable but inherently unequal relationship between husband and wife in a Renaissance companionate marriage.[38] Yet the mutual weaving of proverbs through which Jack and the widow establish and maintain their marriage actually violates the sexual division of labor—the yarn that might prove a good web—which *Jack of Newbury* depicts as inseparable from such portraits of marital harmony. The irresolvability of this tension is particularly resonant given the situation of Renaissance widows.

Propertied widows occupied a conflictual position in late-sixteenth-century England. For example, within craft guilds, the widows of master craftsmen often continued to manage their husbands' shops. Yet their ability to do so was contingent on a number of factors, including their husbands' wills and shifting guild regulations. Although commentators hasten to stress that Jack of Newbury's second wife, Joan, was "liberally provided for," his will does name their son, John, as his "true lawful and sole executor" and as the recipient of "the residue of all my goodys not gevyn and bequeathed." Given the terms of the will, that "residue" seems to include Jack's trade. These terms are fairly unremarkable, given the existence of an adult male heir, yet many men without grown sons actually willed their workplaces or the tools of their trade to another male

---

38. For a lengthier discussion of Renaissance companionate marriages and for appropriate citations, see 67–68 in chapter 2 of this book.

relative or even to an apprentice. Husbands might have been more likely to do so in those occupations where wives tended to be official partners yet not intimately involved in the family's productive and commercial enterprises. Even a woman who retained control over her husband's trade generally was compelled to forfeit her guild privileges if she married someone who was not a member of that craft. And, increasingly, guild regulations restricted the amount of time that any widow might retain control over her husband's trade. In other words, the situation of propertied widows made visible, more generally, the degree to which the conditions of Renaissance women's existence—including their authority and their control over the means of production—were often dependent on their male relatives and on their limited access to institutions such as guilds. These conditions were challenged by the widows of master crafts-men who argued publicly—albeit generally as individuals and in the interests of their children—for their right to retain control over their husbands' shops. And they were challenged by widows with property who, in comparison to their husbands, tended to will more of their estates to women and to name more women as executors of their wills.[39] In short, the situation of these particular widows threatened to make not only visible but visible as oppressive structures that, more generally, helped to shape Renaissance women's conditions of existence.

Jack of Newbury sidesteps the threat posed by propertied widows. For example, the widow's late husband seems to have willed her his entire workplace, and she manages it capably and without apparent restriction. She seems to have no male relatives or children who might jeopardize her claim, or that of her future husband, to that shop. And Jack is conveniently a member of her husband's craft. Nonetheless, when, during their exchange of proverbs, the widow hints that she would consider

39. For discussions of widows and the English guilds, see Lacey, "Women and Work," 37–38, and Prior, "Women and the Urban Economy," 96–97, 102–10. Wiesner, "Spinsters and Seamstresses," 194–95, discusses the practices of widows and of guild officials in Germany. King, *Women of the Renaissance*, 56–62, discusses these practices throughout Europe. Susan Dwyer Amussen, *An Ordered Society: Gender and Class in Early Modern England* (Oxford: Basil Blackwell, 1988), 81–86; Barbara J. Todd, "The Remarrying Widow: A Stereotype Reconsidered," in Prior, *Women in English Society, 1500–1800*, 70, 72–74; and Sue Wright, "Employment of Women," 112–15, describe the wills of male property owners, particularly master craftsmen. For accounts of John Winchcombe's will, see Gray, *Newbury and Its Environs*, 78, and Money, *History of the Ancient Town and Borough of Newbury*, 203. Amussen, *An Ordered Society*, 91–93, discusses the wills of propertied women. Quotations are from Gray, *Newbury and Its Environs*, 78, 78 n, and Money, *History of the Ancient Town and Borough of Newbury*, 203.

Jack a proper suitor, he replies, "for I haue heard say, that manie sor-
rowes followe mariage, especially where want remaines" (9). Yet, envi-
sioning their potential marriage, Jack is not concerned that he would be
wanting financially but, instead, that he would be wanting in domestic
authority:

> For well he perceiued that his Dames affection was great towarde him:
> knowing therefore the womans disposition, and withall that her estate was
> reasonable good, and considering beside that he should finde a house
> ready furnished, seruants readie taught, and all other things for his trade
> necessarie, he thought it best not to let slip that good occasion, least hee
> should neuer come to the like. But againe, when hee considered her
> yeares to bee vnfitting to his youth, and that she that sometime had beene
> his Dame, would (perhaps) disdaine to be gouerned by him that had
> beene her poore seruant, that it would proue but a badde bargaine,
> doubting many inconueniences that might growe thereby, hee therefore
> resolued to be silent rather than to proceed further. (11–12)

In other words, given the logic of the tale, Jack rightly assumes that his
former master's shop will be permanently transferred to him.

In fact, the widow prepares her servants for that transfer when she
invites the three unlucky suitors to dinner and dismisses each for "one
nearer hand" (8–9). "Well my masters," the mistress then tells her servants, "you sawe that this day your poore Dame had her choise of husbands, if shee had listed to marrie, and such as would haue loued and
maintained her like a woman" (19). And, after the unpublicized wedding
of Jack and the widow, when the servants laugh in surprise to find an
apprentice seated "in their old masters chaire," she cautions, "I tell
you . . . he is my husband, for this morning we were maried, and therefore hence forward looke you acknowledge your duty towardes him"
(21). Jack instructs them in how to fulfill this injunction: "I am not
thereby so much puft vp in pride, that any way I will forget my former
estate: Notwithstanding, seeing I am now to holde the place of a Master,
it shall bee wisedome in you to forget what I was, and to take mee as I
am" (21). Deloney writes that "the seruants hearing this, as also knowing
his good gouernment before time, past their yeares with him in dutifull
manner" (22).

In keeping with Jack's earlier assessment of their potential marriage,
the widow is the only member of her household who refuses to heed his

instruction. "I am now in very good case," she tells him after their marriage, "that hee which was my seruant but the other day, will now bee my master: this it is for a Woman to make her foot her head" (22). She neglects her household responsibilities, reminds him of his youth and of his former status as her servant and, finally, claims "that by my gadding abroad, and carelesse spending I waste no goods of thine" (22). Her disobedience is signaled—and fueled—by her inclination to trade proverbs not with Jack but with other neighbors, particularly with women:[40] "Some said that shee was matcht to her sorrow, saying, that so lustie a young man as he, would neuer loue her being so auncient. Whereupon the Woman made answer, that shee would take him downe in his wedding shooes, and woulde trie his patience in the prime of his lustinesse: whereunto many of her Gossips did likewise encourage her" (22). In spite of the widow's ominous assertion that she wastes "no goods of thine," the emphasis on her neighbors and gossips sidesteps the direct threat posed by propertied widows and filters that threat through a more general stereotype about Renaissance widows. Whether in a position to successfully conduct their legal and economic affairs or impoverished and dependent on poor relief, those widows were often represented as dangerous because they combined sexual experience—and sexual appetite—with the absence of a male guardian.[41]

Jack had drawn attention to this unsettling combination even before their marriage. After the widow and Jack traded proverbs about her suitors, he had remarked, "No maruell . . . you are so peremptorie seeing you haue so much choice" (9). Within Deloney's narrative this choice is remarkable not in its range but in its location solely in the widow's hands. Throughout the rest of *Jack of Newbury*, parents and employers are consistently consulted in the selection of a husband and in the designation of a dowry. For example, when Jack asks Joan to be his second wife, "the maid (though shee tooke this motion kindly) said shee would do nothing without consent of her Parents" (26). Her parents, in turn, sell all of their cattle in order to offer a dowry which, however modest, demonstrates their conviction that Jack is a desirable match. In one of

40. The *O.E.D.* suggests that the term gossip—particularly when referring to a baptismal sponsor—designated either men or women; in *Jack of Newbury* all of those gossips whose gender is identified are women.

41. Constance Jordan, *Renaissance Feminism: Literary Texts and Political Models* (Ithaca: Cornell University Press, 1990), 299–300; Todd, "Remarrying Widow," 54–92; and Linda Woodbridge, *Women and the English Renaissance: Literature and the Nature of Womankind, 1540–1620* (Urbana: University of Illinois Press, 1984), 20, 177–78, 255–62.

the tale's ballads, the "faire flower of *Northumberland*" suffers after betraying her father and country by offering herself and her own dowry to a faithless Scottish Knight (43–47). And, finally, Jack matches his pregnant servant, Joan, to the dishonorable Sir George.

This latter match provides a useful counterpoint to the marriage of Jack and the widow. Deloney explains that, before consulting her employers, Joan had attempted to enter into her marriage contract without the help of a male guardian: "This lustie wench hee so allured with hope of marriage, that at length shee yeelded him her loue, and therwithall bent her whole studie to work his content: but in the end she so much contented him, that it wrought altogether her owne discontent: to become high, she laid her selfe so low, that the Knight suddenly fell ouer her, which fall became the rising of her belly" (82). Yet when Joan tells Sir George that she is pregnant, her lover responds:

> Why thou leud paltrie thing . . . commest thou to father thy bastard vpon mee? A way ye dunghill carrion, awaie: heare you good huswife, get you among your companions, and lay your litter where you list, but if you trouble me any more, trust mee thou shalt dearely abie it: and so bending his browes like the angry god of warr, he went his waies leauing the child breeding wench to the hazard of her fortune, either good or bad. (82–83)

Deloney explains that, knighted for his service in France, Sir George was one of those "whose valours farre surpassed their wealth" (82). Although this impoverished god of war actually lived on Jack's hospitality, the two lengthy passages cited above associate the unfaithful knight with the conventions of romance literature. In fact, Jack lures Sir George into marrying Joan by appealing to the knight's conviction that he inhabits the terrain of that literature:

> Hauing earnest occasion to come vp to talke with a bad debter, in my iourney it was my chance to light in company of a gallant widow: a Gentlewoman shee is of wondrous good wealth, whom grisly death hath bereft of a kinde husband, making her a Widow ere shee had been halfe a yeare a wife: her land, sir *George*, is as well worth a hundred pound a yeare as one penny, being as faire and comely a creature as any of her degree in our countrey. (83)

Sir George does not recognize himself as the "bad debter" in Jack's tale. Nor will he recognize the pregnant Joan beneath the supposed widow's "faire Taffetie gowne, and . . . french hood" (84). Instead, he is intrigued by the tale of a gallant widow and of her kind husband's grisly death. And he is predisposed to interpret widows as an unproblematic category—and, in this case, as an unproblematic source of landed wealth.

After Sir George marries this purported widow "in presence of many gentlemen," Jack rebukes him for his earlier behavior and offers, as a dowry, not the land "worth a hundred pound a yeare" (83) that the knight had expected but a sum generally associated with the marriage of wealthy yeomen and tradesmen: "Came you to my table to make my maid your strumpet? had you no mans house to dishonor but mine? Sir, I would you should well know, that I account the poorest wench in my house too good to be your whore, were you ten knights . . . vse her well. . . . [A] hundred pounds for thee: And let him not say thou comst to him a begger" (86). The clothier does supplement this dowry with the promise of two more years of charity, during which time Sir George might "take his diet and his Ladies at his house" (86).[42]

Unlike the anachronistic Sir George, Jack insists on the unsettling nature of Renaissance widows. For example, after trading proverbs with his future wife, he links her unwomanly control over speech to her unwomanly control over sexuality: "No maruell . . . you are so peremptorie seeing you haue so much choice" (9). Yet, the mutual weaving of proverbs also signals that she is willing to make him if not her guardian then, at least, the sole recipient of her speech and the sole object of her sexual appetite. For example, the tailor might bemoan her reluctance to offer her suitors a "direct answer" (18), yet Jack is not at all confused by that indirection. When the widow invites her three suitors to dinner, she says, "And now . . . to make the boord equall, and because it hath beene an ould saying, that three things are to small purpose, if the fourth be awaie: if so it may stand with your fauours, I will call in a Gossip of mine

42. Amussen, *An Ordered Society*, 111–17; A. L. Beier, *Masterless Men: The Vagrancy Problem in England, 1560–1640* (London: Methuen, 1985), 52–54; Ralph A. Houlbrooke, *The English Family, 1450–1700* (London: Longman, 1984), 80–83; and Wrightson, *English Society*, 84–86, for discussions of desertion and illegitimacy in late-sixteenth-century England. Punishment of the pregnant woman was generally most severe when she was not economically self-sufficient and thus would depend on local resources for her support and that of her child. In other words, without Jack's intervention, Sir George, temporarily residing in Newbury because of his own need for charity, would have extended that local charity to Joan and their child. Average dowries are discussed by Alan Macfarlane, *Marriage and Love in England: Modes of Reproduction, 1300–1840* (Oxford: Basil Blackwell, 1986), 264.

to supplie this voide place" (17). By this point in the tale, for Jack, who had traded proverbs about the three suitors and the "one nearer hand" (8–9), the place of the proverbial missing fourth is far from void "for well he perceiued that his Dames affection was great towarde him" (11).

As this playful substitution of the gossip for Jack suggests, within the logic of Deloney's tale, it is not surprising that it is her female friends who later encourage the newly remarried widow to undermine Jack's authority—reinforcing her own fear that she has disempowered herself by obtaining not only a male guardian but a guardian more lusty than she.[43] Even Jack's second wife will temporarily threaten their marital harmony by trusting a woman's proverbial wisdom over his. That woman criticizes Joan for offering her servants "such superfluities, that they spoyle in manner as much as they eate: beleeue me were I their Dame, they should haue things more sparingly, and then they would thinke it more daintie" (72). When Joan follows this advice, Jack rebukes her with his own proverbial wisdom: "I will not haue my people thus pincht of their victuals. Emptie platters make greedy stomackes, and where scarcitie is kept, hunger is nourished: and therefore wife as you loue mee let me haue no more of this doings" (73). Although Joan does acknowledge his authority over their household, she is not convinced that her friend is, in Jack's words, an "old gossip, dame dayntie, mistresse trip and go," and a "light braind" housewife (73). In fact, she responds to Jack's suggestion that she avoid such companions by asking, "Leaue her company? why husband so long as she is an honest woman, why should I leaue her company? Shee neuer gaue mee hurtfull counsell in all her life, but hath alwayes been ready to tell me things for my profit, though you take it not so" (73).

Their disagreement—and the structural role of gossips in Deloney's tale—turns on the various sorts of authority relations that were signaled by the word gossip. According to the *Oxford English Dictionary*, during the late sixteenth century, a gossip could have been a close friend, particularly the female friend for whom a woman would ask when giving birth or the friend entrusted to serve as a child's sponsor at baptism. A gossip could also have been an older figure with some authority to offer spiritual or secular advice, including someone who literally had served as one's baptismal sponsor. Finally, a gossip could have been anyone, usually a

43. Woodbridge, *Women and the English Renaissance*, 224–43, argues that, during the Renaissance, gossips were prominent in depictions of speech among women that was not monitored by men.

woman, "of light and trifling character," especially someone "who delights in idle talk, a newsmonger, a tattler." Although *Jack of Newbury* does seem to restrict gossips to women, these sixteenth-century definitions remain otherwise potentially in play. According to Jack, however, it is the latter definition that best describes his wife's friend. A few chapters later, this "Mistris many-better, dame tittle-tattle, gossip pinte-pot" (78) vindicates Jack's definition of the word. She drunkenly denounces Joan and Jack to their servants; criticizes Joan for wearing the french hood, silk gown, chain, and bracelets that mark Jack's position as "Burgesse in the Parliament house" (70); and reminds the servants about the relative youth and modest backgrounds of the couple. For example, she tells one servant, "Your Master . . . ? I knew your Master a boy, when he was called *Iacke* of *Newbery*; I *Iacke*, I knew him called plaine *Iack*: and your Mistresse, now she is rich and I am poor, but tis no matter, I knew her a draggle tayle girle, marke yee?" (79). In short, the gossip abuses the authority that her age and long acquaintance with the Winchcombes might have granted her and proves herself to be, in the least, a poor adviser and a poor friend.

The tale answers her challenge to Jack's domestic harmony and masculine authority with a shaming ritual. After her drunken outburst to the servants, the gossip is carried through Newbury in a basket. Shaming rituals such as this one were based on an assumption that the unchecked disruption of masculine authority within a single family might have placed in question the more general Renaissance hierarchy of men over women and on an assumption that order within the family was analogous to order within the state.[44] When the gossip is deposited at her house, she gives credence to both of these assumptions: "And as her husband tooke her out of the Basket, shee gaue him a sound boxe on the eare, saying: What you Queanes, do you mocke mee, and so was caried in" (81). Her final outburst demonstrates that she is a scold who has usurped her husband's authority. His inability to maintain domestic order has allowed her to endanger the authority relations between Jack and Joan. And, in turn, by questioning Jack's authority within his family, the gossip also has questioned the authority relations between masters and servants and between burgesses and those they govern.

The marriage of the widow and Jack temporarily threatens to become,

44. For a lengthier discussion of the analogy between order within the family and order within the state and for appropriate citations, see 71–72 in chapter 2 of this book.

like that of the gossip and her husband, a matter of community concern. After the gossips encourage the newly remarried widow to undermine Jack's authority, the couple display their domestic disorder through a public dispute that turns, literally, on each partner's ability to enter their house and to sleep in their marital bed. Yet this dispute, during which Jack and the widow trade proverbs about "birds and beasts" and about "the people of *Ilyris*" (24), ultimately reasserts Jack's status as the sole recipient of the widow's speech and the sole object of her sexual appetite. This trading of proverbs eventually results in the concluding portrait of their harmonious marriage, and of the widow's eventual death, that I cited earlier. As I have argued, however, that portrait actually demonstrates an irresolvable tension in the narrative. This tension marks the tale's simultaneous participation in two very different sites of struggle over the conditions that shaped Renaissance women's lives. *Jack of Newbury* insists on the sexual division of skilled and unskilled labor and on its necessary relationship to marital harmony. Yet Jack and the widow weave, and reweave, their web of marital harmony through a form of mutual authority—made vivid, once again, in the trading of proverbs—which that model refuses to accommodate. By emphasizing this refusal, the tale sidesteps the direct threat that propertied widows posed to Renaissance gender relations and reinforces, instead, a more general stereotype about verbally and sexually empowered widows.

Afterword:
Reading the Culture of Renaissance Criticism—History, *Copia*, and Commodification

As I suggested in my introduction, new historicism has provided an occasion for debates among Renaissance critics about the most persuasive methods of cultural analysis. These critics confront, explicitly or implicitly, what Jean E. Howard calls the challenge of doing "an historical criticism in a postmodern era."[1] In this afterword, I analyze how Karen Newman's *Fashioning Femininity and English Renaissance Drama* and Richard Halpern's *The Poetics of Primitive Accumulation: English Renaissance Culture and the Genealogy of Capital* respond to that challenge.[2] By placing in tension Newman's feminist and Halpern's Marxist accounts of a single rhetorical gesture, Renaissance *copia*, I consider the versions of cultural and historical criticism that each author promotes. This entails examining how these critics read *copia* and its role in mediating the relationships among the cultural, the economic, and the political. And it entails examining the rhetorical gestures that characterize their own disparate reading practices. In other words, this afterword extends, to writing by two contemporary critics, the sort of formal analysis that I brought to bear on writing by Puttenham, Sidney, Shakespeare, and Deloney.

1. Jean E. Howard, "The New Historicism in Renaissance Studies," *English Literary Renaissance* 16:1 (Winter 1986): 19.
2. Karen Newman, *Fashioning Femininity and English Renaissance Drama* (Chicago: University of Chicago Press, 1991), and Richard Halpern, *The Poetics of Primitive Accumulation: English Renaissance Culture and the Genealogy of Capital* (Ithaca: Cornell University Press, 1991). All citations refer to these editions.

I do not assume that Newman's and Halpern's work is—or could be—representative of the range of feminist or Marxist approaches to cultural and historical criticism. Instead, I ask what their particular versions of feminism and Marxism might tell us about the relationship between literary form and Renaissance social struggle, about the shifting conjuncture of forces that comprised the dominant culture and the relationship between dominant and subordinate groups in Renaissance England, and about the peculiar role that Renaissance historical criticism occupies within contemporary cultural studies. Fredric Jameson has argued that cultural studies is "perhaps best approached politically and socially, as the project to constitute a 'historic bloc,' rather than theoretically, as the floor plan for a new discipline." In the preceding chapters, I examined the formal gestures through which Puttenham, Sidney, Shakespeare, and Deloney attempt to conceal potential sites and forms of collective politics. And I considered those notions of literary form and Renaissance social struggle through which critics have approached their writing. I now extend my analysis by asking how the very process of interpreting Renaissance literature might figure into the competing visions of collectivity and social change that Jameson labels "the desire called Cultural Studies."[3]

Although Newman acknowledges the strategic importance of the category "women," she argues that it also tends to essentialize sexual difference and to offer universalized models of women's oppression. She focuses, instead, on the production of femininity through "local and specific formations" of gender (xix). Because "gender was a significant way of *figuring* social relations in early modern England," Newman explains, her "perspective on gender will be multiple, intersected by perspectives of race, sexuality, and what we now term class" (xviii, xix). She describes this project as an attempt "at once to dislocate the hegemonic status of 'patriarchy' in feminist readings of Renaissance texts *and* to show how gender has sometimes been displaced in new historicist readings preoccupied with the politics of colonialism, monarchy, and the elite" (xix). As I indicated in this book's introduction, I am not interested in reducing the diverse practices that have been labeled new historicist to any single model of cultural criticism. But I am interested in how the discussions surrounding these practices serve as one site, within Renaissance studies, for debating the nature and significance of resistance to a

3. Fredric Jameson, "On 'Cultural Studies,'" *Social Text* 34 (1993): 17.

dominant culture. For example, in considering the displacement of gender in new historicism, Newman joins those for whom the often vexed relationship between Renaissance feminism and Renaissance new historicism suggests the necessity of addressing, more generally, the relative importance of gender as a category of analysis, the interpellation and potential agency of gendered subjects, and the relationship between contemporary critics and the histories that they construct.[4]

Drawing on work in new historicism, cultural materialism, and feminist theory, Newman outlines a reading practice in which gender is a governing category and through which she hopes to avoid the narratives of successful domination that she finds far too prevalent both among those feminists who emphasize an unerring and unchanging patriarchy and among those new historicists who emphasize the processes of recuperation. Newman explains that she creates a conversation among various sorts of texts—reading both Renaissance stories and contemporary stories *about* the Renaissance as "hermeneutic arenas in which we contend not for a material ground that is not language, but for meaning and its effects" (143). Her readings stress how the instability of Renaissance images often "resists both the critical lament of the victim characteristic of some feminist work and the new historicist's resigned claims of 'containment' as well" (11). In this way, her study of femininity "threatens the 'literary,' the 'historical,' 'women'" by analyzing all three as "shifting relations rather than fixed categories and values" (146).

Yet, in the final paragraph of the book's epilogue, Newman offers what she terms a "melancholy coda" to her own reading practice:

> In my university, and in the secondary school curriculum in New England at least, any text from the Renaissance, however marginal, however decentered—ballads, jigs, penny histories, long ignored and forgotten plays—produces "canonical effects." That is, any text from an historical period before the French revolution is construed as "canonical." History

4. Walter Cohen, "Political Criticism of Shakespeare," in *Shakespeare Reproduced: The Text in History and Ideology*, ed. Jean E. Howard and Marion F. O'Connor (New York: Methuen, 1987), 33, 38; Peter Erickson, "Rewriting the Renaissance, Rewriting Ourselves," *Shakespeare Quarterly* 38:3 (Autumn 1987): 327–37; Catherine Gallagher, "Marxism and the New Historicism," in *The New Historicism*, ed. H. Aram Veeser (New York: Routledge, 1989), 42–47; Carol Thomas Neely, "Constructing the Subject: Feminist Practice and the New Renaissance Discourses," *English Literary Renaissance* 18:1 (Winter 1988): 5–18; and Judith Newton, "History as Usual? Feminism and the 'New Historicism,'" *Cultural Critique* 9 (Spring 1988): 87–121.

itself, mere *pastness*, produces canonical effects. Similarly, the turn to history, however textualized, however problematized or theorized, produces a similar "history effect" that is powerfully conservative and that explains why cultural studies is being institutionalized as the study of contemporary mass culture—not popular culture of the past, only the present, a present that continues to include the nineteenth century so as not to jettison Marx or Freud. Given the commanding force of what I have termed the history effect to construct any cultural production of the past as canonical, is political criticism possible in the Renaissance? (146)

This melancholy coda gestures toward at least two familiar conceits. The first of these is the new historicist's apology for the limitations of her critical framework. Such apologies generally address the role of new historicism within Renaissance studies, the role of its practitioners within the academic marketplace, and the role of intellectual movements among college and university faculty within larger cultural movements. Critics have argued that apologies of this sort produce the effect of an autonomous, unified, and politically self-conscious subject—an effect at odds with their authors' larger claims. Whatever their limitations, these apologies have helped to make the politics of academic institutions a focus of discussion within Renaissance studies. Newman's melancholy coda retains this focus on institutional politics. Yet it interrupts the subject of the new historicist's apology by gesturing toward a second conceit—the feminist's personal narrative. As Newman's use of personal narratives in the early chapters of the book suggests, her feminism does not accord them an absolute authority; instead, it sanctions them both as a legitimate form of reading and as legitimate objects to be read. In the next few pages I analyze how Newman's concluding narrative performs the possibility of Renaissance political criticism by emphasizing the dialectical relationship between the construction of Renaissance culture and that of contemporary culture. And I analyze how the style of that performance—a style informed by recent feminist discussions about postmodernism—helps to establish a field within which we might envision collectivity.

I will begin to sort through Newman's melancholy coda by turning briefly to her earlier description of the reading process which defines the "task of a political criticism." That process entails reconstituting literary works by rereading canonical texts in noncanonical ways that reveal the contingency of so-called canonical readings, that disturb conventional interpretations and discover them as partisan, constructed, made rather than given, natural and inevitable. Such strategies of reading are particularly necessary in drama because the dramatic immediacy of theatrical representation obscures the fact that the audience is watching a highly artificial enactment—in the case of *Othello*, of what a non-African and a man has made into a vision of blackness and femininity, of passion and desire in the other, the marginal, outside culture yet simultaneously within it. (93)

Thus when Newman claims that the turn to history confers "canonical effects" on all Renaissance cultural production, she is suggesting not that their "pastness" necessarily situates Renaissance texts within a particular canon of works to be read and taught but, instead, that this very pastness makes those texts resistant to the process of reconstitution.

Within this context, I find Newman's melancholy coda striking. By casting her concluding comments as "melancholy," Newman emphasizes that this sort of self-reflexive *apologia*, however politicized, however contextualized, risks producing a privatization effect that is as powerfully conservative as the "history effect" which plagues Renaissance culture. In an earlier analysis of seventeenth-century discussions about Arbella Stuart, Newman wrote: "Contemporaries always mention her propensity for study and claimed it made her melancholic, a common result, according to Renaissance humors theory, of too much study and learning. The melancholic, of course, was said to favor solitude and to be prone to distraction. The frequently repeated claim that Arbella Stuart died mad figures her political transgression in private terms, within the medical discourse of female hysteria" (142). In other words, by labeling her concluding comments a "melancholy coda," Newman acknowledges that those comments might be read not as a political gesture but as a distracting instance of private hysteria—as the critic's too-studied conversation with herself. More specifically, by drawing on a seventeenth-century connection between melancholia and female hysteria, she suggests that this conventional reading of the critic's political concerns would contribute to a twentieth-century definition and production of femininity.

What are we to make of a book that is determined to avoid both the "critical lament of the victim" and "resigned claims of 'containment'" and yet ends with this melancholy lament *about* containment? Or, in Newman's terms, what are we to make of a coda which announces that we are likely to construe both it and all Renaissance cultural production as canonical? One answer lies in the coda's framing sentences. Newman begins her concluding comments with a declarative statement: "A melancholy coda" (146). She closes with an ominous question: "Given the commanding force of what I have termed the history effect to construct any cultural production of the past as canonical, is political criticism possible in the Renaissance?" The framing statement and question actually render unstable the coda's larger lament about containment. For example, by labeling her comments a melancholy coda, Newman urges twentieth-century readers, responding to her *apologia*, to marshal the very categories that she claims governed seventeenth-century responses to Arbella Stuart. By situating those seventeenth-century responses "within the medical discourse of female hysteria," Newman locates them within a discourse that she claims was only medicalized *as* female hysteria during the nineteenth century (58). And by asking whether political criticism is "possible *in* the Renaissance" (146, my emphasis), she again troubles any easy distinction between "pastness" and "presentness." In other words, by constructing her melancholy lament, Newman attempts to *re*construct the very "history effect" that tends to canonize Renaissance culture.

In so doing, Newman not only attempts to make possible political readings of Renaissance culture but, more important, suggests that the resistance of Renaissance culture *to* those readings has been one crucial element in constructing "a present that continues to include the nineteenth century so as not to jettison Marx and Freud"—a present that, by definition, *is* hospitable to political criticism. In short, she suggests that the institutionalization of cultural studies, as she defines it, has depended, in part, on the canonization of Renaissance culture. Newman is not claiming that Renaissance studies and cultural studies are in direct competition for institutional space; instead, she is claiming that the difficulty of "reconstituting" Renaissance culture calls into question the apparent ease with which cultural critics reconstitute "contemporary mass culture" (146). In other words, the concluding coda implies that cultural studies, precisely when its objects of analysis are experienced as "the present," risks producing the sort of "canonical effects" (146) that Renaissance audiences derived from the "dramatic immediacy of theatrical representation" (93). In this way, Newman suggests that her "strategies of reading are particularly necessary" (93) for analyzing not only Renaissance theatrical practices but, in so doing, the twentieth-century practice of institutionalizing cultural studies.

That practice, Newman also reminds us, defines cultural studies as the "study of contemporary mass culture—not popular culture of the past, only the present" (146). Her sentence's movement across the dash signals both the cultural power of the distinction between the "contemporary" and "the past" and the analytical irrelevancy of the distinction between "mass" and "popular." The sentence introduces and undermines two possible contrasts—between "mass culture" and "popular culture" and between "contemporary mass culture" and "popular culture of the past"—before settling on a contrast between popular culture of the past and that of the present and on an equation between "contemporary mass culture" and "popular culture of . . . the present" (146). As I have explained, the terms of Newman's melancholy lament emphasize the institutional and critical relationship between Renaissance studies and cultural studies by exploring the possible consequences of our assumptions about what is "past" and what is "present." Newman's sentence contributes to that larger project. Yet, by marshaling the language of mass and popular culture, its discussion of temporality also suggests how Renaissance criticism might contribute to recent debates about the possibility of collective resistance to a dominant culture.

The gradual unraveling of Newman's sentence implies that popular politics does not emerge in tension with its "other"—the "mass"—but, instead, emerges as an articulation of mass culture. In other words, the popular is neither politically nor temporally distinct from the mass. In twentieth-century Britain and the United States, for example, popular culture cannot avoid the form of commodification that characterizes late capitalism. Some critics have rejected this interpretation of contemporary culture and attempt to locate instances of authentic popular culture which coexist uneasily and tenuously with a commodified culture of the masses. Others have accepted this interpretation and yet argue that it makes contemporary popular culture if not an improbability then, at least, probably less authentic than a popular culture that preceded the effects of late capitalism, a popular culture like that of the English Renaissance. Newman's discussion of temporality would caution against this sort of nostalgia and its simultaneous production of Renaissance and contemporary popular culture—implying, instead, that popular culture is always a site of struggle and contradiction and that critics must attend to the very specific sites and forms of cultural production and consumption which make possible a range of collective identities and a range of political alliances within any hegemonic bloc. In this way, Newman's sentence challenges those critics who—schooled in the culture of late capitalism—have too quickly equated hegemony with the pervasiveness of the commodity form and thus, more generally, have too quickly relinquished the possibility of resistance to a dominant culture.[5]

My reading has emphasized how Newman's melancholy coda performs an answer to its own concluding question—responding that political criticism *is* possible in the Renaissance. The coda formulates this response, in part, by situating Renaissance studies within contemporary debates about collective politics. I turn now to the style of the coda's performance in order to analyze what versions of historical criticism and cultural analysis are promoted—and foreclosed—by Newman's reading practice. That style approximates what Newman defines as a heteroglossic mode of Renaissance composition. She describes how this form of writing helped organize knowledge about Renaissance marriages:

> Catholic and early reform writers organize their texts according to the rhetorical principles and practices of *copia*. . . . Writers used commonplace books and the *florilegia* to "stock" the imagination with "matter" . . . to produce a heteroglossic richness different from later modes of composition. That richness depends on the play of signifiers, on aural echoes, verbal associations, on a productive process of difference and deferral in which meanings proliferate on many cognitive axes—sensory, psychological, intellectual—on what Derrida has termed *différance*. (20)

A subsequent mode of composition—"methodizing"—organized Puritan marital texts around the "taxonomy of dichotomized categories" (23). Within these texts, because of its emphasis on "polarized and hierarchized categories," methodizing "promoted rigid sexual divisions

---

5. For discussions about mass- and popular-culture criticism, see John Caughie, "Popular Culture: Notes and Revisions," in *High Theory/Low Culture: Analysing Popular Television and Film*, ed. Colin MacCabe (New York: St. Martin's Press, 1986), 156–71; Fredric Jameson, "Reification and Utopia in Mass Culture," *Social Text* 1 (1979): 130–48; George Lipsitz, *Time Passages: Collective Memory and American Popular Culture* (Minneapolis: University of Minnesota Press, 1990), 3–36; and Colin MacCabe, "Defining Popular Culture," in MacCabe, *High Theory/Low Culture*, 1–10. For a discussion about popular culture and the dangers of equating hegemony with the commodity form, see Michael Denning, "The End of Mass Culture," in *Modernity and Mass Culture*, ed. James Naremore and Patrick Brantlinger (Bloomington: Indiana University Press, 1991), 253–68.

more prominently than earlier rhetorical forms based on *copia*" (25). In short, unlike *copia*, methodizing naturalized and codified binary thinking. Although Newman claims that methodizing helped reinforce gender binarisms and although she associates those binarisms with a monologic masculinity, she does not argue that this or any form of composition has a single, inevitable cultural effect. She does argue that the gradual Renaissance shift in modes of writing about marriage signals a "newly mobilizable means of managing and regulating sexual difference" (26) and thus a shift in how women "are interpellated as social and sexual subjects" (25). For example, by attending to this shift, Newman challenges those who have claimed that Catholic definitions of marriage were more oppressive to Renaissance women than subsequent Puritan definitions.

What does it mean, then, to suggest that Newman's *twentieth-century* mode of composition approximates Renaissance *copia*? Newman relies on Mikhail Bakhtin's description of novelistic discourse when she defines *copia* as a heteroglossic mode of composition. Yet *copia* achieves its heteroglossia through mechanisms that are somewhat different from those described by Bakhtin. "The ideal of *copia*," Newman explains, is "more akin to a postmodernist aesthetic that values the elaboration of unsubordinated details over structure" (23). By emphasizing the value of local readings and of unsubordinated detail, Newman situates her mode of composition within a particular conjunction of feminism and postmodernism. At this conjunction, feminist critics strategically engage postmodernism less as a philosophical framework than as a series of local practices. These critics are attentive to the ways in which, writing from within a postmodern culture, they help shape the terms within which members of that culture might understand the nature and possibility of collective action. For example, in her influential "A Cyborg Manifesto: Science, Technology, and Socialist-Feminism in the Late Twentieth Century," Donna J. Haraway explains how a struggle "against perfect communication, against the one code that translates all meaning perfectly," against "universal, totalizing theory," might be conducted, in part, through a heteroglossic mode of composition. "Cyborg imagery can suggest a way out of the maze of dualisms in which we have explained our bodies and our tools to ourselves," she writes. "This is a dream not of a common language, but of a powerful infidel heteroglossia." This "postmodernist, non-naturalist mode" of writing embraces "partial, contradictory, permanently unclosed constructions of personal and collective selves" and promotes "*pleasure* in the confusion of boundaries and . . . *responsibility* in their construction." For Haraway this is an insurgent mode of composition precisely because it is produced by the contradictory subject positions assigned to women and "is about the power to survive. . . . The tools are often stories, retold stories, versions that reverse and displace the hierarchical dualisms of naturalized identities."[6]

Within this critical tradition, I find most compelling those feminists who caution that postmodernism is neither univocal nor internationally omnipresent, that even women whose lives evince apparent formal similarities—formal traits often associated with a postmodern aesthetic—might be situated quite differently in relation to modernism, to commodification, and to the effects of a late-capitalist global division of labor. This caution emerges from an attention to the relationships among systems of oppression. For example, Rey Chow sees the future of feminist postmodern automatons in the "careful rejection of postmodernist abandon as a universalist politics." That rejection, she stresses, "goes hand in hand with its insistence on the need to *detail* history, in the sense of cutting it up, so that as it gains more ground in social struggle, sexual difference becomes a way of engaging not simply with women but with other types of subjugation."[7] As this brief discussion suggests, postmodern practices occur under very particular historical conditions.[8] Newman acknowledges that specificity when she suggests that the heteroglossia of Renaissance *copia* is "*akin to* a postmodern aesthetic" (my emphasis). Yet, if she dismisses the notion that Renaissance and contemporary heteroglossia might be identical by suggesting that they are "akin," she does not address explicitly the nature of their kinship or its methodological significance within her own reading practice.

6. Donna J. Haraway, "A Cyborg Manifesto: Science, Technology, and Socialist-Feminism in the Late Twentieth Century," in *Simians, Cyborgs, and Women: The Reinvention of Nature* (New York: Routledge, 1991), 149–81. Quotations are from 176, 181, 181, 150, 157, 150, 175.

7. Rey Chow, "Postmodern Automatons," in *Feminists Theorize the Political*, ed. Judith Butler and Joan W. Scott (New York: Routledge, 1992), 101–17. Quotations are from 114–15.

8. In *Postmodernism, or, The Cultural Logic of Late Capitalism* (Durham: Duke University Press, 1991; paperback ed., 1992), Fredric Jameson considers practices often associated with postmodernism actually to be "postmodern" only when they are elements within a cultural dominant and not when they are simply "one cultural style or movement among others" (3–4). It is with this in mind that I discuss the conjunction of feminism and postmodernism in Newman's work.

Newman's recourse to an unexamined kinship is even more prominent when she analyzes another example of Renaissance *copia*—the "series." The "series" is a formal category through which Newman brings together the Renaissance fashion system, the language with which contemporaries described that system, and the forms of Renaissance writing which contemporaries dismissed as resembling extravagant dress. These connections turn on the relationships among fashion, femininity, composition, and commodification. Newman claims that "the argument for 'class' as the hegemonic category of fashion analysis in the early modern period dismisses too easily the relation of gender to sartorial extravagance" (111). She argues, first, that "dress was less a signifier of *class* or degree, as commentators on fashion and social historians have usually claimed, than a signifier of *difference* itself" and, second, that

> as fashion became available first to the middling sort, and then increasingly to the working classes, the differences it claimed to signify were challenged, and other means of marking difference within the fashion system were produced. The anxiety produced by these challenges to traditional, hierarchically organized systems of difference produced new modes of organizing the fashion system.
>
> Sexual difference, as a seemingly essential, ineffaceable category became the overdetermined imaginary for organizing social distinctions. (120)

Renaissance writers often attacked "sartorial excess" by producing "lists of fashion details that are always relegated either to descriptions of the female characters or the feminized gallant or fop" (122–23). In addition, contemporaries labeled this "frequently deployed grammatical series"— with its focus on "details"—as itself feminine (123).

Newman asks why, given this construction of femininity, the supposedly "manly" (126) rhetoric with which Ben Jonson condemns the fashion of sartorial and rhetorical excess "is as elaborately figured and periodically complex, as characterized by exaggeration and by the detailed series, as the 'effeminate' language he berates" (127)—why his "hegemonic rhetoric" (127) is preoccupied with a femininity against which he rails and yet from which he derives pleasure. Focusing on that rhetoric, Newman argues that Jonson's characteristic "*copia* enacted through the grammatical series" (139) implicitly produces an "etcetera." In other words, the series is an inherently incomplete form; it asks the reader to recognize its governing logic and to contribute appropriate—

but inevitably insufficient—additional items. For this reason, the series is a particularly appropriate vehicle for representing the Renaissance relationship between women and consumption. Like the Renaissance fashion system, the grammatical series offers what Newman calls "commodity pleasures" (140)—producing an experience of scarcity, and a desire to overcome that insufficiency, precisely by seeming to be excessive or abundant. In this way, the grammatical series, again like the Renaissance fashion system it helps organize, produces a circumspect system of oppressive relations: "The series seems to democratize things: separated only by commas or the semi-colon, the items of a series hurtle along pell-mell seemingly without distinctions, enacting a sort of grammatical commodification; but instead of erasing differences, the grammatical series, like commodification itself, systematizes privilege and difference" (140). In the paragraph that immediately precedes her melancholy coda, Newman acknowledges that her own reading practice participates in the logic of the series. She describes her criticism as an effort to mobilize "a variety of texts and stories—theoretical, canonical, archival, historical, from Marx and Stow, Derrida, Foucault and Baudrillard, Shakespeare and Jonson, Elizabeth and James, the Venetian ambassadors, Agnes Waterhouse, *to name only a few*" (146, my emphasis). In other words, her readings create a conversation among texts which, in turn, produces a critical desire to introduce additional, comparable interlocutors. For Newman that desire marks one link among contemporary, nineteenth-century, and Renaissance cultures—the centrality of "commodity pleasures" (140).

As Newman's discussion of Jonson, Marx, and Stow suggests, this link does not imply that commodification and sexual difference operate in a single unchanging dynamic. Yet it does suggest one axis around which Newman considers contemporary, nineteenth-century, and Renaissance cultures to be "akin," again, without addressing the nature or significance of that kinship. Newman moves from her analysis of Jonson, Marx, and commodification to her analysis of Arbella Stuart by way of a curious distinction: "I would like to end with an episode in what I would term cultural politics rather than cultural poetics" (140). This proviso announces Newman's reluctance to engage the issues that Renaissance critics have raised when discussing cultural poetics. These critics generally explore how intertextual models of reading operate at the intersection of historicism and formalism—examining both the methods by which their readings negotiate the boundaries among synchronic cultural discourses and the logic with which they address, or avoid addressing, the relationship between synchronic and diachronic social systems.[9] In Richard Halpern's reading of Renaissance culture, what I have called Newman's "recourse to an unexamined kinship" might also be understood as one instance of those turns, within historical narratives, which, according to Halpern, signal "both a history to be written and the limits such a history must observe" (67).

Situating his reading practice within "the various attempts at historical renarration at work in Renaissance studies today" (1), Halpern organizes his readings around the concept of "primitive accumulation." In so doing, he "highlights the distinctiveness of a Marxist narrative of transition" (2). Halpern explains that he calls his book "*The Poetics of Primitive Accumulation* not to oblige myself to refer repeatedly to a specifically economic narrative but to mobilize the genealogical force of this narrative and to articulate it with other areas of the social formation—political, cultural, ideological" (13). In this way, Halpern argues that the long tradition of understanding sixteenth- and seventeenth-century England as, in some way, a transitional period makes Renaissance studies an ideal site for reconsidering the *narrative practices* that underpin contemporary historical criticism and cultural analysis.

Marx's discussion of primitive accumulation narrates the process of separating the direct producer from the means of production—a process that undermined feudalism and made possible the consolidation of capitalism. Drawing on this discussion, Halpern claims that "economic modes of production are crucial categories for an understanding of historical (and hence cultural) process. It is not to impute to them a mysterious omnipotence that installs them at the heart of all historical phenomena, but it is to grant them a specific and powerful materiality that is worthy of notice" (14). For example, by attending to that materiality, Halpern is able to isolate "regions and models of power which are accessible to Marxist but not to Foucauldian or new-historical analysis" (2). He explains that new historicists generally focus on the visibly coercive exercise of power: "Some more recent new-historical work has shifted its gaze from the dazzling sight of the king, but a kind of after-

9. Stephen Greenblatt, introduction to *Renaissance Self-Fashioning: From More to Shakespeare* (Chicago: University of Chicago Press, 1980), 1–9, *Shakespearean Negotiations: The Circulation of Social Energy in Renaissance England* (Berkeley: University of California Press, 1988), 1–20, and "Towards a Poetics of Culture," in Veeser, *New Historicism*, 1–14; and Louis A[drian] Montrose, "Professing the Renaissance: The Poetics and Politics of Culture," in Veeser, *New Historicism*, 15–36.

image persists in its *model* of power, which is still predominantly juridico-political, and therefore focuses on relations of force or sovereignty (more or less subtle) between unequal, hierarchical subjects: husband and wife, father and child, master and servant, colonizer and colonized" (3). Halpern does not deny the significance of this model of power in Renaissance society, yet he argues that "capital replaces the visible or patent form of sovereign political power with an invisible and resolutely *latent* form of economic domination" (5). Within the capitalist mode of production, surplus value is extracted in the economic realm without the need for direct political or legal coercion. "As a result," he explains, "capital operates a historically unprecedented form of social power which is opaque to analysis by models derived from the political, legal, or even (it turns out) economic sphere, if the economic is conceived of merely as a sphere of exchange" (3–4).

Halpern adds that Nicos Poulantzas's analysis of the transition from feudalism to capitalism extends these "'latent,' fugitive, or nonsovereign forms of power even to the juridico-political mechanisms of the state itself. For the capitalist state secures and reproduces political dominion precisely by *not* exercising violence or class power, save in exceptional instances, and by limiting the right of others to do so" (7). By bringing together Marx's economic narrative with the juridico-politico narrative that Poulantzas derives from it, Halpern redescribes the relationship between economic exploitation and political and legal power during the Renaissance. In so doing, he makes accessible to cultural critics a form of social power whose visibility depends on attending to feudalism and capitalism as "both economic and social modes of production" (1). For example, Halpern acknowledges that Renaissance society actually "predates . . . all but the most nascent forms of capitalist production," yet he argues that "certain political, legal, or cultural domains were able to anticipate those of a capitalist formation even in advance of capitalism *as such*" (9). He also notes that "early forms of capital—in particular, merchant's capital—were already firmly entrenched by the beginning of the sixteenth century" (9). In the latter case, however, he distinguishes among the spread of commodity production under merchant's capital, primitive accumulation, and generalized commodity production under capitalism. Merchant's capital "helped effect a late mutation of feudalism" by relocating feudal relations in "the sphere of exchange" (71, 74). Primitive accumulation effected an absolute decoding of feudalism by violently—and decisively—separating direct producers from the means of production (74). And capitalism's generalized commodity production produced a class structure in which the "extraction of surplus value survives within, and often thrives on, the politico-juridical equality of all classes" (159). As Marx's account of primitive accumulation and Halpern's account of anticipatory cultural domains suggest, this is by no means an unproblematic, chronological movement between "stages" of history.

Halpern stresses that Marx produced his account of primitive accumulation when confronted by a theoretical dilemma—the inability of a "structural account of capitalism" to "explain its *origins* as a mode of production" (62). In response to that dilemma, "Marx offers an *economic* prehistory of capital rather than a history of the transition to capitalism" (10). Marx's economic prehistory "serves a theoretical purpose by illustrating that the elements of capitalism, in their genesis, lack any direct structural relation to one another or to the mode of production they will help to compose" (66). Halpern argues that this turn to genealogy within a narrative of transition is a resolutely antiteleological gesture which is a "sign of a certain lack within theory when it confronts the concrete of history" (11) and which "signifies both a history to be written and the limits such a history must observe. Its vocation is to provide not a conclusive narrative but a useful one" (67).

Yet these limitations do not lead Halpern to forfeit the "entire [Marxist] machinery of periodization and transition" or "the concept of *relative* autonomy, which still assumes a social totality" (11), in favor of absolute autonomy and Foucauldian genealogy. In fact, Halpern argues that "to have 'succeeded' in such a project [fully theorizing a transitional process] would have been to impose an iron grid of necessity on history. The determinism for which Marxism can legitimately argue is more modest; it agrees with the etymological sense of the word as a limit on the field of the possible rather than an irresistible compulsion in any one direction" (11). This notion of determinism informs Halpern's understanding of the relative autonomy of cultural regions. Halpern argues that, in practice, a reliance on absolute autonomy too often "ends up homogenizing the social field" and thus precludes theorizing "the conditions under which regimes of power replace each other" (12). He adopts a Marxist theory of relative autonomy in an effort to avoid this tendency to homogenize. He explains that "for Althusser, relative autonomy signifies that each level or instance of a social formation—political, ideological, cultural, economic, etc.—possesses its own characteristic structures, temporalities, and effectivity" (6). For example, in his reading of Thomas More's *Utopia*, this concept allows Halpern to account for the noncongruence between "the depredations of absolutist monarchy and the displacement of the agricultural populations" (157). The concept of relative autonomy also allows him to specify how forms of culture that generally are not considered either economic or politico-juridical might participate in the transition between modes of production. A Marxist theory of relative autonomy

> enables one to maintain that even if a cultural discourse is *not* directly inscribed in power—that is to say, even if it does not form part of a "strategic" formation—it may nevertheless generate effects of domination or, for that matter, subversion by means of its (nonstrategic and purely structural) relation to other, relatively autonomous areas of the social formation. . . . [Althusserian Marxism] allows that pertinent political effects may arise from *purely conjunctural* formations, even if these are not "strategic." (8–9)

Halpern locates *copia* and, more generally, "the ideological effects of Tudor schooling . . . under this category" (9).

Halpern argues that Tudor schooling is a "relatively autonomous process that nevertheless has pertinent (but merely conjunctural) effects on economic class divisions" (15). Within late feudal society, he explains, "freedom is conceived of as difference from or transgression of law. This mode of power by no means disappears under capitalism, but it is supplemented by other modes for which the differential subject is not an impediment but a conduit" (43). Tudor schools combined juridical with mimetic forms of learning; the first supported the dominant feudal form of political authority, the second distributed "individual differences within a regularized system" (45) and, in so doing, "began to recast cultural domination into forms that would suit a new kind of ruling class" (45). This latter form of learning involved a new, bourgeois style of humanist literary production that "deploy[ed] a normalizing social order based on the production of empty heterogeneity" (44). Halpern concludes that "the transitional labor of the schools can thus be located at the sometimes tense intersection of these two systems, which both reproduced a more traditional model of cultural authority and helped to lay the basis for a new one" (45). Erasmus's version of *copia* contributed to that new model of cultural authority. Halpern explains that "reading for copia tended to decode the poetic text by atomizing its larger structures of meaning and ideological content and by resolving it into generative strategies of style, on the one hand, and dissociated bits of elocutionary material, on the other" (47). Erasmus encouraged this textual disintegration "as a way of reducing the authority of individual writers, thus freeing the formation of a personal style from the slavish imitation of a single prestigious model" (49). In this way, *copia* neutralized the foreign ideologies of many such prestigious models and offered a regularized system within which a variety of individual styles might be produced.

In his analysis of imitation, Halpern addresses what Newman labels linguistic and sartorial extravagance. He understands these two fashions as two "modes of imitation" (41)—arguing that "the humanist 'fashioning system,' like the fashion system it both resembles and feeds into, extends its power through the production of *negligible* differences that bind the subject to it without challenging its boundaries" (43). There is, he stresses, no predetermined "realm of the fashionable." Instead,

> the general realm of the fashionable is always given a specific inflection by the subjects who enter into it. This differential character is not, however, a mode of resistance to the system but one of its principal lures, allowing the subject to claim a space within the larger framework of a collective representation. Fashionability propagates itself through the formation of nonidentical "individuals," who are nevertheless created within the confines of a governing system. Indeed, there is no original model that *can* be copied fully. (42–43)

In this way, fashion registers and reinforces "class distinctions, even in the absence of legal regulation" (40).

Yet Halpern's reading practice, unlike Newman's, also emphasizes the distinctions between linguistic and sartorial modes of imitation. He stresses that literary style—"and this is its crucial difference from the fashion system it *formally* resembled—could circulate at other levels of the social edifice, largely for the simple reason that it was a more affordable (though by no means universally affordable) mode of display" (44). As a result, the two modes often produced quite different official and unofficial responses and participated in different ways in Renaissance social struggles. In short, by drawing on the concept of relative autonomy, Halpern's readings emphasize that what Newman labels "commodification" actually operates in a variety of not always compatible registers.

This emphasis is particularly vivid when, later in his book, Halpern distinguishes the *Utopia*'s managing of lack, excess, and consumption from that of *King Lear*. More envisions a natural "zero state" (174) whose perfect equilibrium between use and need would eliminate the destructiveness of what Newman calls "commodity pleasures" (140). By "rooting out sources of potential excess" (174), More replaces the specters of lack and surplus with "useful or rational consumption" (174). Halpern writes that "More's devotion to the moral economy of use value represents an important bourgeois strategy for wresting economic and cultural power from the aristocracy. What *Utopia* cannot imagine in any coherent way, however, is the socialization, rather than the elimination, of destructive expenditure" (174). *King Lear*, on the other hand, addresses an aristocratic crisis—"the increased reliance on economic consumption as a class marker during a period of decreasing or at least stable revenues" (267). The play's tragic form relies on the consumption of a destructive expenditure whose socialization it, too, cannot imagine and whose quiet elimination it cannot tolerate. These readings are part of what I have described as Halpern's more general attention to the synchronic and diachronic specificity of cultural regions. Wary of those who argue "that *everything* is an economy, to figure all of culture as an expanded or general process of circulation" (14), Halpern emphasizes that he draws on theorists who "try to expand the boundaries of Marxist political economy while still respecting them and who therefore open up lines of connection with other cultural areas without simply erasing distinctions" (15). And he criticizes those versions of Renaissance cultural analysis which assume "a realm of the 'early modern' which is somehow always-already-there yet always still in progress. Local, institutional transactions are analyzed without asking what global conditions, if any, serve as their condition of possibility" (12). In other words, although Newman and Halpern concur that "meaning and its effects" (Newman, 143) are a crucial site of social struggle, Newman's reading practice stresses a material ground that *is* language, while Halpern's reading practice stresses the specificity of and relationships among different modes of materiality.

Yet, if Halpern models his readings after Marx's discussion of primitive accumulation in order "to maintain theoretical and genealogical narratives in a state of creative tension" (13), he also models those readings after Marx's "mongrel combination of theoretical and polemical concerns" (62). Halpern argues that "Marx himself employed the term [primitive accumulation] both as a mocking trope on Adam Smith's notion of 'prior' accumulation *and* as a serious concept in its own right" (61–62). In Marx's account, Smith authors an ethical prehistory of capitalism in which the thrifty prevail over the imprudent; Marx substitutes for this narrative about innate capacities a narrative about the violent expropriation of land. Halpern points out that ethical accounts of the transition from feudalism to capitalism actually predate Smith. In fact, he argues, Tudor education contributed to one version of this ideological narrative. For example, Erasmus's version of *copia* helped to distinguish the deserving, capable writer—the producer of an individualized style—from the undeserving, "slavish" (49) imitator. In this way, *copia* promoted the myth of primitive accumulation and its "collusion between a narrative of social mobility and a discourse of capacities"—a collusion that rewrote process as essence (88). Yet Halpern also points out that Smith was decidedly *un*sympathetic to ethical accounts of capitalism and, like Marx, sought a structural account of economic behavior. Finally, Halpern argues that *Capital*'s nineteenth-century readers would have been aware of Marx's egregious—and uncharacteristic—misreading of Smith. Thus Marx's narrative of primitive accumulation performs the errors of an "'ethical' conception of history" that, unlike *Capital*, "takes a free and volitional subject as its basis and starting point" for analyzing the dynamics of capital (87).

In his introductory chapter, Halpern offers his own version of such a performance. First, he explains: "Instead of defending against Foucauldian and new-historical critique, launching a counterattack against them, or 'subsuming' these movements within a Marxist project, I prefer to begin by arguing the *complementarity* of Marxist and non-Marxist approaches. This I do somewhat polemically by isolating regions and models of power which are accessible to Marxist but not to Foucauldian or new-historical analysis" (2). Then, later in the chapter, Halpern announces that his polemic, like Marx's, depends on a misreading:

> If there is a polemical point here, it is that the new historicism has tended to avoid the materiality of the economic in order to focus on political or sovereign models of power. Yet it is not quite true to suggest that the economic has been entirely ignored. The more recent work of Stephen Greenblatt, in particular, has tended to invoke a model of economic circulation (or "negotiation") and to understand cultural production as a process of inter- or ex-change among different levels or regions of the social edifice. (14)

In other words, the style of these introductory comments imitates what Halpern will characterize as the mongrel form of Marx's narrative about primitive accumulation. In this way, the style announces, in Halpern's words, that unabashed "'return to Marx'" with which he claims to risk "the *appearance* of an outmoded orthodoxy" (62, my emphasis)—the appearance, according to the distinctions produced by *copia*, of merely imitating his prestigious model. If the task of primitive accumulation "is to provide not a conclusive narrative but a useful one" (67), this risk taking suggests that such a narrative actually might perform in excess of its usefulness precisely by appearing to be outmoded or out of fashion and thus risking its author's symbolic capital.

In the following paragraph, Halpern argues that fluctuations in symbolic capital must be understood in relation to "the specificity of the economic" (14). He argues that theories of symbolic capital—like "Greenblatt's 'poetics of culture'" (14)—too often lose sight of that specificity:

> The boundaries between economic and noneconomic regions are not merely imperfectly permeable but also asymmetrically so and . . . capital in the restricted sense defines the conditions under which other kinds of cultural material or "energy" can enter its domain. . . . For the economic changes that began to favor the gentry over the aristocracy not only set limits to the extent of aristocratic expense or display; they also interrupted the circuit through which these older forms of symbolic capital could be reconverted into liquid wealth, while creating entirely new domains of cultural capital (literacy, education, and others). . . . To say that a ruling class secures its dominance through symbolic as well as material means should not, then, be taken to impute a perfect equivalence between these. (14–15)

In other words, capital places a limit on the field of possible *relationships* among these relatively autonomous realms—not by consolidating a general primacy of the economic realm but by helping to determine that realm's characteristic structures and effectivity. Within this framework, by appearing to risk its author's symbolic capital, the style of Halpern's introductory comments suggests that he writes his narrative of primitive accumulation from within the dialectical relationship between utility and expenditure that defines the commodity form. In other words, if Marx's polemic performs the errors of an "'ethical' conception of history" (87), Halpern's introductory polemic performs the contemporary necessity of addressing the specificity of the economic realm when writing cultural criticism and when, in the process, attempting to "think the present historically."[10]

10. Jameson, *Postmodernism*, ix.

🍏 Index

Mouffe, Chantal, and Ernesto Laclau, 4n, 25n. 19, 55n. 11

National identity, construction of, 15, 35–38, 58–63, 94n, 100–101, 101n, 138–40; in relation to regional identity, 62, 80, 94–95, 99–105, 131, 140–48
Neale, J. E., 29n. 23
Neely, Carol Thomas, 80, 81n. 3, 106n. 27, 169n
Neill, S. Diana, 129n. 3
New historicism, 1–2, 6, 167–70, 179, 185
Newman, Karen, 9–10, 167–79, 167n. 2, 184
Newton, Judith, 169n

Outhwaite, R. B., 99n

Parker, David, 129n. 3, 129n. 4
Parker, Patricia, 13n. 3, 101n, 106n. 27, 107n
Parsons, 97–98; and *The Merry Wives of Windsor*, 86–87, 99–102. *See also* Courts, ecclesiastical and secular; Defamation
Parten, Anne, 106n. 27, 113n
Patterson, Annabel, 47n
Pätzold, Kurt-Michael, 129n. 3, 129n. 4
Pechter, Edward, 2n
Pittenger, Elizabeth, 107n
Plett, Heinrich F., 13, 13n. 3, 14n. 4, 15n. 6, 16n. 7, 17n. 9
Postmodernism, 167, 170, 175–76, 176n. 8
Poulantzas, Nicos, 180
Primitive accumulation, 179–87
Prior, Mary, 114n, 152n. 30, 152n. 31, 159n
Pro-women writing, 2, 8, 25n. 19, 71, 108, 108n; arguments appropriated by the *Arcadia*, 68–71; on equity, 9, 68, 68n. 19; on rape, 68, 73
Puttenham, George, and *The Arte of English Poesie*, 2–7, 11–42, 11n, 43, 167

Quilligan, Maureen, 44n

Raitière Martin N., 44–45n. 1
Ray, John, 24
Rebellion, 5–6, 53–55, 56, 62–63, 141; and anti-enclosure activity, 53–54, 53–54n. 8, 54n. 9, 114; and apprentices, 133–36, 146–48; contemporary accounts of, 134–36, 141, 147–48; depiction of, in the *Arcadia*, 6–7, 45–46, 49–53, 56–62, 70–71, 75; and England's seventeenth-century revolution, 5, 54, 54n. 10; fear of, 70–

71, 99, 146–48; Sidney's ideas about, 44–45. *See also* Collective politics and hegemony, models of
Rees, Joan, 101n
Reuter, Ole, 129n. 3, 129n. 4
Revisionist history, 5–6, 6n, 141. *See also* Collective politics and hegemony, models of; Rebellion; Social status
Ribner, Irving, 45n. 1
Ringler, W. A., Jr., 47n
Roberts, Jeanne Addison, 106n. 27
Robertson, Jean, 47n
Rollins, Hyder E., 129n. 3, 129n. 4
Rushton, Peter, 79n

Sanford, Hugh, 46
Scalingi, Paula Louise, 108n
Seymour, Jane, 144
Shakespeare, William, 13, 14n. 4, 178; and *King Lear*, 184; and *The Merry Wives of Windsor*, 2–7, 9, 62, 75, 77–125, 77n. 1, 131, 167; and *The Winter's Tale*, 39n
Shaming rituals, 9, 78–79, 91, 96, 102–3, 118, 122, 146–47, 165; and *Jack of Newbury*, 165–66; and *The Merry Wives of Windsor*, 80, 85–86, 93, 101–2, 112, 122, 124
Sidney, Mary, 46, 47n
Sidney, Philip, 13, 14n. 4; and the *Arcadia*, 2–7, 9, 45–75, 43n. 3, 167; letters of, 57–58, 57n. 15, 58n; reputation as a courtier, 43–45
Simons, John, 129n. 3, 129n. 4, 131, 131n. 8
Sinfield, Alan, 2n, 16n. 7, 45n. 1, 68n. 19; and Jonathan Dollimore, 1n
Skretkowicz, Victor, 47n
Slack, Paul, and Peter Clark, 95n, 96n. 15, 99n, 104n, 105n, 136n. 15, 140n. 17, 144n. 21, 146n. 23
Slights, Camille Wells, 80, 81n. 3, 82n. 7
Smith, Adam, 184–85
Smith, Hilda L., 23n, 27n. 21, 47n
Smith, James D., and John E. Hill, 24n
Social mobility, 6, 81; and *The Arte of English Poesie*, 7, 16, 32–35, 37–42; and the court of Elizabeth I, 15–16; and experience of economic exploitation, 55, 130n. 5; and *Jack of Newbury*, 128, 136–37, 142–43; possibilities for, 35–37, 136, 136n. 15, 142. *See also* Authority relations; Class, definitions of; Social status
Social status: and the *Arcadia*, 59–63, 71–75; and experience of economic